The Best of The Minneapolis Review of Baseball

Volume I, 1981-1987

Edited by Ken LaZebnik & Steve Lehman

Designed & Illustrated by Andy Nelson

Forewords by
Garrison Keillor
& Eugene McCarthy

 Wm. C. Brown Publishers

Acknowledgments

We gratefully acknowledge our friends and advocates at William C. Brown Publishers for all their assistance and support: Ed Bartell, Tom Doran, and Karla Blaser.

We want to take this opportunity to finally thank the folks who donated their time, talent, expertise, and dollars to keep the **MRB** rally alive during our tumultuous early innings: David Unowsky and the Hungry Mind Bookstore; the irrepressible Julian Empson and Tom Bartsch of Save the Met (now Ballpark Tours, Inc.); Jack Reuler, Charlie Moore and the gang at Mixed Blood Theatre; Cuno Barragan; Jon Kerr; Mike Smith; Mary Flanagan; Deb Palma; Joe DiMaggio (of Erskine, MN); Elio Chacon; Margaret Hamburger and Kamman Art Printing; Steve Dierkes, a dear friend and terrific guy even though he doesn't really like baseball much; Dave Moore, Hot Stove League Banquet MC and crowd control specialist extraordinaire; Wes Westrum; David Tripp, Don Leeper, Ellen Watters, and Stu Abraham (Culpepper Press); Calvin Griffith; and the wonderful and amazing Judy Gilats of Peregrine Publications (we'd never have made it without you, Judy).

Thanks to Carol Koop, Virginia Pappas, Kevin Morrissey and Judy (again) for their word processor wizardry in preparing this book.

For supporting us through the long nights of labor, we thank our oldest friends and supporters: our moms and dads and families. Thank you, thank you, thank you to Kate and Kathy; you know why.

We especially acknowledge all the readers of the **MRB**, with many of whom we've corresponded, debated, reminisced, exulted, commiserated, exchanged research and stories (apocryphal and otherwise), and shared outrage, all-time line-ups and a common passion. Without you, this whole enterprise would have been a lot less fun, financially ruinous, and entirely pointless.

And finally, to the talented writers and artists whose hard work graces the **MRB** pages past, present, and future, our deepest gratitude. You *are* **The Minneapolis Review of Baseball.**

— K.L., S.L., & A.N.

THE ROSTER for *Base Paths: The Best of The Minneapolis Review of Baseball*

FOREWORDS

The big boom in sensitive male writing about baseball is an offshoot of the men's movement, I suppose, or whatever it's called when men get together on weekend retreats to weep and hug and beat drums and put on antlers and fart in the moonlight, the movement that led to Robert Bly's seminal work on toilets, **Iron John**, and I hope this doesn't sound negative because *sensitive male writing about baseball is really wonderful.* Anybody who doesn't think so is a fat pig.

But why does so much sensitive baseball writing have to be about East Coast baseball? There are tons of frothy reminiscence about the Giants, the Yankees, fanhood as the door to manhood, the bond with Dad and Uncle Al, New York When New York *Was* New York, the doubts, the fears, the disillusion, etc. And the sensitive writing about the Brooklyn Dodgers and the Athens that was Ebbets Field and then O'Malley's perfidy of 1957 and the loss of innocence and the end of America's Golden Age and the death of tailfins and the inevitable slide toward Vietnam and Richard Nixon and George Bush would fill two tank trucks. I say, *Give us a break. They're gone. It's been thirty-some years. Try therapy. Try drinking more liquids. You want to know what sorrow is, move to Philadelphia.* And then there are the acres of existential bushwa about the Boston Red Sox and the complicated, unknowable agonies of Sox fans for whom victory is only a prelude to eventual defeat and ultimate loss.

No, I am all for sensitive baseball writing, but where is the SBW on the Pittsburgh Pirates and the Toledo Mud Hens or the St. Cloud Rox? It doesn't stand a chance. A guy who writes, say, a sensitive coming-of-age story about growing up with the Detroit Tigers or the Kansas City Royals and ships it to an editor in Manhattan doesn't have a prayer. The editor is astonished. "Are there *cities* out there on the plains?" he asks his assistant. "Do they *have* baseball there? I thought they just went in for square dancing and shooting squirrels and rasslin' pigs." And the story is rejected, even though it's great. Or *fairly* great. It's like when Buddy Holly went to Columbia Records in New York and auditioned for Mitch Miller. Miller was an oboeist and his idea of a great singer was Gordon MacRae.

It's a dreadful situation in America, with all the media on the Right Coast or the Left Coast and most of the brains and wit and saavy in the Big Middle. Of course, Roger Angell is the exception here, the one that proves the rule. He is the Father and the Apotheosis of Baseball Literature, the writer to whom all others must be compared, and he lives in New York. But only because he was born in New York. If Roger Angell had been born in Minneapolis, he would be there today, following the Twins and listening to Herb Carneal, the classiest play-by-play announcer in Amercia, and writing for **The Minneapolis Review of Baseball**.

Thank goodness the **MRB** came along when it did and gave writers from the interior a place to put their thoughts about baseball. The best stuff from the magazine's first years is gathered in this book, and it speaks elegantly for itself, and is worth several readings. Poetry and reporting and SBW on the St. Louis Cardinals and the Cubs and White Sox and of course the Twins and our beloved old Met Stadium and the incomparable Calvin Griffith. Here is the remarkable Red Shuttleworth, the only catcher in the Texas League to become an English professor in Nebraska, and here is the best critical essay to date on Leonardo da Vinci's attempts to design baseball.

Unfortunately, the **Review** did not come along in time for older men such as myself. Years ago, I could have written an essay about the Minnesota Twins and their loss to the Dodgers in the 1965 World Series and how this marked me with a sense of bitter fatalism, but there was no **MRB** around and so I went into fiction instead. Fiction was not like baseball at all, didn't serve as a bond with my dad and Uncle Al, wasn't an agony to me, wasn't allegorical, wasn't a repository of my hopes and dreams — fiction was more like stoopball. You stand and hurl a tennis ball at the front steps and you catch the rebound and make big plays and narrate the whole thing under your breath. Fun, but nothing to write memoirs about.

— Garrison Keillor
February, 1991

* * * * * * *

The game of baseball is revealed in this anthology in all of its levity, simplicity, complexity and profundity. Like no other game, baseball is a challenge to essayists, novelists, playwrights and poets. Sociologists look to it as a model of social behavior. Scientists seek to explain the physics of the game. Even the moralists, the philosophers and the theologians find meaning in baseball. The moralists point out that in baseball, as distinguished from most other games, some person is always responsible, for both good and bad. Hits and errors are recorded. Earned runs are recorded, walks, strikeouts. The books are balanced. Philosophers have noted that baseball is played in a unique spatial frame, projected from the point of home plate in a ninety degree angle, running to infinity, whereas other games are played within defined areas, rectangular, near rectangular or oval. Baseballs never absolutely go out of bounds. They are either fair or foul. Baseball also has a singular relationship to time. It is above or outside time. Most other games are arbitrarily divided into measured quarters, halves, periods. They are controlled, even dominated by time. Baseball ignores time. An inning theoretically can go on forever. And a game. *Time out* is not taken in baseball, time is *called*. Theoretically, *time* in baseball can be called *forever*.

The religious aspect of baseball is manifest in the special role of the umpire. Umpires have to be dealt with absolutely. They are not asked to settle disputes as are referees. Umpires make judgements. The word is derived from the Old French word *nompere*, "one who is alone and without a peer." "Refuse not," the medieval philosophers warned, "the *umpeereship* and judgementes of the Holy Ghoste."

And so the game goes on, essentially the same, whether played in Mudville or Manhattan.

— Eugene J. McCarthy
February, 1991

IN THE OWNER'S BOX

I started the Minneapolis Review of Baseball for two reasons:

1. To provide a journal of writing about baseball.
2. To supply a rallying point for fan opinion.

Most sport magazines try to tell their readers what happened and let them know why. We aren't going to try to do either. The Minneapolis Review of Baseball (let's get in the habit right now of calling ourselves MRB) will be published quarterly: a Hot Stove Edition (we start at home), an Opening Day Edition (first base), an All-Star Break Number, and, rounding third, on our way home, a World Serious Edition.

Obviously we are not a news source. We can't give our readers much insight into players' psyche. I've never been in a major league locker room. I don't know how to interview a player, and doubt if I'll ever try. We're fans, who like good writing about the game. There's an ever-increasing amount of literature and reminiscence about baseball being published, and we seek to offer a quarterly that will review and publish baseball fiction and reportage.

In addition, we'd like to supply fans with a vehicle for expression. For example: MRB takes a strong stand on the issue of breaking the leagues into three divisions (we're against it), and we hope to use what limited means are at our disposal to convince the owners a majority of fans are against it. (For a further comment on this issue see our editorial centerpage.)

So we have a fan's eye journal. We invite letters from far-flung correspondents: our roster, unlike the big leagues, is open to all.

Ken Lazebnik

THE MINNEAPOLIS REVIEW OF BASEBALL

A JOURNAL OF WRITING ON BASEBALL

Volume 1, Number 1   Hot Stove Edition
Winter 1981   50¢

INTRODUCTION

The Minneapolis Review of Baseball

In the fall of 1980, in the living room of his basement row house apartment in Minneapolis, Ken LaZebnik showed me a small mock-up of folded notebook paper. It was for a journal he was thinking of putting together, a journal of writing on baseball from a fan's perspective. Five years earlier we had taken a course on baseball literature at Macalester College. We both passed, but neither of us won MVP (Most Valuable Paper), which was an essay on the '64 Phillies entitled *In the Days of Wine and Rojas*. That class provided us with the first inkling of a connection between our twin loves of baseball and literature. Ken proposed to combine the two, creating a quasi-literary quarterly in which baseball fans from any walk of life could express their opinions on and abiding affection for the National Pastime.

Volume 1, Number 1 of **The Minneapolis Review of Baseball**, typed out on a Selectric at The Mixed Blood Theatre Company (where Ken was employed as an actor), appeared in January, 1981. It was 28 pages long, written almost entirely by Ken and his relatives, and each copy was priced at less than it cost to produce. The first page looked like the this: (See reproduction at left).

The cover of this issue – depicting a batter whose swing has sent the head of the catcher hurtling into the outfield – was drawn by college pal Steve Dierkes, and at $2 a year we proclaimed ourselves "The Cheapest Magazine Subscription in America!" (We later amended that to "Only the **Watchtower** is Cheaper!") Crusty octogenarian sportswriter Staff Writer made his debut in that issue as well. The general format, in fact, is still more or less intact. We quickly found ourselves publishing a community of eccentric correspondents and baseball lovers: construction workers, professional poets, cab drivers, college professors, a retired diplomat, and anyone else who writes well and fervently about baseball.

In its first years, Ken and I would go to our anarchist printer and fold, staple and trim the issues ourselves to save money. We'd then adjourn to the Keys Restaurant, eat enormous amounts of carbohydrates and work it off playing pinball – altogether, a terrific avocation for young men.

At times, the **MRB** seemed to produce itself. We were never able to give it complete attention, since we never got paid, but we spent every spare minute opening mail, pasting labels, collating pages, and reading manuscripts, and we never seemed to lose enough money to force us to stop doing this thing that we enjoyed. We likened the **MRB** to a needy child always crying for our attention (this comment came before our children were born, usually as we leaned over a pinball machine). But it was our love, and it never occurred to us to walk away.

We started to get noticed in the press – ironically, the strike of 1981 was the best thing that could have happened to an infant publication. With nothing else to cover, we got written up in the local papers and **The Sporting News**.

In 1983, we began The Hot Stove League Benefit Banquet to defray the losses we were incurring. It was the brainchild of Julian Empson, who had formed and directed Save The Met, a lobby group against the building of the Metrodome. He redirected that group into a bus tour service to outdoor ballparks after the battle was lost. It was on one of those tours that we met artist Andy Nelson, whose *pièce de résistance* at the time was an extensive series of baseball murals in Joe DiMaggio's bar (the Joe DiMaggio of Erskine, Minnesota). Andy quickly revitalized the journal with his cover art, story illustrations and beautiful, professional design, and became a third partner.

In 1984, Ken left for New York City and announced that it was now my turn to lose money on the magazine. I set up an office in the utility closet of the Ramsey County Morgue (where I work as an investigator). The **MRB** continued to be published haphazardly, often intermittently – throughout marriages, divorce, children and other jobs (it was always pleasure rather than a meal ticket). Then, in the spring of 1990, **The Minneapolis Review of Baseball** was purchased by William C. Brown Publishers of Dubuque, Iowa. They were starting a line of baseball books and we all just seemed to fit in well with one another. Andy and I stayed on to produce the magazine just as always, except now it comes out on time. The journal is better than ever and 1991 represents our tenth anniversary.

The **MRB** has always been an eclectic journal and one produced as a labor of love. Through these labors we've met a wonderful group of people, of baseball lovers.

What better way to celebrate a tenth anniversary than with an anthology selected from our first six years? (We included a couple of things from year seven, too — consistency has never been our strong suit.) We've arranged this book in the manner of a year of our quarterly, following the seasons from spring to winter.

Steve Lehman, Editor-in-Chief,

     with Andy Nelson, Art Director & Illustrator,

     and Ken LaZebnik, Founder & Consulting Publisher

For
Bethany and Shannon,
Sam and Will,
and Jack

THE MOMENT, pen & ink drawing by Andy Nelson. Cover art for The Minneapolis Review of Baseball, Vol. 6, No. 2

SPRING

A Meditation on Playing Catch

Dave Healy

As I write this, the lamb-like days of March are giving way to cruel April, with its alternately proffered and retracted promises of spring. Of all the rites of spring, surely none is more exquisitely gratifying than that first game of catch.

Yes, the shoulder will be sore tomorrow, will rebel at movements it has not been asked to make – save for an occasional hurled snowball – for lo these many months. But that won't hit full force till later. Now all that hits full force is the thrown ball finding its way into the waiting glove with a sound impossible to capture orthographically. "Crack" suffices reasonably well to suggest the sound of bat meeting ball. But what does ball meeting glove sound like? Thwack? Thunk? Not quite. Actually, the word "catch" itself isn't bad, the initial velar stop giving way to the softer sibilant in a way analogous to the combination of hard and soft resistance offered by the well-tended mitt.

Playing catch offers a convenient opportunity to reflect on the folly of human activity. I have a friend who dismisses all forms of sport as "silly, really, perfectly silly." He is quite right, of course. Viewed from any sort of reasonably pragmatic perspective, the games we play are ludicrous, indeed. And playing catch has the added distinction of not even being a game, at least not in the sense of promoting competition and producing winners and losers. It is a perfectly useless activity – pure play.

One could argue, perhaps, that playing catch is preparatory to playing real games – i.e., baseball or softball – that the participants are honing their skills or loosening up for a contest. People do play catch for those reasons, but as often as not they play just for the hell of it – in a way that very few people hit golf balls at a driving range of tennis balls against a wall just for the hell of it. There is no rival in our culture for the time-honored post-Sunday-dinner-out-on-the-front-sidewalk catch.

Games are, by definition and consent, nonutilitarian. This is part of the reason my friend dismisses them. They don't accomplish anything: They exist purely for their own sake. Most games in our society, however, at least produce winners and losers. As such, they have a certain entertainment value. But playing catch is not even competition. Nothing is more boring than watching people play catch.

Indeed, there is something Sisyphean about the whole business. Sisyphus, it will be recalled, was the legendary Corinthian king condemned to roll a huge a stone up a steep hill in Hades, only to have it roll down again as it neared the top. But Sisyphus was *condemned* to engage in this activity, as a punishment for betraying a secret of Zeus. Catch players do what they do voluntarily. Why?

It is interesting that we say playing catch, rather than playing throw. Only half the activity is described, and judging from the relative status accorded to pitchers and catchers, not the more important half. But there is really no reason to quibble over which activity, throwing or catching, is more important, for playing catch demands both. To throw is to launch, to set forth, to commit to the air, to release, to aim. It is the masculine to the catch's feminine. To catch is to receive, to enclose, to take in. To play catch is to do both – each participant both a giver and a receiver, both offering and accepting. To play catch is to experience both the yin and the yang of life.

Which perhaps is another way of saying that playing catch is interactive. One does it with someone else – most often, perhaps, with a single partner, but sometimes with more. Indeed, there is no theoretical limit to the number of participants. Playing catch demands accommodation to the abilities of one's partner(s) and is a reminder that life is intrinsically and inescapably social – an ongoing exercise in reciprocity and mutuality. Mutuality because the object of playing catch is not to win, but to play. Indeed, competitiveness threatens rather than facilitates a game of catch.

The language of catch players is affirmative, conciliatory, apologetic. "Nice grab." "My fault." "I'll get it." A good catch is cause for mutual rejoicing: It elevates the catcher and redeems the thrower. A miss is a shared failure: "I should've had it." "No, you didn't have a chance."

One can, of course, play catch with oneself, just as one can scratch oneself. How infinitely more pleasurable, though, to be scratched by someone else.

But what is it about playing catch that is pleasurable? What itch does it scratch? The experience may well be archetypal, part of our racial memory. Indeed, it is not difficult to imagine that catch was the first game humans played. Perhaps, then, playing catch activates something primal, is a response to some deep, unconscious urge at the core of our being. Perhaps.

It seems likely, though, that if there is such an urge, it involves more than catch playing. "A thing worth doing is worth doing well," we say. But what makes a thing worth doing? Perhaps a thing done well is worth doing, and is satisfying, for its own sake and nothing else. Wouldn't it be interesting if Americans, that most pragmatic of peoples, discovered that utility is not the only, or best, measure of an activity's value? That in such useless endeavors as playing catch we experience true freedom, freedom from the compulsions of practicality, of winning, of competition – the marvelous, liberating freedom of inutility?

Carolina League Old Timers Game, 1980

Paul Shuttleworth
for Miles Wolff

Their dead arms cock and toss
ghostly looping baseballs.
With golf course tans,
observable paunches,
and bored teenaged children
in the stands,
they trade anecdotes
their wives will never hear.

In the dugouts,
young minor leaguers
giggle, not recognizing
how it is they will gather
their own aged summers
into a blue weather
three-inning old timers game
where the trails cross
past pink slips, real jobs.

In our dugout,
Joe Cowley farts
and says Enos Slaughter
is obscenely fat.
Out on the mound,
Tommy Byrne kicks at
the rubber with new spikes.

Gallagher tells me
not to watch too long.
I have to warm up
our starting pitcher,
a bonus baby
West Point drop out
whose hard one explodes
like a grenade as it
crosses the plate.

But I want to memorize
this grassy field in May sunlight,
the baggy flannel uniforms,
the bald, blunt head of Enos Slaughter
as he grins and signs a ball,
the blonde, nearly bare-breasted woman
interviewing Bob Veale for TV,
her buttocks tense and snug
in grey designer jeans.

I want to memorize
the quizzical expression
on Tommy Byrne's face
as he adjusts his grip
on a batting practice ball,
the pheasant-brained
radio announcer eating
his fourth hot dog,
the wide-open happiness
of middle-aged baseball players
who never expected this
residue of poise and grace.

It's good to sit here
out of old timers' way
with my glove in my hands.
When the years have been piled on
and I'm nearer some mortuary,
I'll stand over there, just behind
home plate with the gear on
one last blood-pulsing time.

And I'll look over here
to the dugout to see myself
young again, lean, my hands
tight with impatience.
I'll look over one spring day,
then turn around, squat and catch
my finest innings even if
I resemble a beached sea lion.

The True Origins of Baseball

Dear Editors:

In W.P. Kinsella's **The Iowa Baseball Confederacy**, Leonardo da Vinci descends to a ballpark in a hot-air balloon and explains that he is the true inventor of baseball. Oh, it sounds so perfect, so right to have such a distinguished father, we think. But it's only Kinsella's fiction and the mind quickly nods, distastefully perhaps, back to the tradition of a third-rate Union general.

But what if. . . ?

In 1985, renovation began on the oldest commercial building in Minneapolis: the Upton Block. Built in 1855, the Upton hadn't seen the light of commerce in over half a century. During reconstruction, workmen found a 3'x4' wooden casket sheltered in a first floor corner where Gringolet Books now resides, and Gringolet owner Michael Leimer claimed the casket under Minnesota's Unowsky Rule.[1] I was directed to take care of the casket and its effects.

History on the wooden box is skimpy. This much we do know: It was owned by a 19th century art dealer named Vados Carmason who ran an unsuccessful gallery on Minneapolis' East Bank. Carmason left the area soon after the Civil War and his obituary in the March, 1887 Hannibal, Missouri , newspaper listed him as an advertising agent. No one knows why he left the wooden box in Minneapolis.

When I pried open the casket, I was astonished to find a group of prints and artifacts. If they proved authentic it would be The Find of the Century; the evidence irrefutably showed Leonardo da Vinci invented Baseball! Somehow, experts had to be found to test the articles. But where? Then, I remembered a

---

[1] Attached as a rider amendment to the 1983 Minnesota State Budget and passed during the last day of legislative session, the Unowsky Rule stipulates that it is the right of an individual to claim and protect any baseball artifact from the wanton and gutless destruction perpetrated by the state legislature, city councils, or any commercial venture.

conversation.

My friend Shawn Mahoney once told me about an oddball museum he visited in Milan, which, he said, was at the end of long back alley. One evening, full of Chianti and rigatoni, probably more of the former, Shawn stumbled on the place and snooped about like any good American tourist. The ramshackle room featured a handful of rare prints and objects supporting the theory that DaVinci created bocci ball. The curator, one Marco Seerup, dropped some questionable remarks about Leonardo also being the father of baseball. Signore Seerup was the guy who would know what to make of the evidence.

The articles were insured and shipped to the L'Bocchi Musi in Milan the next day. Three long weeks later we received a telegram at Gringolet from Signore Seerup who excitedly authenticated the Carmason cache. The provenance of the casket itself, Seerup said, came from the same age and area around Ferrar that the wooden bat model was made. Copies of the evidence were painstakingly made in Milan as payment for his research. The originals I requested to be securely sent back to the States for additional chemical analysis at the Sydd Finch Memorial Museum in Cooperstown, New York.

With the Finch Museum's further confirmation a month later, the only thing remaining was to publicly announce The Great Discovery. On May 1, 1986, in pointed defiance of the Soviet Union's May Day celebration, Gringolet Books formally announced and displayed The Glorious Truth: Leonardo da Vinci , Father of Baseball. Like a cherished clutch hit to break a ninth-inning tie, that very day Mr. Kinsella visited Gringolet to see what his prophecy had wrought.

There are, of course, loose threads to this yarn. Is there a da Vinci - Doubleday-Carmason connection wandering around in the murky pages of time? Did Albrecht Dürer have a hand in inventing the game as the evidence seems to suggest? Does this tell us more as to why the Italian people are hot-to-trot about baseball? Did "Slammin' Sammy" Scheidt ever find the ballpark? And just who did win the very first baseball game?[2] These questions I leave to historical detectives to ponder. For my part, association with these artifacts is a fan's life fulfilled.

On behalf of Michael Leimer and the Gringolet Books Gang, it is my pleasure to present The True Relics to **The Minneapolis Review of Baseball's** responsible hands.

Wayne N. Farr
Minneapolis, MN

P.S. When in Italy, visit Milan.

---

[2] Already there are opposing theories as to who won The First Game. The artist's supporters point to Holbein's great speed in the field and on the base paths as an asset tilting in their favor. Those who believe the writers won indicate that their team had considerably deeper power in the lineup. No one argues that Chaucer against Dürer must have been one helluva duel.

Three Baseball Cap Designs

As recorded in "The Last Inning" and "Josquin de Pres
Hit By Pitch", Leonardo favored the middle one.

(lead on parchment)

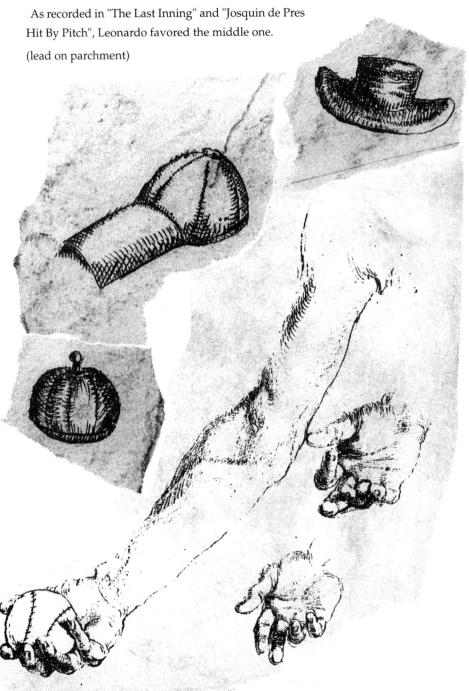

Analysis of the Pitching Arm

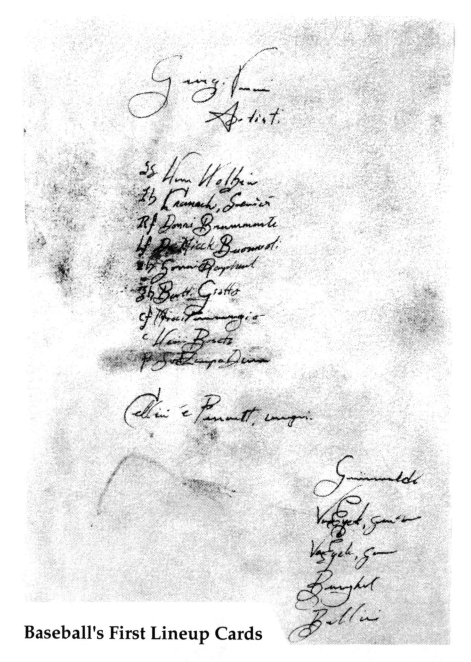

Baseball's First Lineup Cards

Although the final score of the first baseball game ever played has been lost, the lineup card for the teams miraculously survived. The rosters — artists and architects versus composers and writers — read like a veritable Who's Who of the era. Vasari's card is written in his hand whereas the scribe of Dante's is uncertain. It has been variously attributed to Cervantes, who served as third base and pitching coach, or Langland, who jokingly wrote himself in the lineup as Piero Ploughman, one of his fictional characters.

Leonardo himself, of course, was well-qualified to play with either squad. It has been suggested that he originally was scheduled to compete with the writers but withdrew at the last minute, perhaps the result of an unwillingness to allow himself to be so narrowly identified. This would account for the one less player on the writers' bench. However, notes in Frescobaldi's diary indicate that Samuel "Slammin' Sammy" Scheidt was scheduled to play but got lost on the way to the park. In either case, history records Dante's team minus one player.

Lineup Cards (Translated)

Georgi Vasari
Artists
SS - Hans Holbein
1B - Lucas Cranach, Senior
RF - Donni Brammante
LF - 'Da Micch' Buonarroti
(Michelangelo)
2B - Sonni Raphael
3B - Buddi Giotto
CF - Micci Carravaggio
C - Heini Bosch (Heironymous)
P - Sudzampa Dürer (Albrecht)
(The Italian "sudzampa" literally
meaning "southpaw".)

Bench:
Grunewald
Van Ecyk, Senior
Van Ecyk, Junior
Brughel
Belleni

Danny Alighieri
Composers & Writers
2B - Larri de Medici (Lorenzo)
LF - Eddi Spenser (Edmund)
RF - Miki de Cervantes (Miquel)
1B - Franki Petrarch
CF - Hank Schutz (Heinrich. Whoever wrote
the lineup card mistakenly wrote down
'Schultz' then corrected it.)
3B - Claudio Monteverdi
SS - Piero Ploughman (Piers)
C - Frank Rabelais
P - Geff Chaucer (Geoffrey)

Bench:
Jack Grimmelshaussen
Chris De Troyes (Chretien)
Billi Byrd (William)
Orland Gibbons

Claudio & Perrault, Umpires
(The Perrault listed as an uimpire was the brother of the more famed Charles Perrault
who is known to us for the earliset Mother Goose rhymes. Bellini, having dealt with the
Perrault Brothers some years earliers when designing the Louvre in Paris, had a low
opinion of Charles and would not play if Charles was invited. To prevent offending
anyone, da Vinci wisely invited Claudio while keeping bellini out of the initial lineup.)

(silverpoint on parchment)

Josquin de Pres Hit by Pitch

Josquin was clobbered in practice and missed the first game.
The culprit is unknown.

(charcoal on light vellum)

Out at Second

Hans Holbein's fielding was so impressive Dürer drew this lead and ink cartoon a few days after the first game. Da Vinci would allow no more than a pencil sketch until Dürer received expressed written consent to complete the drawing.

(lead and ink on vellum)

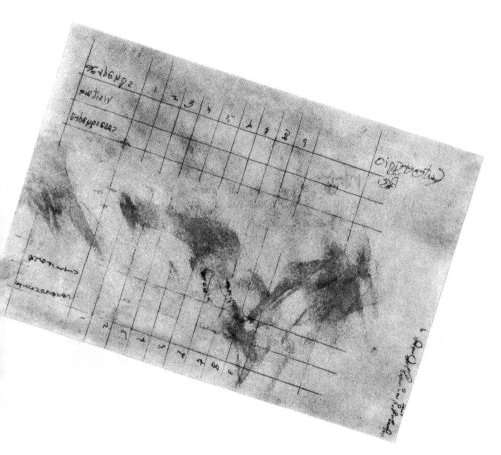

Guttenberg Scorecard

Here, Leonardo toyed with a vertical as well as a horizontal scorecard. The horizontal design was decided upon because the vertical
one was noted as being "Cinese - Dimenticare", "Chinese , Forget It".
The lower righthand corner confirms where da Vinci obtained the
idea of a nine inning game: the nine planets of the solar system (listed,
bottom to top, as "Sun, Mercury, Venus, Earth, Luna, Mars, Saturn,
Jupiter, Neptune"). In the upper right in large letters, characteristi-
cally written backwards, are the words "Gutenberg Scoreboard".
There are no surviving notes as to its dimensions.

(silverpoint on parchment)

Signalling the Catcher

The pitcher portrayed here may be Jack Grimmelshausen,
considered the Phil Niekro of his time.

Van Eyck Making Finger Placement Studies

This silverpoint sketch shows Van Eyck, Senior, studiously analyzing finger placements on a large model of a baseball. Scholars who believe the writers won the first game point to this as the main piece of evidence supporting their theory. If the artists had won, the argument goes, Van Eyck would not have sought a new pitch. An opposing view says Van Eyck was mesmerized by the game and spent the rest of his days studying da Vinci's mathematical wonder.

Lamentations of a Bad Pitcher

Author unknown. Variously attributed to Andy or Joe Gabrieli, or, the minor 16th century poet, Roberto Clemente.

(silverpoint on parchment)

Al poco giorno e al gran cerchio
d'hangbocci son giunto, lasso!
(I have come to a short day and a great
hanging curveball, alas!)

Signore, orche sara di me ne l'altro
dolce tempo novello bocci?
(Coach, what will become of me in the
sweet new baseball season?)

I'fuide nuyo iorcchi, e tornerovvi ancora
per dar de la mia luce accorri bocci!
(I was in New York, and I shall return there
again to give others delight with my fastball!)

Io son da l'aspettar ormai si picchi,
si vinta dal d'muffi e dal strada…

(I am by now so tired from pitching,
so beaten by errors and walks…)

I'ho purletto ne l'antiche boccicarte
che non ebber a sdegnio i grandi eroi
parimenti sequir DiMaggio e Alexander.
(I have, however, read in the baseball digest
that the great heroes did not scorn to respect
DiMaggio and Alexander equally.)

Signore, troppo peccai, troppo, il conosco;
Signor, piu non m'ammiro
del mio atroce picchi.
(Coach, too much I sinned, too much. I
    know;
Coach, I no longer wonder at my appalling
    pitching.)

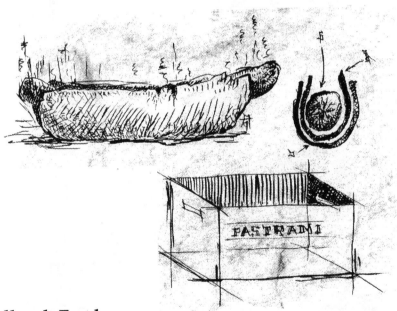

Ballpark Food

The depth of Leonardo's thinking on the game went as far as providing sustenance for the fans. The side view of the "Hot Dog" shows that he had a double-wrap of small flat bread in mind for the bun. The inscription "A.D." under the right side of the weiner was da Vinci's way of thanking the German artist Albrecht Dürer for the idea.

(silverpoint and charcoal on light vellum napkin)

Study for the Proper Way to Warm Up the Ball

Da Vinci's only known sketch for a "Dome of Baseball" which he later defaced, adding the side inscription "Stupid!" Lack of pursuit on the design lead scholars to believe it was the only invention da Vinci considered unsound.

(charcoal and silverpoint on goat vellum, the latter commonly used to tote groceries)

The Last Inning

The badly decomposed cartoon of da Vinci's "The Last Inning" with his friend Dürer as the central character.

(silverpoint on parchment)

The Celtic Claim to the Grand Old Game

Daniel Gabriel

(We got a rebuttal to Wayne Farr's theory: Daniel Gabriel believes that Leonardo da Vinci merely tinkered with a much older tradition, and presented his arguments in a subsequent issue. —Eds.)

* * * * * * *

Perhaps I should just have allowed the matter to pass, but there the article lay, open and festering on my desk top, begging to be refuted. Da Vinci invented baseball? Like Mussolini invented Ethiopia. Such Italianate chest-beating has gone on for far too long. They have claimed title for everything from the invention of perspective to the discovery of America. Isn't it time to cast aside the shroud flung by the Renaissance over everything that preceded their precious little recombinants and explore the real sources of inspiration?

Da Vinci did not invent baseball. The Celts had been playing it for at least a thousand years – possibly quite longer. That this fact should be overlooked by historians is not surprising. The entire Celtic contribution to Western life has long been undervalued and misunderstood.

I shall leave aside such potential evidence for proto-baseball as the 4th century B.C. bronze batting helmet found at the Celtic site of Amfreville in France, or the rock carvings in Val Camonica, Italy, which many scholars believe depict the onset of play between two rival tribes. But even the most rabid Renaissance enthusiast would have to recognize that from the 5th to the 12th centuries the Celts were practically the sole keepers of the flame of European civilization. The Celtic monastery of Bobbio, northeast of Genoa, was still in operation in da Vinci's day. That of St. Gall, just over the border in Switzerland, remains intact today – and features a bronze carving in the southeast transept that depicts two warrior figures with leather, fingered "shields" and a small sphere being tossed between them.

Suffice it to say that Dante, da Vinci, and the scion of all the DiMaggios had Celtic presence on their own soil long before they ever decided to choose up sides. But what of the Celtic homeland? Surely, there, would be ongoing evidence of baseball interest.

In fact, there is such evidence, though much of it is now overlaid by local parochialism and the availability of stout. Each of the Celtic branches has swung off in different directions from the original tree.

The Scots, who were much taken with the accoutrements of the game, eventually abandoned the overall concept to concentrate just on the toting of equipment. Obsessed as they are with strength and weight (who else would call for a "pint of heavy" in a pub?) they gradually increased the heft of the bat and ball and transformed the game into a contest of sheer brute force. Still played at Highland Games, the degenerative form of Scottish baseball occurs in "tossing the caber" (an enormous wooden bat, twice the length of a man, which is flung as far as possible after a simulated called third strike) and in the throwing of an iron ball (the "hammer") to as great a distance as the arm allows.

The Irish were faced with a different set of circumstances. Wood, for one, was in extremely short supply. Bats became valuable, almost totemic, objects. Each player used his own – and only his own, often saving it for years and handing it on down to his son. It was said that an Irishman could hit so long as his bat still had a knob – or even if it was only a knob. The expression still heard today in Ireland "How's your knob?" stems from this belief.

The other uniquely Irish tactic occurred in the infamous "cutting the turf," where wily groundskeepers would slice long lines of peat out of the outfield, leaving a gaping trench which could be leaped by one's own fielders (who knew the location) but often proved the literal downfall of opponents. Many of these local turf-cut fields can still be seen, particularly in central Ireland.

However, it is the Welsh who took baseball closest to their hearts. Many of their bardic chants, with their long name lists and rhythmically repeating statistics, recount the exploits of past batting masters and would-be legends of the mound.

But in Wales, unlike the other Celtic outposts, the game has not died out. Few people in America may be aware of its popularity, but BBC Wales carries live accounts of the annual championships every August and accompanying pub brawls attest to its following. The game differs in many respects from the American version, most notably in the use of upright stakes for bases. These stakes (or a runner attempting to reach one) must be struck with the ball in order to record an out. Similar in construction to a modern cricket wicket, which has three vertical legs topped by a horizontal one, these Welsh base poles provide an intriguing link with the Celts' druidic past.

While many observers feel that the use of bat and ball stems from the ancient sport of hurling (still mightily popular in Ireland, by the by), the base poles seem to mark the first divergence of baseball, as such, into a separate sport.

Research conducted in recent years – principally by Matthew McCortney O'Brien – has led to speculation that the long-mysterious circles of standing stones in Celtic territories from the Orkney Islands to Brittany are, in fact, baseball fields with permanent stone base poles set in place. Large, spacious fields with smaller slabs, such as Avebury, are likely to have been real "hitter's parks," while Stonehenge, with its massive, all-but-enclosed monoliths, was specifically constructed with an eye toward pitching duels. The difficulty of hitting a ball clear of the upright slabs would be greatly increased, and the ease of fielders nailing an out made equally easier. If it is true, as O'Brien believes, that Stonehenge was the site of the annual All-Celtic Baseball Championships during Midsummer's Day, it is no surprise to learn that gatherings there went on for days – it might take that long to score a run.

While it is tempting to diverge further and discuss characteristics of some of the other ball parks, such as the idyllic Maeshowe on Orkney, with its abrupt green swath of grass rising in left field, or the long, almost rectangular Quimper Field in Brittany, I prefer to break off here.

Cricket, hurling, bocci ball or rounders: call them what you will, all are mere variations on the great, eternal game. And I say to the author of *The True Origins of Baseball*, is it really any wonder that the first two great strategists of the game in America were Celtic gentlemen – namely Messrs. John McGraw and Corneluis McGillicuddy?

I rest my case.

Support for the Celts

(Matthew McCortney O'Brien wrote us supporting the Celtic origins of Baseball. –Eds.)

* * * * * * *

To the Editors:

I want to thank Daniel Gabriel (*The Celtic Claim to the Grand Old Game*, **MRB**, Vol. 7, No. 3) for his kind mention of my research in the fledgling field of archeosportology. It's gratifying to me that others now recognize that the diversity of and differences between our American ballparks mimic an ancient tradition, for Wrigley Field is as different from the Metrodome as Stonehenge is from the vast dolmen fields of Rathgáirech. I believe the megalithic sports sites of Europe still offer a wealth of material for further research.

Mr. Gabriel also cites the practice of turf-cutting as an early example of the abuse of home-field advantage. He and your readers may be interested to learn of the recent discovery of an outfielder, found remarkably preserved after centuries, in a peat bog in Co. Kerry, Ireland. His playing position was determined from the size of this crude hog-skin glove, the glare-reducing blackening on his cheekbones, the size and development of the legs from bog sprinting and also from the angle of the knees and callousing of the lateral patella from the extended periods of waiting, half-crouched, with hands on knees in anticipation of fielding opportunities. The poor devil was found on his back, just as he had fallen (as victim possibly of malicious turf-cutting), the tattered remains of a lumpy leather "ball" clutched in the glove of his victoriously-raised arm.

Not mentioned by Mr. Gabriel was my lesser-known theory on the importance of numerology in the early sports rites. Portentous things were thought to happen in threes. Of course one of the most celebrated mysteries of Christian faith is the Trinity, three individual, yet inseparable powers. Even in pre-Christian pagan times the number three was important and nine represented the trinity of trinities, or three squared, the "perfect plural" – a genuinely mystical number. After the advent of Christianity the church continued to foster the rites and helped lend new meaning to some of the old beliefs and practices. Of course the threes became intrinsic to the game of baseball; three strikes, three outs; nine players, nine innings. In the Kyrie Eleison of the Latin Mass we have three bells and a striking of the breast three times, signifying unworthiness, contrition and absolution. This sense of hope and salvation was carried over to baseball, for even after three strikes or three outs one has yet another chance to come to bat. After nine innings there's hope for extra innings, or there's always tomorrow – or next year. There's always hope for the faithful.

A 12th century fragment of the *Táin bó Cuailnge* describes a rite performed by a celebrant named O'Casseigh at a sacrificial stone set before a "gathering of men." The ritual involved the swinging of "the knob" (as mentioned by Mr. Gabriel). In apparent random order, a celebrant would expectorate, grasp at the dirt, rub his palms and tug at his groin (in a gesture thought to signify man's vain hope for immortality through progeneration) and after he had made the sign of the cross, he would approach the sacrificial stone to make his offering. A truly great offering might assure a celebrant a place in the bardic tales – the ongoing history of the race as preserved in oral tradition. The following translated passage is taken from this fragment of the *Táin* :

> I seem alone against all men
> And endure the watchful roar.
> I prepare myself again to battle
> The sphere that grows
> With its fierce approach. . . .
> I slash out with all my might –
> My knob smites only wind.
> And "Three!" they shout
> Their voices full of bitter victory,
> The moment theirs.
> But we shall [be up?] again
> And I will have vengeance
> Before this day's sun has rested.

But in his final offering O'Casseigh again fails at the sacrificial stone. The narrative changes to an omniscient point of view and closes by noting the pervasive gloom of the community:

> Somewhere the sun gives warmth
> And lights the lives of men:
> The wind plays sweet music
> For a laughing, feasting assemblage.
> But [there was] no joy in Mhuidvil [?]
> For great O'Casseigh has struck not.

I believe further research may yield even greater proof to support Mr. Gabriel's position on the "Celtic Claim."

Respectfully,
Matthew McCortney O'Brien

Renewal

Paul Weinman

Each year we'd come back
and the field would still be there.
Sure, the baselines looked worn.
Tired, grass turned grey. Brown.
The batter's box, sullen.
Mound, slope-shouldered old.
But it only needs a birthday ball,
a solid fwak! of first bat –
awkward lunge to the left –
Got it! and that snap to second
from third over to the initial sack
and back to my hand with its sting.
Smell of grass stains
fingering springtime balls.

Opening Day Reports: Chicago, 1981

Philip LaZebnik

(In the spring of 1981 we wrote to friends and family across the country and asked them to attend Opening Day and and then write us a letter — a report on the game from the fan's eye point of view. What follows is a selection of those reports from our first five years. The familial tie is well represented, and our only defense is that before a magazine starts to pay its writers, nepotism may be an editor's best ally.

Met Stadium, the friendly old Erector-set ballpark in Bloomington, Minnesota, passed from view during the course of these years. Our magazine was closely allied with the noble Save the Met organization; its leader Julian Empson will appear later in these pages. Save the Met members ultimately lost the battle against indoor baseball in Minneapolis, but their *esprit de corps* lives on in outdoor baseball tours and in the **MRB's** editorial columns. –Eds.)

* * * * * * *

Of course the Cubs lost their opening-day game. Well, "lost" is perhaps a bit too active a word to use for the particular emotional state the Cubs evinced at Wrigley Field on April 9th. Passive, resigned to their fate, nihilistic – the Cubs had the makings of a good, working, Oriental religion out there on the diamond, but the road to nirvana is not the road to the pennant and so the Cubs lost, by a pathetic, limp 2-0, to the New York Mets.

None of that, however, had any dampening influence on the notoriously blithe and otherwordly Cub fans, many of whom seemed to have achieved nirvana already. Just as Australia broke away from the Asian land mass millions of years ago and developed unique oddities of nature such as the kangaroo and the duckbilled platypus, Wrigley Field, isolated for so many years from the mainstream of baseball, has evolved a new species. For instance, the Cub Fan is autistic with schizophrenic traits. That is, he or she seems oblivious to events occurring in the outside world. Surely, this is nature's kindly way of preserving sanity. As tragedy surges and ebbs down on the field, the Cub fan sits contentedly, smiling and basking in a euphoria which explorers from the outside world can hardly explain in rational terms. The Will to win is alien to the true Cub fan who not only expects to lose – this is mere realism, after all – but, deep in the fan's heart, he or she *wants* the Cubs to lose. A pennant or a World Series victory would totally sever the fan's last tenuous links to reality and leave him or her a vegetable.

On opening day, when Florence Henderson was introduced and sang the

National Anthem, the crowd, I fear, did not receive her to their bosom; indeed, they seemed to find the very concept of "Florence Henderson" amusing and absurd. I was ashamed. When some gentleman took the microphone down on the field and asked for a moment of silence to pray for America and her convalescent President, the crowd seemed to be taking this opportunity to discuss urgent matters they had put off for days. To my horror, Wally Phillips, a local radio celebrity, stepped up to the microphone and asked for another moment of silence for President Reagan. I had not given Phillips enough credit, however: He made it a very short moment. So short that the crowd caught on and laughed. Wally learned his lesson, though, and next asked the crowd to cry out, "Get well, Jim Brady!" and they shouted it out lustily.

Even before the game actually started, my companions and I realized one of the of the hazards of sitting in the lower grandstands: a constant shower of beer dripped from the girders above our seats. However, we were seated below and behind the press boxes, and all through the game various celebrities came trooping across the walkway. Governor (Big Jim) Thompson made an appearance at the bottom of the third. Florence Henderson followed shortly after. Was it an assignation? Perhaps a *ménage á trois* with Jack Brickhouse?

Down on the baseball diamond, the only excitement occurred each time Dave Kingman came to bat. When the crowd stood up and hissed and booed, Kingman would tip his cap and then strike out and the crowd applauded and cheered. Other than that, not much happened down there. The real show, as always, was in the choice selection of Cub Fan Types. There were the Young Loudmouths behind us. When Dave Kingman made his first entrance, one of them shouted, "Get a real job, Kingman." By the seventh inning, this witticism began to pall on me. Sitting in front of us were the archetypical Elderly Couple. They watched the game in moody silence, and then left as morosely as they had come. The Large, Quarreling Family sat to our left, the young Rising Professional With His Blonde Date to our right, and, not too far in the distance, lolled the inevitable Big Fat Slob Who Takes His Shirt Off Even Though It's 40 Degrees With a Wind Chill Factor of Minus 20.

Eventually, and finally, the game ended. The happy crowd swarmed out of Wrigley Field into the surrounding streets and yards and alleys. As I walked the two blocks home, it occurred to me that opening day at Wrigley Field must be pretty close to opening day in Ancient Athens: The crowd knew they were going to see a tragedy. They knew that down there in the arena the gods were going to get angry, and valiant heroes would bite the dust, and everything was going to end in death and destruction. In the stands, the vendors were shouting. "Col' beer! Col' beer!" and those crazy guys from the gymnasium were throwing pot shards down on the chorus, and that fat slob Kallimedes had taken his robe off and was trying to stand on his head, and all was right with the world.

Minneapolis, 1981

Ken LaZebnik

Got a letter from Missouri:

". . . all the trees have burst forth simultaneously in full greenery; forsythia is bright yellow; daffodils are in almost every yard and a bunch is collected on our dining room table to reflect the sunlight . . ."

Got a letter from Kansas:

"Spring is here, with blustery winds, trailing golden willows, green grass, bulbs blooming, yellow forsythia. A person ought to start in Texas and follow spring all the way to Canada."

Spring is coming, heading north. This morning, April 9, I went out to Met Stadium at 10 to buy bleacher seats. By noon the parking lot is already jammed with tailgaters: It's the last outdoor Opening Day in Minnesota (the Dome opens next spring).

Into the Met, left field bleachers. Kids with gloves are catching HRs from the A's batting practice. The turf at the Met seems to be in its usual crummy shape: remnants of football markings, some small torn-up patches, strips where grass was laid.

The field clears, the loudspeaker announces something indistinguishable as 12 new Chevy cars drive around the field.

A marching band forms out in deep center field and, drums beating, marches in to the infield for a ceremony. A lone A's player does calisthenics – consciously or not? – in time to the beat.

The loudspeaker garbles something again, and a guy at a mike in center field sings *God Bless America*. Everyone stands up and shuts up. A friend says, "Why are we standing? This is neither the National Anthem nor the Hallelujah Chorus." Everybody cheers at the end, killing the effect of the Star Spangled Banner.

Friend sings to the anthem:

"O beautiful, for specious lies,

For micro-waves of grain.

For mountain condominiums,

And ski bums on cocaine."

Ready to play ball, Koos on the mound, then a delay as fans are booted out of center field bleachers, which have been closed to make a black background for hitting. Right field bleachers are filling – the place is packed.

Game starts briskly! Koos and Norris are pitching swiftly and well, although Koos starts getting the ball up. The A's third base coach is Clete Boyer, prompting discussion of who was third Boyer brother. Someone suggests it was Charles Boyer.

Game progresses swiftly first 3 and 2/3 innings. Then the weather turns foul. Winds rise. Overcast. People shiver in T-shirts. Koos lets in two runs.

Works his way out of trouble in fifth. Weather continues bad, Twins score in fifth, but A's answer in sixth with a run. Game bogs down. Twins can't hit. Gets cold. Lose.

But we left with memories of: wind; clouds, sun in and out; shadow of Koosman on the mound; cleat marks on the turf. A hot dog wrapper lifting higher and higher in the wind, like it'll never land.

Opening Day next year won't be the same.

San Francisco, 1981

Sharon Walton

San Francisco is famous for making the most of minor holidays. Every city of course goes green on St. Patrick's Day, but only in San Francisco is Halloween a whole day of festivity – where your mailman is Bozo the Clown, and your bank teller is Kermit the Frog. Needless to say, it's not a conducive atmosphere in which to conduct business.

One should also understand that most business in San Francisco is conducted not behind a desk, but over a cocktail, on the golf course, or in the box seats of Candlestick Park. Opening Day of the San Francisco Giants is another de facto holiday. In fact, if a bomb had fallen on Candlestick on April 9, among the 54,520 in attendance, it's very likely that many of the city's chief executives (including the mayor) would have perished, leaving the San Francisco business world in shambles.

Businesses spend lots of money to attract and keep happy their large corporate customers – such clients as Levi Strauss, Crown Zellerbach (they produce most of the toilet paper and paper towels in the U.S.), and Castle & Cooke (Dole Pineapple). One company hosted a tailgate picnic for its favored clients. Let's look in detail at one particular company's expenses for the day.

The tickets to the game itself were reserved seats costing $5.00 (Actually, they weren't very good seats – beneath the bleachers and totally out of the sun). They were purchased as part of a package from one of the largest private clubs in the city. This package included the baseball ticket, box lunch, bus transportation to and from the game, and drinks served aboard the bus. The price of this deal: approximately $20.00 per person.

Even with all the Bloody Marys you can drink and a carefully prepared lunch of chicken, finger sandwiches, deviled eggs, and an apple, what is a baseball game without hot dogs and beer? For those snacks, figure $25.00 per per customer. Therefore, the cost of entertaining four customers (with their four respective hosts) comes to approximately $260. A little more than your average fan might spend at a game, but it's all tax deductible, and it's all good business.

It was the fifth largest crowd in Giant history, and the second largest ever for opening day. The San Diego Padres scored in the first inning, the Giants tied it in the seventh, and the Padres won it in the twelfth. It was basically a pitcher's duel. John Curtis (ex-Giant) went 10 innings for the Padres, giving up only 7 hits and no walks. Vida Blue started for the Giants, and lasted 7 innings allowing four hits, two walks, and striking out six. Greg Minton then pitched four shutout innings; Al Holland then gave up three runs and ended the game.

Friday, of course, was back to normal. Giant euphoria is very short lived (the Giants lost again Friday – and Saturday), and now San Franciscans can settle back for a long season of looking forward to next season. As for being back to business, well, in San Francisco, business is rarely conducted on a Friday – that's when you get ready to drive up to Tahoe to ski.

St. Louis, 1982

Ephram St. Dirx

That was *it*.

I felt a little blasphemous attending a game on the day after Good Friday, the last day of Lent. But then I realized that I suffered the whole 172 minutes. That's enough to satisfy even *my* church.

For one thing, it was too cold. I wore a flannel shirt, a wool sweater and a peacoat, and sat rubbing my fingers. For another thing, I couldn't get seats in the bleachers. All True Americans sit in bleachers; I was herded into the colorless general admission.

But there are other disadvantages of modern baseball. The turf, for instance, looks fake. It has vague, dry tracks on it, and is not even a true grass-green (more like viridiana). Moreover, non-wooden seats, having no clatter, make for a listless seventh-inning-stretch song. Worse, the new stretch type suits make the players look chubby.

Unfortunately, we arrived just as the Opening Day festivities stopped, so we had missed the marching bands and the motorcade: the best part. When we heard the Cardinals entering the field, we tried to rush up the honey-combed walkways of the stadium – but were everywhere impeded by people massing in front of food vendors.

(Why were *they* in no hurry? Throughout the game I noticed a steady flow of people going out and coming back with food. A ball game doesn't last much longer than a movie – yet you never see movie patrons slipping out several times in two hours to return with pounds of food.)

The Cardinals were playing the Pirates. It was appropriate on this Holy Saturday that Whitey Herzog harrowed hell in his search for a decent pitcher. An Easter-egg assortment passed before us: Mura, LaPoint, Rincon, Ramsey, Littell, and Bair. By the third inning the Pirates led 5-0. Now was the time for a Busch.

Busch stadium is, not surprisingly, a beer-conscious place. Two billboards constantly urged us to "Treat yourself like a Most Valuable Player" by filling up with Bud. Another diagnosed the cause of the pitcher problem: "Busch – it's in the Cards."

The game dragged on. The billboard wished Happy Birthdays to various attendant fans, welcomed students, greeted a couple from Swaziland. One message offered "many tanks" to a Chevrolet man for his help in the motorcade – persuading me that I'd missed a truly spectacular and patriotic motorcade – until they changed tanks to thanks.

The organ music was not compelling. The organist led the traditional duddle la dah da-dah charge and played a new threefold cheer: the "dit-dat widdum-waddam bottom chew" part that precedes "and they swam and they swam right over the dam" in the song. The crowd did not know how to respond.

The game got older. Some more runs were scored by both teams; vagrant plastic bags blew about the field. That was IT. No renewed faith in St. Louis, baseball or America. It was such a waste, this game! That's why I could bring myself to write about it.

Mental Tenacity: Boston, 1982

Rob LaZebnik

It was cold and brisk that day. It was partly cloudy that day. It was the Red Sox against the White Sox that day. But, more importantly, it was Fenway home opener that day, and the spectators, hungry for real sport, knew that the game was to be won on shrewd mental tenacity.

The players knew it as well. On the field before the game, Jim Rice nervously stepped over to Yaz and, in a hushed voice, said, "Yaz, I can't remember the last line." Yaz replied testily, "To love that well which thou must leave ere long." Tension was also high in the White Sox dugout as Greg Luzinski quizzed a weary Ron LeFlore over Petrarchan poetic conceits. At last, however, the game began, with Dotson pitching for Chicago and Torrez for Boston.

In the bottom of the first, Kemp of the White Sox cleverly yelled to Torrez (who was winding up), "Hey, Mike, 'Much have I traveled in the realms of gold,'" at which the pitcher was so flustered he gave up a single. Torrez quickly recovered, however, and threw well for five straight innings, allowing no runs. Dotson was equal to the task, as he also pitched five scoreless innings. Finally, in the sixth, Yaz stepped to the plate with two out, pointed to the right field bleachers, and proclaimed, "You will see a new planet swim into your ken." His prophecy proved true; as he touched home, the Red Sox jumped ahead 1-0.

The White Sox, however, soon retaliated, scoring two runs in the sixth and one in the seventh. Boston had flickering hopes in the ninth when Glenn Hoffman scored on a Rich Gedman double, making the score 3-2. But when Rick Miller walked to the platter, with one on and two out, devious Chicago catcher Carlton Fisk taunted him with lines of Falstaff from **Henry IV, Part I**: "'S'blood, you starveling, you eel-skins, you dried neat's tongue..." Miller fouled two fast balls off behind him. Badly-shaken, he could not recall Prince Hal's replys; he listened desperately as Fisk's tirade continued: "You bull's pizzle, you stock-fish!" Miller fouled off the next tree pitches. Finally, Fisk switched parts and, settling down to give the sign, called Miller "This sanguine coward, this bed-presser, this horse-back-breaker, this huge hill of flesh!" Needless to say, the trembling Red Sox outfielder watched helplessly as a Barojas curve sailed over the plate for strike three and a lost game.

In the Boston clubhouse after the game, manager Ralph Houk wearily shook his head and shouted to his players, "You looked like a bunch of romantics out there," and proceeded to toss them all copies of *The Sun Also Rises*. On the other side, however, White Sox manager Tony LaRussa was jubilant. "Atta way, boys," he called, "we've shown them who the high mimetic mode heroes really are!"

So the sun curled down toward the skyline that day. And the Beacon Hill sitting rooms beckoned that night. The players packed up their equipment to walk cat-like out into the fog-filled evening, to journey through half-deserted streets, to turn iambs over in their minds, and to flex their pectorals.

Baltimore, 1982

George Kaplan

The noted poet/first baseman Eugene McCarthy once said: "It will be a good season." As always, he was right.

Opening day in Bawlmer (or Ballimurr to some purists) is refreshingly old-fashioned. Nervous rookies strive to look cool. The proud mayor primps to toss the ceremonial first pitch. Orioles' owner Edward Bennet Williams could have bagged the Chief Justice or even RR himself for this chore, but this quintessential Washington insider – counsel to the **Washington Post**, Richard Helms, and Joe McCarthy – has absorbed the facts of Baltimore life.

Once an International League park, Memorial Stadium is a fan's delight. A nondescript mass of steel and concrete set in a blue collar borough of row houses and saloons, it has nothing in common with the architectural banalities of KingMetroAstro-Dome or Three Veterans Riverfront Coliseum. The groundskeeper is an artist whose masterwork is immune to climate or base hit bunt attempts; only the loutish NFL Colts can harm his daily *chef d'oeuvre*, but not until September. And where else can you get Chesapeake crabcakes, see trees and houses beyond the center field fence, and learn an obscure regional patois?

Whatever happens on the field in 1982 may pale before the saga of Earl Weaver, who says "Those — jukeboxes" the players carry about are driving him into retirement. Owner of a hair dryer, graduate of a course in disco, and a convicted drunk driver, he's certainly tried to come to terms with the 1980s. Down deep, though, Weaver is a throwback: an obscene but meticulous super-achiever who keeps his distance ("We're on speaking terms") from his players. No ambiguity about umpires, though. "Weaver," says Jim Evans, "is baseball's Son of Sam." Evans, replies Weaver, is "definitely incompetent," Hank Morganweck is "the blind one," and Marty Springstead, a long-time nemesis, isn't "smart enough to remember the rule book."

The opener was thoroughly predictable. Wonder Man Sammy Stewart, robbed of the 1981 ERA title on a technicality, relieved a chilled Nicaraguan, Dennis Martinez, in the fifth and allowed only a Brett homer and a hit or two the rest of the way. The O's bopped four long ones, including a Murray slam, a three-runner by Dan Ford, and a two-run shot by Cal Ripken, the Birds' next superstar. So the vital signs look good. Dag Hammarskjold wrote: "Never, for the sake of peace and quiet, deny your own experience or convictions." Both suggest another vintage season for the classiest team in baseball.

Opening Night: St. Louis, 1984

Paul Davis

The rites of spring, the annual rituals under full moon as with ancient Druids and the spill of blood to wed winter to warmer mornings, and young men with clumps of hay ablaze on pitchforks running fields to dance past great bonfires lit to love the sun and ward off drought and barrenness in cattle and to stir fertility in herds and homes. Spring as in woodland frolics of old Celts adorned in sweet greenery up the valleys of the Rhine and Irish young bloods dancing defiance at winter long ago circling Maypoles shouting and ajuice with hope, and later Pilgrims outside Plymouth singing other gods than dogma in wooded glade of Merry Mount. So in technical America of late report, the United States of tax reform and annual debt and Gross National Product, the coming each year of baseball some cool evening halfway into April, the arrival of opening night, as this spring, April edging on toward May under moon full and silvery delicious, the start again in St. Louis, the Pirates of Pittsburgh and the Cardinals at Busch Stadium on Astroturf resplendent and in its newness green as grass real and rural which it isn't.

At the beginning, the bands festooned and blaring across center field catch the eye as they and that in military maneuvers contrast strangely with the moon aloof and cooling where it dangles like a silver watch fob above the cathedral arches of the stadium rising above the din of seated sections, reserved and general admission, gradually filling up.

Then to the microphone steps Jack Buck, radio and television personality, as they say, his hair silver as the moon, his fame almost as great on a local basis, his mission, to introduce the Pirates and the Cardinals. As he does so, the same Jack Buck doing the same introductions is projected on the mammoth television screen above right center field, as to mind comes technology, the way in the age of instant replay and multi reproductions, live, one time only is not enough as, if you have the equipment, use it, and we are indeed not able to trust the real thing, as Jack Buck magnified is somehow more impressive than Jack Buck in the flesh, as we watch him and watch the picture of him, twice we tell ourselves, or we are told, someway more assuring.

Before long the Cardinals come out of the right field gate encased in white automobiles, convertibles all alike, as if from the same agency, one new shiny chassis to each player. Mr. Busch, the owner of the Cardinals, is at the head, driven by a young driver who looks much pleased, Mr. Busch under a big red cowboy hat ballooning above his aging face. Whitey Herzog, manager of the

Cardinals, whose face never seems to age, is second and then the players one by one like gladiators at a Roman circus come waving around the outfield cinder track, while the Pirates (the lions) stand at the mouth of their cave bored and bemused, not quite able to believe what they see but having to believe it, the show business baseball has come to. Then back of home plate as their names are said, the Cardinals come ducking up out of their chariots like again high school boys a little embarrassed, as soon all of them – the Cardinals and the Pirates – stand along the foul lines, the Pirates toward third base, the Cardinals toward first, lined up awkward and overpaid before the mostly lower paid others who cheer nevertheless.

The game itself is a pitching duel, LaPoint and Candelaria 1 to 1 until the seventh when Ozzie Smith homers into the left field seats for 3 and that makes it 4 to 1 and that is it.

Soon after that the game ends and the crowd, many young, some very drunk on the only brew sold in the park, make their way braying and like animals in heat out and down the ramps, some belligerent, some playfully happy, as in the parking garage they blow their horns in a compulsive hue. And to mind come Druids young as these and as spirited, though maybe with religious vision more intact, though maybe not, dashing through fields with flaming forks of hay where cattle scatter beneath moon as round as this in time that seems to circle more than going anywhere else.

Chicago White Sox, 1985

Judy Aronson

April 19

I should write the date more than once to make myself believe that miracles do occur. The Sox have won before on Opening Day without winning the season, but – it's April 19 and it's eighty-for-god's-sake-five degrees at game time. And Britt Burns has struck out seven (including Jim Rice three times),and walked only one, and went nine innings, and of the six hits he did give up, two were to Buckner.

To start at the very beginning, it was warm, with a balmy breeze when I entered the ballpark. The first problem was to decide what to eat. I decided to go with tradition on Opening Day and walked past the new roast beef/corned beef stand to the kosher hot dog lady. Now this is not my tradition mind you, but America's. I personally eat tacos 99% of the time. But it was Opening Day.

Opening Day ceremonies were standard except for the offensive invitation to Illinois' Republican Cub-loving governor to throw out the first ball rather than Chicago's Democrat life-long Sox fan mayor, who being black might have been more offensive to our redneck blue collar true believers. I personally felt baseball loyalty should come before race, but that just makes me a member of another minority.

The first inning said it all: Rudy Law caught Wade Boggs' foul fly like I haven't seen done since Minnie caught one in the old timers game in 1983. Then Burns walked Evans (only walk), and then called strike three on Rice and Easler. And that was the ball game.

In the bottom of the first, Rudy Law (yes, Rudy Law) hit a soft home run to right (last season he got six home runs total). Baines struck out, the only out he made all day. And guess who (remember we're playing Boston), hit a two-run homer, a shot that Rice just ignored? Who? Carlton Fisk.

And so it went. Britt Burns mowed 'em down, and the Sox hit home runs (Baines, Salazar), or only triples (Walker). It was a lovely day at the ballpark. April, April, April, April. I think.

Home Opener: Busch Memorial Stadium, 1985

Jack LaZebnik

We are high, near the roof – last-minute seats – but the view is grand, rich in color and line. The Expos are warming up: easy tosses, wrist-flips, playful misses, the hollow crack! in the batting cage – every batter looks like a slugger.

Six-forty and most of the seats still empty. The batting cage off, the waterhose out, the men raking and smoothing the dirt at the bases. A high-school band walks onto the field (not like the noise and glare of a football opening); it plays a few nice tunes, makes simple formations – almost quiet, subdued. It retires in the same manner: restrained.

Seven o'clock, Jack Buck out there at a microphone to make announcements. "At three o'clock this afternoon – " but the crowd roars; it already knows: Ozzie Smith has signed his contract. Buck names the Expo players; then a funny "motorcade" of new Cameros comes onto the field, Ozzie does his back flip (a pleasure!), the soft moment of tossing the ball around before the game begins.

And it begins! Forsch looks good on the mound, throws strikes, makes 'em ground out and fly out. In the second, Andy Van Slyke hits a beauty into right center; he stretches for three – almost, almost, but a stinging throw and he's out. The crowd changes its roar into a groan – but then, as Andy, his head down, slouches toward the dugout, the roar and applause come up again: He tried, he tried.

The "wave" starts: from the murmur to a roar, strange sound of cheering for no reason; we watch it come – a distraction, a nuisance; it breaks the rhythm of the game for us.

Up to the fourth, a no-hitter. Someone behind us mentions it. "There you go," his companion says. "You've jinxed it." True: a hit. But no score.

Behind us: "All life is like baseball – sweatin' out the competition. You wait till somebody makes a mistake."

Fifth inning, Forsch going along steadily. Law, of the Expos, slashes one out of Ozzie's reach. "Ozzie didn't even try. Give 'em two million dollars and he don't try anymore." Gullickson, the Expos pitcher, gets a single. "Whitey! Whitey, are you in there?" But Whitey leaves Forsch alone. Ozzie catches one nicely. "Ah, for two million you're supposed to make 'em."

Fifth: Tommy Herr whacks one: two runs in! Ozzie makes a great slide home! Terry Pendleton – a hit! Three runs in!

In the sixth, Ozzie dives and scoops, tosses to second: one motion. "That was worth a million right there."

Jack Clark (oh, how they applaud *him* each time – a slugger, at last!) gets his first Cardinal hit. Brian Harper (who's he?) bats for Steve Braun (who started, did well): a double. Andy Van Slyke up. "Andy's not aggressive enough. He's going to get traded if he don't do something' soon." He scores Clark; Harper goes to third. When Lavalliere sends one high to right, Harper crushes the catcher (a flying sprawl): safe! safe!

And then, then, Ozzie! Home run! Ozzie! Ozzie! Six to one!

In the field, two outs, two men on base for the Expos, shot! into right, Andy van Slyke dives, dives, a diving catch! Not aggressive enough, huh?

Behind us: "Look at her. She ain't got no idea of what's going on. She'd done her nails all during the game and already figured out three places to go after. She don't know who's playing." But he's talking over a hit, a steal (out at second), a strike-out.

Our throats are sore, voices hoarse. People start to leave during the ninth; the stadium empties the way it filled. Forsch made it all the way through; the Cardinals slap and hug each other – what a pleasure! We don't even mind the pack slowly circling down to street level, the suffocating crawl of cars out of the park arena, the long wait in traffic before Route 70 comes up and we can find the freedom of the fast lane to Columbia.

It's the Season Again:
Opening Day, Yankee Stadium, 1985

Ken LaZebnik

I stepped just inside a cave-like ramp entrance. On the field below, a military precision parachutist had just landed on the third base side of the pitcher's mound. He had a Chicago pennant and thus helped to identify that these were the Chicago White Sox who ranged along the third base line. The Yankees were then introduced singly. There were cheers for old favorites (Yogi) and boos for the goats of the opening road trip (e.g., Yogi's son Dale). As they filed onto the first base line, another sky diver helpfully floated down with a pennant telling these were the New York Yankees. The politicos present said a few words and received their traditional boos.

As Robert Merrill (not booed) sang the National Anthem, another sky diver floated down toward an X laid out behind second base. He held an American flag. He hit the target precisely, the crowd erupting with cheers mid-song. In true American fashion, we were able to make even the singing of the National Anthem a competition, and we won.

The next task at hand was to "throw out the first ball." Sometimes celebrities do it – the second game at Shea Stadium this year was christened by Rodney Dangerfield. Baseball Commissioner Bowie Kuhn had ruled that Mickey Mantle and Willie Mays, working at casinos, were ineligible to work for a major league team. Mantle could have thrown out the first pitch last year, but to the public at large he was exiled from the House that Ruth built. This spring the new commissioner, Peter Ueberroth, declared the old ban lifted, in much the same way medieval popes would lift ex-communications.

So here it was, Opening Day 1985, and there was a deep roar from the crowd as a film showed on the large screen in right field: Mickey Mantle in his playing days. At the end the announcer said, "Ladies and gentlemen, to throw out the first ball, welcome back Mickey Mantle." And from the Yankee dugout, he came, dressed in a sport coat, looking heavier, but still graceful. He stood alone on the pitcher's mound, the entirety of Yankee Stadium afoot, cheering him. He stood there like a pitcher with no one to pitch to. Then he jumped a bit, as two sky divers, one perched on the other's shoulders, circled out of the blue above him. They had a banner that read, "Welcome Back Number 7," and it was just as well their chute crumpled over and they had trouble getting their sign out.

Roger Maris was announced as the bearer of the ball that Mantle would throw. Maris has born the peculiar onus of being the man to break Babe Ruth's single season home run record who was not Mickey Mantle. Because Maris butted his way into history, fans always disliked him. Even the league president could not accept the reality of what he had done, and put an asterisk by his record. In choosing not to ignore Maris, the Yankees reinforced his image as second banana. Maris, from ten feet away, faked throwing a bullet at Mantle. Mantle ducked. Mantle and Maris hugged; Mick took the ball from the ball bearer and tossed it to Butch Wynegar.

Most of the people in my section missed a good ball game. People around me spent lots of time trying to buy beer. Handing money down a row to a vendor is a sacred tradition of trust at a ball game. The fellow below me gave a teenager who was scooting by him a twenty dollar bill and told him to pick up some beer. The kid came back, with the twenty – no brew to be had.

From behind me came the reassuring commentary of fandom as the game unfolded:

"I can't stand a pitcher who has to rely on being cute for the whole season. (With disgust) Look at his velocity."

"Come on, Willie, get the ball out of your mitt."

"Griffey – look, they give him a lot of line."

"Dale Berra – you won't see two years out of this guy. If Yogi gets canned, he's gone the next week."

"Here's another one to die with this year – Ed Whitson – another piece of shit."

"Get this bum outta here. He's scattered a nice eight hits in four innings. Get this bum outta here. Get in gas can Dale Murray."

"Let's see – oh and two. How can he beat you oh and two?"

The outfield fences at Yankee Stadium have been moved in this year. They look far more generic now, following the same semi-circle that characterized the newer multi-purpose stadiums: in an age that conspires against individuality, another blow struck for conformity. The distant vista from my seat connected with the past more than the interior of the stadium – subway trains rolled by; dirty brown apartments with fire escapes looked unchanged in fifty years. A faded sign on a building beyond right field: "Buy DiNoto's bread and rolls. Long on Flavor. Free win tickets Yankees home games."

Chatter in the late innings:

"It's nice to see someone in this area watching the ballgame."

(Baylor caught stealing by a mile, protests he eluded the tag.) "Automatic. Sit down, Don. Siddown. Automatic baseball. Whatssa guy gotta put in your chops?!"

Righetti, on in relief, brings the crowd to life with his overpowering fastball. Griffey makes a great catch to rob Kittle in the top of the ninth, Don Baylor hits a home run.

Cheers. Late afternoon shadows. Crowds of people walking down wide ramps. Vendors of hats and inflatable bats. It's the season again.

Opening Day '86

E. Wright Blodgett

(The year we began publication, we received a letter from E. Wright Blodgett of Kalamazo, Michigan. We've never met Mr. Blodgett, but over the years we've come to treasure his peculiar correspondence: the creation of a sort of baseball word salad, peppered with references to baseball history, Greek mytholoy, puns, and personal reminiscence. Usually "Blodgett's Blotter" is a letter; this time he wrote an essay on Opening Day. — Eds.)

* * * * * * *

"The inviting green cucumber has most everybody's number." (anon.)

Just a few wandering thoughts to point the way to a few wanderers. Mother nature has the pickle as a sign to the beginning and end of a harvest season. Come umber – the cucumber turns into a pickle in the month known as the ember month. The seasons, baseball and otherwise, pass with their signposts, and we grow too soon old and too late smart. "Call it a day," a common expression, is an actual confession that we count the day too soon. "It is never over until the last man's out."

Too soon they see the moon. Baseball is a festive ritual, American style. It contains a number of pagan events, and thus we are right to declare that baseball shall be played under the sun on nature's grounds. Indeed, the American Declaration of Independence refers to "the Laws of Nature and of Nature's God."

Last year, alas, **The Sporting News**, the self styled Baseball Bible, put out a tract on the glories of Opening Day. And what a travesty of Opening Day we had this year: everything at night. By the year 2022 A.D. baseball will be a fond memory, but not by you or me.

Well, if Uncle Wrigley's Gum Ball don't burst too soon,

I'll write the rune, of an odd-ball game beneath the moon.

June's Innings

Paul Shuttleworth

In the Motel 6 in Corpus Christi,
we unscrew lightbulbs,
chew them up and spit them out.
We chew up all the aluminum beer cans
and spit out the chunks. We leave
our shit unflushed in the toilet bowl.
Maybe if we'd beaten the Sea Gulls,
gotten better pitching, we'd have just
dreamed all this other stuff, Stork.
A week later we tell a cross-eyed
McAllen waitress she ought to model
high fashion lingerie in the Big Apple.
It's the first half of a long season
in the Lone Star League and it's fun
when the lead ball misses the couch
and busts through the stucco wall;
the secretary looks through the hole
in her living room and we smirk,
ask for our ball back, ask if we
can come over for a six-pack.
"Now I really hate baseball,"
she says, but she starts coming
to our home games after we show her
how K-Y Jelly is used in our league.

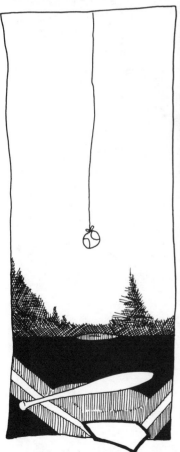

Clockwise, top: Illustration, author, volume taken from. *Baseball With Steve Lyon* (Bill Meissner, Vol. 5, No. 4); *The Resurrection* (section head, 6,2); *Change of Pace* (Jack LaZebnik, 6,3). Illustrations, Andy Nelson. *Base Paths: The Best of The Minneapolis Review of Baseball.*

Two illustrations from *For All the World to See* (Bill Comiskey, MRB 7,2). Illustrations by Andy Nelson. *Base Paths: The Best of The Minneapolis Review of Baseball.*

Just the Facts, Ma'am (Joseph Shadwell, MRB 6,2); *Wrigley Field, 1987: You Can't Go Home Again* (Linda Adler, MRB 7,1); *Ted "Doubleduty" Radcliffe* (cover art, MRB 5,4). Illustrations by Andy Nelson. *Base Paths: The Best of The Minneapolis Review of Baseball.*

Baseball Cards Come to Life (from *The Resurrection of Johnny Callison* by Pete Gunn, MRB 6,1). Illustration by Andy Nelson. *Base Paths: The Best of The Minneapolis Review of Baseball.*

SUMMER

Grounders

Stephen Lehman

My father and I would play catch in the yard and sometimes my mother would call out, "You're tearing up the grass." My father would tell her, "We're not raising grass here, we're raising boys."
– Harmon Killebrew
August 12, 1984, Cooperstown, New York

In summer, I ran too hard
for careful grounds work, and the grass
grew long on the front yard
where my father and I played catch,

and I took grounders and practiced my throw.
Right in the breadbasket, he implored,
but I was wild, high and low
and sick with fear, and my bony arm sore.

On the short hop, I'd grope
with gloved hand, blindly, for the ball,
as if a fate deferred by childish hope
could still be grasped, or never faced at all.

Always I quit first and went inside,
my face flushed with cowardice;
but he retrieved when I threw wide,
and moved me on by his sacrifice.

We stood apart. Stranded across the space
between us – flesh and the years –
the loneliness of his love beat his face,
and furrows wore there by my tears.

My head is down now, heart planted fast;
nor do I now ask what love can yield:
We did not grow but grass
on that rough infield.

Basket Catch

Bart Schneider

It was in '58, the year they moved out,
the year Mays had his windows smashed, midseason,
for hitting only .329, the year Toothpick
Jones lost his no-hitter in the bottom of the ninth,
that I became a fan.

I was seven.
My Dad was forty and liked to carry on
about Johnny Antonelli.
Night games, he'd pace the breakfast room floor
with his fiddle, and when the going got bad,
when the Redlegs had runners on the corners,
he'd blister a few double stops,
a towering *partita*,
as if he was Kluszewski himself in the on deck circle.
Look at that lumber.
Stop him Johnny.

Occasionally, in the middle innings,
there'd be this strange calm come over him.
Was he contemplating his life – that dance
between emotion and restraint –
now that Davenport was caught napping at first,
and Felipe Alou left standing, bowlegged at the plate?
There is no solitude like baseball.

My father's miseries arrived with the early summer
as the Giants went into their June swoon,
and Arthur Fiedler came to town.
Stuck in the pit, three weeks
of show tunes, waltzes, fairy music.
Enough to ruin a man's soul.
He hated the crowds.
They're the lowest common denominator,
the easy listeners, the lousy pretzel nibblers.

He loved the bleachers though.
HEY, BURGIE!
Especially when the lowly Phillies came to town.
BURGERMEISTER!
Let 'em pitch Robin Roberts.
A LOAF OF BREAD!
Let Ashburn hit for the cycle.
A POUND OF MEAT!
We'll still take 'em.
AND ALL THE MUSTARD YOU CAN EAT!
HOT DOGGIES!!!

We were out in right field, one day,
when Willie Kirkland misjudged a fly.
The crowd all over him. A fat man
full of beer, chanting:
dumb nigger, dumb nigger, dumb nigger
Reluctantly, Kirkland began to climb the fence
'til Mays loped over from center and cooed at him.
This is how the world is, rookie.
HEY BURGIE!
I was a child, sucking my thumb
against all that was harsh,
peeking through the planks of bleachers
to that horrid place little boys
could fall to in a flutter
of hotdog wrappers and old scorecards.
My Dad glared at fat man,
and led me by the hand to center field,
called to Mays in a voice
only he and I could hear.
Give us a basket catch, Willie.

Wild Pitches

Philip Dacey

You've been holding back
long enough, Son.
Stop aiming the ball.
Let your power,
that animal,
out. Don't worry
about hurting me.
I'm in my father-squat
behind homeplate, like a frog,
nothing and nobody
can stop that story.
Not even you. The whole world
squats so, just waiting
for you to throw the ball
as if you meant it,
an angry word,
an idea
to change the world,
a declaration
of love. It's true
some pitches will go wild.

At first a lot will.
But remember,
God is somewhere
with a mask and protector
for his chest and nuts
and catches every
wild pitch there is.
He's a scrambler.
So let that arm uncurl
and snake out
like the snake that girdles
the world. Whip-snake,
diamonded and poisoned
to the point where
the wildest pitch
is the one that stays
in the hand.

My Child

Paul Weinman

Kahlin's throw back had always been too hard.
I'd still be seeing the breath of that last ball
when another would suddenly appear
fast, too close to face, my eyes still at plate.
My hand without consent suddenly springs up,
snatches with a sharp snap that hardness –
its crack to my glove, instantly, a thing alive.
Now to study the stride, angles of arms,
stroke of bat at air of the next man up.
Then, for Kahlin to tell me, hand at crotch
directing me to throw a curve, fastball,
change-up with just a flip of fingers.
I give that ball its identity – its selfness.
Each pitch is my creation, mine to protect
with whatever speed, sweep, or change of pace
I know that ball to need to survive the swing
of him at bat. Not a catcher in Kahlin clothing.
Not that squat ugliness of random pads, plastics.
This ball rocked in my hand will take my smell,
my sweat, my fingers tight to seams –
my child for the next 60 feet 6 inches.

Blodgett's Blotter

Dear Ken,

So you have lost a diamond, Bloomington, MN or where ever as the old I.Q. chestnut goes and how you go about finding it. Well I went about it as I was taught. One of the gym class lost a locker-key and the student-coach to-be(2b) had us join hands and walk acrost the lot. Upon given the "thing" I ask'd where did you find the field? Cooperstown! In school all rooms had east day light and one (person) sat facing north with the east to their-right. Right? In a Christian world all fields are laid out in squares and only in Moslem places are such things found. I know this but was un-he-did. Well ball diamonds have little diamonds in the corner of the infield call'd bags Bases if you will and finding the one at home is the game. NAME of the GAME.

Now on to *The Portsider* the diamond is laid out so the pitchers' leftside is to the south so that they are called "southpaws." Of course if the infield is turn'd so the chucker left arm is on the seeside in the East he's a Portsider.

Well, Ken, as we know now the "Twins" have a new owner. The old haymarket, Charley Bennett Park, Navinfield, Briggs' stadium, Tiger land was given for one dollar (1$). Uncle Walt's brother was a railroad man and his son Harry become Henry Ford's bodyguard-righthandman. Uncle Bert Blodgett was a railroad man too, in Detroit and help out to (2) gether the first Cadillac. I'd love to put cobblestones around "the thing" and call it Cobb's little acre the infield I mean.

I am getting ready to watch this year's All-Star game the first I have been able to see in years in that I've been at the Big Mac Bridge on the Fourth for five years. The resurgence of the Minny team reflects the fortunes of Det., under new ownership much improved. But the domino theory haunts me! "Bump off the 1st domminnow and they all fall down." Cobb's Little Lakes had a certain ring to it.

Someone express'd the desire to know how "Twilite Ed" Killian got his name. I know Eddie Killian he ran a clothing store here in Kazoo after his O.B. days. It is Ed came on in the fading hrs., of daygames.

Between the dark and the daylite,
When the day is beginning to dawn
Comes the start of the day's occupation
That is known as the trip to the john.

Between the dark and the daylite,
When man is beginning to yawn
Comes the end of the day's ocupation
That is known as the trip to the john.

We have this summer some baseball stories told in the movies. *The Natural*, and *The Slugger's Wife*. How would you narrate the modern player on a scale of one too ten?

Too concern'd with his retirement,
The pitcher wants to retire him now
Wants to but don't know how.
And he retires and the D.H. makes his bow WOOha!

E. Wright Blodgett

Bleacher Bum Tour Cuts Swath
of Diamond Dementia Across Three States

Ken LaZebnik

(After the Dome opened in Minneapolis, Julian Empson's Save the Met began sponsoring outdoor baseball tours. This chronicle attempts to capture the glorious anarchy of one of his early trips. –Eds.)

* * * * * * *

July 16, 1982. Julian wears a Bleacher Bums Holiday T-Shirt and a straw hat with a photo button of the old Met. "Baseball's been bery bery good to me." We throw cups, plates, charcoal, into his station wagon and race off for dry ice. Our group is gathering in the Midway Center parking lot. Our Lorenz bus is there, as well as the one-hundred-pound bag of peanuts Julian has purchased for the trip.

There is a cluster of people wearing baseball caps and "Hello My Name Is" name tags. Tom Bartsch is selling his specially prepared "Bleacher Bum Holiday" T-Shirts. WCCO-TV is there. We mill about. We pose for a group picture.

"Board the bus!" Julian goes over his checklist, and then a general cheer as Lloyd, our veteran bus driver, pulls us out of the lot.

First order of business on the road is introductions, with a word on the individual's favorite baseball experience. White-haired Alden Mead rises, wearing a Cardinal cap. The shout goes up: "It's Red Schoendienst!" Alden cites as his favorite baseball experience the All-St. Louis World Series of 1944. (Alden's brother, by the way, is the author of the excellent reminiscence of WWII ball **Even the Browns**.) Gerry Esselman recalls teaching Tom Burgmeier English: "I told him, Tommy, you'll never amount to anything if you don't study your English. Now he's making $300,000 a year as a major league baseball player and I'm just an English teacher." I relate the unfortunate incident of my mother being struck in the nose by a foul ball off the bat of Ted Simmons.

A quick check of occupations represented showed "unemployed" heading the list, closely followed by librarians.

The bus ride to Beloit, Wisconsin, is about six hours. What do baseball fans do for six hours? Same thing they do for sixty – talk baseball. Baseball is a verbal game. After a full day of watching two games, I passed by a group of five talking outside the hotel door. I learned later they talked until six in the morning.

Triva questions abounded: Who was the pitcher who hit Tony C.? (Ken Tatum? Jack Hamilton?) What's an All-Star team of players whose careers were destroyed with a single pitch? (Starting pitchers: Herb Score and Dizzy Dean.) An All-Star team of plane crash victims – Clemente, Hubbs, Munson, et. al. A jailhouse team. Who was the last switch-hitter to win the American League MVP? (Trick question: the answer is switch-hitting pitcher Vida Blue.)

We arrive in Beloit, stop to get groceries for our tailgating, and get directions from a gas station for the ball park. We come in what appears to be a new parking lot addition, off the first base side of the park. Unload and break out the grills. From our vantage point we can see the Beloit players clubhouse – a trailer parked along the side of the field.

We eat a quick meal sprawled among grills on the blacktop. Then, the $2 tickets are passed out and groups of three and four start making their way into the park.

The Beloit park is totally satisfactory, giving a fan everything he or she looks for in a minor league stadium: an outfield fence consisting of advertising panels; a grandstand behind home plate and bleachers to either side of that; a water fountain that serves both players and spectators just on the fans' side of a fence separating field from stands. More than once during the game a player had to wait for a kid to get a drink before he could get his.

I picked up a deck of Beloit Brewer baseball cards, handsomely produced by Fritsch Cards. The vast majority of the players had career stats of one year, generally at Butte, Montana. Most were born after 1960. I filled out the line-up of my scorecard and a gentleman next to me noted that many of the players had already moved on. Typical of the people there, this man, and his family, had a thorough knowledge of the team. At one point the Brewers executed a suicide squeeze. The man said, "That's the first time we tried that." His daughter: "No it ain't. Brad tried it once when Gomez was up." I sat just above a group of young women whom I guessed (correctly) to be wives and girlfriends of the players.

They were pretty, had clear eyes, neat hair cut in a Farrah Fawcett style, wore clothes that were a cut above the average fan's, and looked, in sum, stunningly young.

The home fans were very quiet in the early going: One doesn't yell at friends who are screwing up. Our group, however, felt no such constriction and there was the eerie effect of a grandstand full of silent people with one small corner raising hell. There was no organ, so at one point we bleacher bums started yelling the da-da-da-da-da-dah! that precedes "charge!"

The Brewers scored their first run in the fifth, and when they did a beautiful sound arose suddenly from the night air. It took me a moment to realize what it was. It occurred spontaneously and sounded like scores of little cymbals: it was the fans stamping their feet on the aluminum grandstand.

The next afternoon – Chicago Cubs territory. Judy Aronson was our point person. She ventured early to Wrigley and bought 46 bleacher seats for us. In the Wrigley bleachers, you know that the outfielder can hear you.

The fans at Wrigley are well-informed and, in marked contrast to the quiet scholars of Beloit, are raucous. I sat with Judy near three older women who didn't hesitate to tell Bump Wills what a disappointment his fielding had been.

The Cubs couldn't seem to do anything with dispatch and snap. It was all just a little off. The Braves biggest liability seemed to be Claudell Washington in right field. Judy told me when he played for the Sox the fans in right put up a banner: "Claudell Washington Slept Here." True to form, he let a fly ball bounce off his glove through sheer nonchalance.

Judy gave me a scouting report on each Cub, and they proceeded to demonstrate her analysis as if on cue. Ryne Sandberg, her "baby," fielded smoothly at third; Keith Moreland let balls get by him with alarming regularity; Jay Johnstone made each fielding play a little adventure; Larry Bowa was in the game until the last out and taught the Cubs not to quit.

I've been anesthetized by years of Twins-style booster announcing so it was refreshing to hear Harry Caray rip a Cub player in a completely prejudicial fashion. He execrated the performance of Dickie Noles, for an error rightfully charged to Bill Buckner. Buck threw the ball ten feet beyond Noles, who was covering first base. "Noles should have had his glove up there. He was slow getting there to begin with. Boy, let me tell you – when Noles is good, he's good – when he's bad, he's terrible."

Dallas Green is attempting to begin a "new tradition" with the Cubs, exploiting a leggy woman as "ball girl." Before, this task was carried out by a man, a chubby Andy Frain usher squatting on a folding chair near home plate.

En route, I read Thomas Boswell's account of baseball in Latin America and it prepared me for County Stadium: The fans of each team sit on opposite sides of the stadium and hurl incredible abuse at each other.

The Brewers were playing the White Sox, the stadium was packed (about

30% Sox fans up for the game) and, as is typical, beer was flowing freely. People in our group came away with negative feelings. "They aren't baseball fans. They're frustrated people who have nothing to do so they go to the ball park and get drunk."

The Brewers, over that night's game, and the afternoon the next day, demonstrated they were simply a much better team. Jim Gantner was hot that weekend and they easily dominated the Sox. Sunday's crowd was more relaxed and likable, and everyone felt a sense of purgation as we entered the (now fairly foul-smelling) bus. Three games: power hitting Braves in Wrigley Field, Brewers twice in County Stadium. How many home-runs would you guess? Answer: Exactly one – struck by Aurelio Rodriguez.

On the ride home I asked Alden and Karin Mead if they had their baseball quota for a while. Karin looked surprised: "Why, no, we'll watch the game Monday night as we usually do."

The Portsider

Staff Writer

You can't bang plastic. Least ways, you aren't inclined to. Hard plastic, I'm talking here. I was in Milwaukee County Stadium on a seat cushion giveaway night once, and the fans pounded those soft fanny savers against one another until I thought the reverberations would splinter the grandstand awning.

I've been thinking about ballpark noise ever since I visited Fenway in July. Yes, for an old codger I get around some. My old buddy Michael Welch works for the Jimmy Fund there. (No, it's not a collection for Jimmy Piersall; it's for genuine little kids.) He got me tickets and I decided it was time to revisit the old park.

I hadn't been back since I played there – old ballplayers don't haunt the graveyard. My first appearance at the Fens I got fanned twice by the Bambino himself. In today's world I suppose that's no disgrace. Garagiola would point out it was a "lefty-lefty matchup." I thought it was a humiliation. That big old grin of his when that curve broke over – the quick "Strike three!" of the ump, the pug nosed heckler in the box seats . . .

Noise. Sound. Losing the thread here. I'd forgotten how much noise gets rolling around an old ballpark. You'd think those new stadia that hold 60,000 would get more volume, but the old parks condense sound. It echoes under the grandstand, giving it a deeper bass. It's got more body.

And seats. Seat banging. That's what started me up on all this. Gosh, if I hadn't forgotten that sound until the Sox were down three runs in the bottom of the twelfth. There were two outs, and then a runner got on. Jim Rice stepped up. I looked out at the big clock in the outfield. The hands were about to fold onto twelve when Rice lofted a home run into the net in left center.

Lord, what a drumming! I looked around, and thousands of seats were being slapped, banged – flapped is the right word. Everybody on their feet; every seat tom-tommed against its seat back. It was contagious. It got the blood going in a way that all the Mitsubishi screens and loudspeaker trumpets never will. With all that tympani, something was bound to happen.

Baylor's up next, and he hits a major league pop-up – which the Angel third sacker drops. Now, I'm not saying that the joyful roar of the fans squeezed the ball out of that glove. But, I must say that fans can holler and bang seats whenever they please, but the video screen is mandated to shut up before each pitch.

And so it went. Dwight Evans walked. Rich Gedman came up and fell behind 1-2. He fouled off five pitches, the crowd giving him a drum roll each time, until he singled in the tying run. Evans to third. New pitcher for Angels.

Before the new man threw one pitch, as he went into his windup in this cacophony – I saw Bob Boone rip off his mask and step in front of the umpire to argue. The pitcher had balked. The run was waved home. Red Sox win.

I was hoarse. It wasn't from yelling "Charge!" off the cue of the video screen. And it certainly wasn't responding to a cartoon telling me that somebody wants more "NOISE." This was the kind of good old-fashioned noise that won a ballgame.

The Baseball Lover

Bill Meissner

So far it's a no hitter.
She's still on the couch staring at quiz shows,
he's in the corner, oiling his glove
with his tongue.

This is the tension of extra innings –
all day he's waited on deck,
counting the circles chalked
on his brain.

She complains he wears his yellow baseball cap
too much. Sometimes he even sleeps with it
on his face like an egg yolk,
while her breathing makes the sound of wind
through empty bleachers.
All night dreams flow from the cap's brim:
He's sliding toward home plate
and the slide never stops – through the dugout,
under the grandstand, across the sandlot,
into the skin of his childhood,
the seat of his pants burning
like birth.

At the commercial he switches on the Braves game.
Someone is trying to steal home –
his legs
are the wings
of anxious birds.
He will never
move in slow
motion, not
even in the
replay. Here
comes the pitch
here comes
the runner,
he slides
next to her on the couch,
begins whispering sweet baseball scores
into her ear.

Notes from the Heart: Comiskey Park 1983

Judy Aronson

(In 1983 Judy Aronson sent us handwritten letters — thoughtful, analytic, ecstatic — detailing the ups and downs of following the Chicago White Sox. Her remarkable fan diary continues in the MRB today, but she's never had more fun than the year the Sox finally won something. —Eds.)

* * * * * * *

PENNANT FEVER

Pennant fever is a disease of the mind and body that through mass hypnosis can halt all normal activity for one million or more people. Children are not as susceptible as adults and over-30 adults are more susceptible than under 30. The symptoms are lack of focus on everything except magic numbers; inability to make plans beyond October; dirty houses; barren gardens; and the need for a haircut. There are some minor side effects like looking for good omens in everyday activities, running through batting orders in your dreams, being no longer able to eat anything except hotdogs, going to Wrigley Field only to scout Andujar's pickoff move to see if it could get Julio or Rudy, reading **USA Today** to make sure the eastern media isn't grooming some lesser god than Kittle for Rookie of the Year (a not uncommon trick as Hrbek watchers know), worrying that you won't get a ticket for Hoyt's twentieth win, wondering if it's legitimate to ask your doctor for tranquilizers to see you through October, or whether you should just go ahead and become an alcoholic.

April

The Sox can win the pennant, but the variable is the management (field and ownership). So far LaRussa and friends have (on the negative side) traded Pat Tabler and (on the positive side) snuck rookie Greg Walker into the line-up as DH instead of Luzinski against a right-handed starter – he got three hits.

I cannot begin to elaborate on LaRussa's incompetence as a manager, beginning with his choices of 25 from among 40 or so at spring training, to his insecurity (kowtowing to Carlton Fisk and Greg Luzinski), failure to back up his players, constant searching for one scapegoat per loss, and the effect of all of the above on his daily line-up choices. When he does do the right thing – like play Rusty Kuntz (the best white center fielder in the majors) against left-handed pitchers, he does it a year later than the fans (and Piersall) suggest it, and comes up with rationalizations to explain it away. He is so afraid of Luzinski that he won't platoon him with left-handed hitter Greg Walker, who is an incompetent first baseman, especially compared with low hitting lefty Mike Squires, a Golden Glove, and with sufficient fielder, extraordinary right-handed hitting Tom Paciorek. Fisk used his clout rightly last year in getting LaRussa to dump Jim Morrison, a lousy fielding, erratic hitting third baseman, and wrongly in getting LaRussa to dump Steve Trout, a potentially brilliant pitcher but one without the patience to pitch a three hour game, which is the only kind of game Fisk catches.

Now, I know you're going to ask about Kittle. What can I say about a guy who came on strong the first couple of weeks because he can hit a major league curveball. Now they are up and in fastballing him, and it will take him a few days to make the adjustment. He's great, and the management doesn't like him.

Some history: Two years ago the LaRussa-Piersall feud started because Jimmy, as official part-time outfield coach was bearing down on the showboating Chet Lemon. LaRussa, ever ready to defend strong-minded players (Lemon, Fisk, Luzinski), fired Jimmy. The next year, Jimmy, being courted muchly by the owners to tout Sportsvision (Pay TV of Sox games – Jimmy loves money, his and others, as much as he loves good fielders), was kept happy by being an influential voice in the Sox minor league outfield coaching system. On his advice they kept Kittle down on the farm to learn, under his tutelage, left-fielding. Which means, among other things, that the guy knows how to field a position. The only error he has this season is very dubious scoring, unlike Kemp last year, who so badly misplayed his position, that he didn't get errors: He wasn't near enough to the balls that flew over his head.

There was talk this spring of trading Kittle. Unlike Walker, he doesn't wear a mental three-piece suit to the park. On the spring's first Einhorn call-in show (10 a.m. Sundays and guaranteed to start your day wrong), all the callers started out by saying: "I am a season ticket holder and don't want to see Ron Kittle traded." The message got across, but he had the double curse of being a Piersall protege and of being a bit of his own man. My favorite Kittle quote came when a reporter, while discussing Kittle's 50 home runs in the Pacific Coast League last year, felt obliged to point out that Edmonton *does* have a small ballpark, and the PCL *is*, after all, *only* a minor league. Kittle's response: "Who *else* hit 50 home runs there last year?"

I love Ron Kittle, but he will not be happy in Chicago!

July

Let's talk about psychology and baseball. PRK (Pre-Ron-Kittle), a more sober and law abiding team than the Sox couldn't be found. After unsuccessfully trying to trade RK in the spring (most prominently in a package for Buddy Bell), the Sox tried to keep him out of the limelight, so reporters wouldn't feel forced to interview and quote him. But since benching RK led to losing games and lower attendance, management capitulated and RK plays everyday, is quoted everyday, brings people to the ballpark and has caused a minor revolution in the team psychology. Paciorek drops his one-liners once again. Lamp resurrects his Cubdays famous burlesques of teammates and foes. And twice in the same week LaRussa has not only smiled, but laughed, and (I swear!) tried to "clown" around. Fisk and Luzinski have regained the ebullience that they showed their first few months with the Sox, before LaRussa taught them how to be low key, and while I can't quite swear to it, I think I almost saw Baines smile.

A low-key Carlton Fisk has been a low-hitting Carlton Fisk. Since the RK era was established, Fisk outdoes Pete Rose in never-say-die baseball. For three years whenever the Sox were behind in late innings they followed LaRussa's lead in abandoning today's game to rest and plan strategy for tomorrow's. But now Fisk keeps them playing for today and there are no more routine seventh, eighth and ninth innings. You can't turn off the radio (we don't have free TV you know), or leave the ballpark early to beat the traffic anymore. And the Bull is rising to RK competition by both trying to outdo him in quantity and quality of homeruns and by working with him in batting practice. RK has made 25 individual talents into a team, by the oldest uniting gimmick in the world: a sense of humor and therefore a sense of perspective. LaRussa PRK would call for game plan plays which were rarely correctly implemented. Now the players, less intense, more a team, execute them all.

For the first time in three years sitting through a ballgame is not unpleasantly tense, but pleasurably scary. Now we know all errors charged to our players are bad calls by umpires or official scorers. The tension in each game is caused by the close plays on the field, not by the tense postures of the players on the field. ARK (After Ron Kittle) CYA (Cover Your Ass) stopped. The pitchers stopped blaming the infielders; the batters stopped blaming the wind. Instead everyone started playing baseball. I fully expect this season to see the hidden ball trick, someone steal home, an outfielder fall over the high bullpen fence, a triple play, a no-hitter, and everything else that can occur in baseball, and hasn't been seen in Comiskey Park since 1959.

A ballpark is a mood. Comiskey Park is loved despite its unbelievably dreary facilities, because the field is unbelievably symmetrical, functionally perfect, and, after all, when you are in your seat, this is what you see. Behind you are depressing ramps, ugly washrooms, poorly designed concession stands, martial law rules, and dusty, dirty streets and parking lots.

Midsummer Musings

You've Come a Long Way Baby:

Time Warp – 1933 1953 1983. Judy Johnson and Carl Hubbell. Bob Feller and Minnie Minoso. Dave Stieb and Dave Winfield.

"If Judy were only white he could name his own price," said Connie Mack.

123 hits, 14 HR, 72 R, 63 RBI, 56 BB .306 (Gil McDougald)

173 hits, 10 HR, 112 R, 76 RBI, 72 BB .326 (Minnie Minoso)

In 1951, who was white and was named Rookie of the Year, and who was black (and also led the league that year in triples and stolen bases) and came in second . . .

In 1983 in an All-Star Game, who was black and went 3 for 3 and scored the game-winning run and wasn't MVP . . .

We got to Dave Stieb the other night, and I didn't enjoy it. For one thing, I don't care who wins the East, and if I thought about it at all, would prefer it to be Milwaukee or Toronto, as part of my grand dream of the media finally recognizing the Midwest for any reason, but (before this sentence gets too impossible to retrieve grammatically), after Stieb's utter bravery and show of guts in the All-Star game, I just have to face the fact that I never want to watch him pitch poorly. I don't like my heroes to fail, which happens occasionally, or age, which happens inevitably.

Twenty-five years of collecting books and reference material on many, many subjects, and it all comes down to one book, Reichler's, on our bookshelf. Shall I finally discard my **Oxford Companion to English Literature, Bengali-English Dictionary, MGM Stock Company, Tynan's Reviews,** Volume Two of **The Way Things Work**, MacNeill's **Rise of the West, A History of the Lyric Opera** and **The Minneapolis Homeowner's Guide**?

I shouldn't be allowed to go to any more Old Timers Games. I went to my deepest piles of papers and found the notebook/scoresheets I kept from 1953-1956 including the July 13, 1954 (from TV I assume) scoresheet for the All-Star Game held before 68,751 at Cleveland. Al Rosen went three for four, with 5 RBI. Mantle (who I carefully recorded as an "S" – switch-hitter) went 2 for 5. Nellie Fox was one for two with 2 RBI. But another, equal star of the game was Bobby Avila, ten years the Cleveland second baseman, who was a lifetime (11 years) .281 hitter (courtesy Reichler), only by virtue of his 1954 league-leading .341. In the All-Star game he went 3 for 4 officially. The fifth at bat was a sacrifice fly, scoring two runs and getting two RBI. What a great year he had.

So I started thinking about second basemen.

Eddie Collins 1906-1930

Frankie Frisch 1919-1939

Charlie Gehringer 1924-1942

Billy Herman 1931-1947

Rogers Hornsby 1915-1937

Napoleon Lajoie 1896-1916

Jackie Robinson 1947-1956

are the listed second basemen in the Hall of Fame. If you remove Robinson (who played second base for less than half of his ten year career), you find no second baseman in the Hall of Fame who has played since 1947. [Written prior to the inductions of Joe Morgan, 1963-1984, and Rod Carew, 1967-1985, in 1990 and 1991.]

In the 1950s, as today in the 1980s, the American League had special breeds of second basemen. They were the sparkplugs of their teams in the field or on the bases or both. Since 1950, one high hitting second baseman in each league has been an MVP. The second baseman is never rested, he plays every game, he is most often in the sacrificial part of the batting order, he is often the only player on his American League team who is expected to know how to bunt. Without statistics, it still seems that he is also rarely traded. He is the glue. His pivot makes the flashy shortstop's assist become a double play. Dauer, Remy, Grich, Garcia, Cruz, Trillo, Whitaker, White, Gantner, Castino, Randolph, Lopes, Bernazard, Tolleson. In 1983, there's not a dud in the whole league. But we thought the same in 1951: Coleman, Avila, Doerr, Fox, for the top four teams, yet none are Hall of Famers, and the 1950s loved their second basemen, were proud of them, and they were the heart of the team. But when their legs give out, second basemen don't hit hard enough to be moved to first or DH and artificially extend their time.

Of course it's just coincidence that Tony Bernazard's broken leg was followed by the White Sox abandoning the 1982 pennant race. How could a .256 hitter be that important? Easily, when he bats second, switching to his weaker side when called upon to sacrifice behind the runner. Easily when he plays every game. Easily when he draws the second most walks for the team only behind the DH cleanup batter. Easily when he is also second on the team for doubles, first in runs scored, third in stolen bases, the only starter switch-hitter, etc. But second basemen do everything well, and come in first in nothing, certainly not home runs, hits, and RBI, the glamour categories for MVP and the Hall of Fame.

August

More about winning. It's such an unusual subject for a Chicago sports fan that it leads to unlimited analysis. A team player is not a sacrificer; he's the man who executes. The ball is thrown to the correct base. The ball is thrown to the fielder, not beyond him. The ball is caught whenever it is theoretically catchable, etc. It sounds so simple, but it's been a long time since Chicago has seen this kind of play.

And more. The strike zone on your batters gets smaller, and for your pitchers gets larger. Winners are supposed to be better so therefore they are better at judging balls.

And more. Everyone on the team wants to join in the winning. No one wants to be left out. So everyone plays smart, and pays attention when they're not in the game, so they are really and truly ready when they do play.

And more. Outsiders come to Comiskey Park. They need directions to get there. They *like* the team mascots. They watch the Diamondvision scoreboard more than they watch the diamond, and they don't know the players' numbers. They only know how to go wherever the action is: Oak Street Beach, Chicagofest, Watertower Shopping Mall. They cultivate tans which go higher up their arms than shirt sleeves. I even saw a beachball game in the grandstands.

And more. After scorning my childish enthusiasms for a ball team, friends and acquaintances now look upon me as a source of information on the current main topic in the city.

I apologize for not recognizing the symptoms earlier: an uncontrollable desire to watch baseball 24 hours a day, difficulty in focusing on work or housework or on what friends are saying, constant consulting of sport pages. It's pennant fever. I suppose I can be excused for not realizing sooner. It's like the first virus of the winter which is rampant before you know you have it. It's been too long since the last attack to remember the early warning signs. For me it's been since 1959, since I was otherwise occupied in 1977 when it last spread through Comiskey Park. But the omens are right. It was a very hot summer in 1959; we had a conservative Republican President, etc. It can't be coincidence, it must be fate. The only negative pointer is that last winter was mild whereas in 1958-59, we had heavy snowfall. Can this be important? Is it something to worry about?

September

I am higher than a kite on baseball, baseball, baseball! Not only are we the Best in the West, Winning Ugly, but the bill for my playoff tickets arrived in today's mail, awaiting my return from Wrigley Field, where the **Summer Stock Murder** (long-running hit musical by Stan Day and Philip LaZebnik) cast sang the Star Spangled Banner, while I waited in the dugout, using willpower to resist grabbing ass off of Jay Johnstone and Mel Hall as they passed me to take the field.

Earlier I had hung out between the dugout and backstop while the Astros took batting practice. I sort of strutted back and forth, pretending to be needed, as I felt the grass under my feet and the sun on my back (and the bat in my hands and the ball coming toward my glove – wait, that didn't happen!), and I watched Vuckovich (Cubs coach) tape the lineup card on the dugout wall and the bat boys unload towels, and the bats and the helmets, and Vince Lloyd interview the pitching coach, and on my important errands down the dugout runway, passed a coach sneaking a cigarette. Thirteen hours later, and I'm still flying.

This summer has been too full of perfect days. Kittle home runs. The Old-Timers game at Wrigley Field. The Old-Timers game at Comiskey Park. The All-Star Game. Bull's home run over the left field roof. The dugout at Wrigley Field. And, of course, Hoyt, Hoyt, Hoyt. The meanest man in the major leagues. It's as if there's an attempt to compensate me for the fact that I held a ticket for the seventh game in 1959, when the Sox lost it in six! The omens are everywhere: most days over 90 degrees temperature since 1959. Most home runs hit by a catcher since 1959 (Fisk vs. Lollar), and, oh no, I can't handle this, an announcing team of four, two of whom are Don Drysdale and Early Wynn, reunited after their 1959 confrontations, only this time, both are on te same side.

And for the second time in thirty years, I've made a bet on baseball – that Kittle would get 100 RBI. 81 down, 19 to go. What more do I want? The whole thing! Two million attendance (we're almost there), Rookie of the Year – Kittle; MVP – Fisk; Cy Young – Hoyt; and the *big flag* to fly. I'm not totally greedy. Even though I now hold three playoff tickets, and four World Series, I'm willing to give up a game or two if we can win it in less.

The media correctly refer to us as a pitching team, but they also think of us as a power team. Mostly we steal our runs — some by stolen bases, but mostly being opportunists. Julio Cruz and Rudy Law rattle the opposing players and mistakes are made — mental as well as actual; opposing pitchers strike out Luzinski or Kittle and relax enough for Walker or Fletcher to hit a double or walk or otherwise get our men on base. We are very, very sneaky. Twice this year two men have scored on one sacrifice fly. At least three times our vaudeville team of Fletcher and Cruz have pantomimed plays, decoying runners into stopping where they were, and not where they could have reached. Our batters get infielders to move out of position by pretending to bunt or not bunt, pull or spray.

My personal suspicion is not to credit the natural legal craftiness of our lawyer-manager, but the street smarts of Carlton Fisk. He is a past master of getting the pitch called by the umpire where his glove is (not necessarily where the pitch crossed the plate). He knows exactly how to safely get hit by a pitched ball. He also knows how to behave at the plate when Julio or Rudy are on first base. Patience is his middle name. He can find something in his eye that halts the game the precise amount of time needed by a reliever to warm up. Or if he has done that already, he knows how to get "stung" by a foul ball requiring recuperation time, or how to signal imperceptibly that the trainer should stall for the reliever by checking an invisible incipient blister or hangnail on our tiring starter's hand. Need I go on?

Once RK loosened LaRussa's iron deadening grip on the team, the experienced "specialists" began sharing their tricks and the whole batting order became unpredictable in their actions. After Paciorek told him how, RK even hit a wrong way home run. Vance Law has become indistinguishable even by my educated eye from Fisk as he approaches the plate. Every mannerism is duplicated. Baines is picking up Rudy Law's shallow fielding and has increased his range toward center.

Our bullpen is still undependable. We have two left-handers of use only against left-handed hitters, and three right-handers good only in long relief, but no right-handed stoppers and no left-handed long relievers, which means we're in trouble anytime there is less than two out and left-handed hitter coming to bat with men on base. I personally think the Sox will pay an astronomical price in the next two weeks for Ron Davis or some other right-handed stopper.

Because, although we've convinced the press we are a power team, we are really the usual, punchless, defensive Sox team. We score more than one run for every two hits we get. We're talking low team numbers on extra-base hits. We're talking walks, and errors and sacrifices and an extra base reached on throws, stolen bases and singles clearing the bases. We're talking grounding out, flying out, striking out for 5,6,7, innings until those barely visible moments between their starter's weakening and their manager's pulling him, and into the gap we squeeze the runs needed to win.

Our only .300 hitter is our only left-handed pinch hitter. They call us a power team and we only have two players with more than 100 hits. We have three home run hitters who all specialize in solo home runs, successfully softening up the pitcher for our Punch and Judy runs batted in. The pitcher invariably walks the next batter, who invariably scores somehow. And the solo home run has turned into a three or four-run inning with little punch displayed. And it has taken twenty minutes to the out, thoroughly resting our faltering starter and giving him the energy for another two innings.

If we can't successfully confuse the opposing team, we at least have our ace in the hole: to confuse the radio audience who thereby forget and forgive the loss. I'm talking of course about my beloved Early Wynn, who will never get his paperwork in order, but who always has his priorities straight. The pitcher has the right to the outside half of the plate, and any disputes over this should be ruled in favor of the pitcher. His recent joy over Burns' forkball could not be matched. After a couple of years, he now grudgingly will point out those weakness in the opposing pitchers which might aid the Sox batters.

As he mixes incomprehensibly all metaphors, he magnifies our delight in our starting rotation, unmatched in either league. He applauds the high inside fastball, he gloats in the sneaky sinker, he loves rattling off the now in, now out, now fast, now change magic of the good ones.

So where will it end? Maybe in County Stadium Milwaukee, or in Comiskey Park against Baltimore. In County Stadium our solos won't match the men on base for Cooper or Simmons, and Yount can stop our terrorism on the infield. We can intimidate the Milwaukee pitchers, but there isn't enough outfield for us to get that extra base. And we can't intimidate the Baltimore pitchers, but if we get enough rest (rain? travel day?) to use our four best starters five times, it might not matter if we can only get one run a game. It won't be dull or routine.

Atlanta or LA will be no problem, but NL East is more defensive and more apt to spoil our game.

This is a year in a million.

Late September

Pennant Fever is people at the ballpark saying "Excuse me" and "Please" instead of "Nice tits, lady" and "Sox suck" chants as you leave the park.

Pennant Fever is 45 days with temperature over 90 degrees and sitting through ten of them in the sun field without complaining.

Pennant Fever is "Winning Ugly" courtesy of Doug Rader, and "Miracle on 35th Street" courtesy of Kevin Hickey and Tom Paciorek.

Pennant Fever is hours per week of TV and Radio sports coverage, and front to last page newspaper reports.

Pennant Fever is the Bears having empty seats, the Cubs drawing 10,000 against St. Louis, and 40,000 coming to Comiskey Park to see if the thunderstorms will end.

Pennant Fever is Jimmy Piersall refusing call-in questions critical of LaRussa.

So, we go back to 1959, when a no name Sox team with outstanding pitchers took it almost all the way. The difference this time: four players with more than 75 RBI, three players with more than 25 home runs, two players with more than 50 stolen bases, and wow, is this a *team*; two late innings Golden Glovers (Aurelio Rodriquez and Mike Squires) to hold the lead, which is why we have no fastball, only sinkerball/slider relievers.

What can't we do? Pick men off first. Bunt. Throw out a runner from left or center. Pinch hit against a left-hander (though only an idiot manager would send up a left-hander to face Fisk, Paciorek, Luzinski and Kittle).

What can we do: score runs per hits at a .560 ratio vs. opposing teams' .500.

Much of this season has been unbelievable (that is, at the time I cannot believe what is happening), but last night topped the "I-can't-believe-its." After losing the night before 11-0, on September 10th California arrived at the ballpark mean, just out and out ornery, and for eight innings made the Sox look second rate. California scored six runs and fielded like champions. Zahn gave up only one run on seven hits, cutting off one Sox rally after another. But neither four California pitchers nor a 93 minute rain delay in the ninth could stop an ugly Sox rally: two walks, one hit, one sacrifice, one rain delay, one pop-up, two hits and another Sox rally ties it (by this time well after midnight). An hour later, three brilliant Sox fielding plays, our non-extinguishing fireman Barojas going five almost impeccable innings, and California running out of left-handed pitchers. Baines lifts a high fly ball just clearing the right field wall. Sox win. 43,000 started the game; 2,000 saw it end.

The tying runs scored on a double by "Booter" Hill, our second string catcher, brought in to face the left-hander brought in to face our fourth string left-handed first baseman. What was even more impressive is that this game was played with our 25-man playoff roster only – no ringers from Triple AAA have played, and knowing how superstitious LaRussa is, none of them will probably play until after the division is officially won in the middle of this week.

The Fisk contribution is pride. The team has now won 12 in a row at home. This team won't let us down. We feed them and they feed us. They use Comiskey Park as a musician uses a fine instrument: the fences, the foul lines, the winds, the grass.

Against left-handers, we win conventionally, with our strong right-handed batting order. But against righties, we lead off with Rudy and steal games. Even though he bats 60 points higher from the right, Julio from the left gets a jump toward first that eliminates double plays, causes opposing team errors and gives us our strange approach to getting runs. It's not as relaxing, but it's much more fun when we face the right-handers.

October

Do I have the energy to call Einhorn's talk show tomorrow and remind him that he told me in May that he couldn't play Fletcher and Walker as well as Kittle because no team ever won the pennant with more than one rookie?

The only time I ever heard Einhorn admit a mistake was in the spring when he admitted Rodriquez' leaving was a mistake. In August he got him back. It's a shame he didn't also get Almon and Tabler and Harry Caray to return. I'd put money on three consecutive pennants with that line-up.

The cats will be so happy when the season ends and the scoreboard leaves my lap vacant for them. Ordinary books aren't wet with ink.

Expert advice indicates it will take all winter to come down from my October high. I don't know if my house can go twelve months without being cleaned. And I know I'll run out of safety pins and have to get new clothes. The ink stains will fade from my fingers. Old friends, with no interest in baseball, will come back into my life.

I have never heard or seen an exciting game pitched by Bannister. When he is winning, I can easily doze off. He is extraordinarily boring, especially when he has his best stuff and I am sitting in right field, and he isn't letting any balls leave the infield.

When Koosman pitches I can puff on my cigarette and sip my beer between the time the ball leaves his hand and crosses the plate. I can also mentally review my entire life (*a la* drownings) during a game that Koos pitches. It isn't dull of course because lots of balls leave the infield, most of them carrying terrifyingly far.

Dot is best watched from close in, as is Burns. The difference is one of nerve: It takes more of it to watch Britt.

Hoyt can be enjoyed any time from any part of the park and, win or lose, is fun to watch.

The whole park groans when anyone is summoned from the bullpen. It's like playing Russian roulette. When they are good, they are very, very good, and when they are bad, they are horrid. But without the bullpen, the Chicago writers would have nothing to theorize about. Does Barojas need more or less rest between outings? Can Agosto pitch successfully to right-handed hitters? Should Dennis Lamp be a starter? This last question because he is the most erratic of our relievers – the best and the worst. Why is Tidrow even on the squad? If Lee Smith played for the Sox rather than the Cubs, would there be any doubt about the outcome of all post-season play? If I had wings, could I fly?

Questions to be resolved during the winter:
Can you become a permanent junk food addict from one season of hotdogs and popcorn?
Does beer *taste* good off-season?
Does the Dan Ryan Rapid Transit have stops other than 35th Street?
Does the number 44 represent my age or only Paciorek's jersey number?
Is there life after post-season?
Will Barry Spector ever speak to me again? He hasn't since the beginning of August when the Sox took a wide lead over the rest of the Division. *I'd* be happy for *him* if the Cubs were winning.
Do the following words have non-baseball meanings: clutch, ugly, awesome, right side, left side, Bull (market? china shop?), roofer?

The Day After
The roller coaster has come to a stop. To be precise it stopped in the seventh inning of the fourth game when the 24th or 25th player on the Sox roster did not score from third. We were unsuccessful in stealing our 101st game. We only had 100 in us. Friday night had been bad enough, only purged by my swimming 25 pool lengths and a mile and a half brisk walk the next morning. But hearts can break when your bad luck pitcher (Britt Burns) — probably, won-lost record notwithstanding, your best classic pitcher — goes nine scoreless innings and loses because his heart can go ten, but not his arm.
The heart of this team was its pitching staff, who rarely were given more than a two-run lead to work with, who knew they had to go nine innings every time out or turn their lead over to the not so tender hands of the (oh, it hurts!) bullpen. Unlike almost every other AL team, only one reliever ended the season with a lower ERA that the Big Four starting staff.
The highlights of the season: LaMarr Hoyt every outing. The Bull at the City Pep Rally high-fiving the Mayor. Harold's first smile. Midnight plus 10 on September 10-11, the bottom of the ninth, one and a half hours rain delay over and the 23rd player, Marc Hill hits a double to tie the score and send the Sox and California into extra innings, and slightly after 1 a.m. Harold hits a homer in the bottom of the 12th and the remaining 2,000 (out of 43,000) smile at each other with silly miracle grins, and some happy soul shouts in the night: "Eat your heart out Harry Caray."
Chicago had a winner.

Mystery Baseball

Philip Dacey

No one knows the man who throws out the season's first ball.
  His face has never appeared in the newspapers,
    except in crowd scenes, blurred.
  Asked his name, he mumbles something
    about loneliness,
    about the beginnings of hard times.

Each team fields an extra, tenth man.
  This is the invisible player,
    assigned to no particular position.
  Runners edging off base feel a tap on their shoulders,
    turn, see no one.
  Or a batter, the count against him, will hear whispered
    in his ear vague, dark
    rumors of his wife, and go down.

Vendors move through the stands
  selling unmarked sacks,
  never disclosing the contents,
  never having been told.
  People buy, hoping.

Pitchers stay busy
  getting signs.
  They are everywhere.

An outfielder goes for a ball on the warning track.
  He leaps into the air and keeps rising,
    beyond himself, past
    the limp flag.
  Days later he is discovered,
    descended, wandering dazed
    in center field.

Deep under second base lives an old man,
   bearded, said to be
   a hundred. All through the game,
   players pull at the bills of their caps,
   acknowledging him.

One man rounds third base, pumping hard,
   and is never seen again.
   Teammates and relatives wait years at the plate,
     uneasy, fearful.

Hitting as a Contagious Disease

Ken LaZebnik

This season, more than most, has shown the avalanche quality of baseball. Last year's pennant winners saw their teams suffer chips and cracks of injuries, then the loose shale of slumps, and, scrambling among falling rock, a sudden slip from the mountain of first place. The Mets, to reverse the metaphor, have seen superior pitching and power hitting send their snowball rolling into the victory column with ever accelerating speed.

Roger Angell recently explored the vicissitudes of a team's performance, its upswings and downturns. He sought a cause and came up with many different explanations. I went to Shea Stadium recently and narrowed the discussion to the team psychology of hitting. The Cards were playing the Mets. What could I learn of the Cardinals' team hitting slump? I was prompted by the very idea of causation – is there a cause to a team's slump, or is it simply concomitant variation, invariable sequence and such? So much in baseball seems sheer luck. Is it simply luck? Is it simply luck that virtually all the Cardinals hit so well last year and so poorly this?

My first stop was the visiting manager's office. Whitey Herzog was chewing on a cigar and bent over the sports pages of **The Daily News**.

"Well, hitting is a contagious thing. But then Willie doesn't hit for Ozzie, and Tommie doesn't hit for Jack. Hitting is mental. Hell, everything in baseball is mental. What did Casey Stengel say? 75% of baseball is mental and the other 50% is physical. When a batter's going well, he's concentrating on the pitcher. When he's in a slump, he's thinking about where his arm is, or where his leg is on the swing ... I've always said there are three categories of good hitters:

1. Great physical hitter, 2. Crazy guys who don't care what they did the last time up, and 3. The ignorant, who forget what they've done."

Our discussion drifted from the 75% mental into the 50% physical:

"What I look for in a young hitter is if he can keep the bat back. Moving your body forward and keeping the bat back is the key to hitting . . . Then there's always fear. If Willie Mays wasn't scared, he'd have hit .700. Hell, throw anything within three feet of him and he'd jump."

And a parting word of advice for young hitters:

"Get comfortable and when you see something white, swing at it."

I walked out onto the field, which this particular Saturday had been transformed from a baseball diamond into a media circus. The Mets were filming a video, and a camera crew was tracking Mookie Wilson sliding head first into second, and then grooving on a the lyric, "Let's go, Mets go." Ed Bradley of *60 Minutes* was on hand, interviewing Ron Darling. Frank Cashen was leaving a trail of reporters, and Johnny Bench, there to do a CBS radio broadcast of the game, was talking with Ray Knight. Sensing a hitting schmooze-fest, I tracked down Tony Kubek. (It was also on NBC Game of the Week — natch).

Kubek was alert and articulate:

"Hitting is a contagious thing. That can be explained in part because we know that a pitcher generates less velocity when pitching from the stretch. When a man gets on base, the next batter will be facing fast balls that aren't quite as fast. And, of course, with men on base, holes open up in infield . . . Hitting is a physical act, but it's triggered by a mental process. You work on physical details in batting practice – but in the game you have to not think about those things. It's really very simple. As the old saying goes – see ball, hit ball. That's hitting in a nutshell."

Gene Shalit, for some obscure reason, was wandering around home plate. Joe Piscipo had a camera crew trailing him and his son; apparently he was part of the Mets video. I caught up with Johnny Bench after Lenny Dykstra demonstrated his golf swing.

"I tell kids to look for the ball out of the pitcher's hand and in a zone you like. You can get the pitch to hit."

And, as far as a team slump, and team psychology?

"If two guys in the middle of the lineup aren't hitting it can start a landslide. Other players try to pick up the slack; they press and try to hit home runs when they may not be home run hitters."

On a batter's relationship with a pitcher:

"Hitting's like dancing with a girl – you have to go with them. If they're a good dancer, you dance better. But you have to be in rhythm with her."

Johnny Lewis is the Cardinals' batting coach. We sat in the Cards quiet dugout. Across the infield, a camera rolled in front of the Mets dugout, as the Mets chanted, "Go, Mets, go."

"What's the thing I look for in a hitter? Number one is bat quickness. Bat speed and balance – the balance of the swing. Mental concentration is important – the concentration of doing your homework. What type of pitcher are you facing? What does he throw in certain situations? What is that pitcher's best pitch? Does he have a pattern? Pitchers make mistakes – hit the mistakes . . . Confidence is very important; it enables you to relax and execute."

How can one learn relaxation and concentration?

"Repetition. Mold your swing to a point where you can relax. Then you have the confidence your swing is there. Now good hitters, like Hernandez over there, have that confidence for three strikes. Some others only have it for two . . . It's my job to take the individual and work with what he has. We're a contact hitting club. Earlier in the season when we were getting 10 K's a game – that's not our game. . . . It's an individual game, it starts from within. If I could pinpoint just why somebody gets into a slump . . . Hey . . .

Lewis laughed. We were watching the Cardinals warming up. Suddenly, I heard Whitey's voice: "Between me and Johnny you've got enough dope there to write ten or fifteen chapters."

I had the dope, but not the synthesis. There's an element of mystery at the core of hitting that seems to be related to the unconscious, to confidence, to seeing the ball – the same ball – better at times than at others. Maybe the mystery is simply that there is no cause for hitting streaks and slumps.

The Encyclopedia of Philosophy told me, "Many scientists dispense with the idea of a cause; it is `anthropomorphic' in origin and replaceable by less esoteric concepts such as concomitant variation and invariable sequence." Rich Gedman joined their ranks in the next day's paper when explaining a game winning home run: "I wasn't really looking for anything because the count was 3-1. I'm not really sure what I was thinking. It's a hit and miss thing. You just gotta go up and get your hacks."

And yet, more than one person said, "Hitting is contagious." Maybe that's the metaphor – hitting as a contagious illness. We know when one person is sick those around him are exposed and vulnerable to his disease. Not everyone will catch it, and those who do will suffer in varying degrees. To be sure there is an element of mystery in the onset of illness – why this person? Why now? Perhaps because that person was prepared for it, and his chances increased until they united with the moment.

And, from the point the batter sees the ball out of the pitcher's hand, relaxes and concentrates, sees it in the zone he likes, molds his swing toward driving the ball, and sends it flying into the open field, the causal chain is in motion.

The Oracle of Ruth

Dana Christian Jensen
For my father

Adore the one who makes you rise screaming.

He stands alone
with his stick,
immortal in those clothes;
he stands alone
resting on our voices,
stares into a nation's sky
and points to the far distant walls
as though he knows.

He steps in,
nine opponents approach.
He meets their offering,
gliding over heads
and outreaching hands
the live hide and string,
into the crowds gathered beyond the fields,
insane with triumph,
the power of one human
to run freely in a circle,
to love and be congratulated
before disappearing into the dug out earth,

before the game goes on.

A Fitting Shrine

Harley Henry

I was well into what must pass as my adulthood when I acquired the awful knowledge that baseball-as-we-know-it was not invented by Abner Doubleday in Cooperstown, New York in 1839. At the time, the revelation that the "immaculate conception" theory of baseball was jingoistic fraud seemed to me but another example of the ugly fissures and feet of clay that Americans were discovering in their institutions and idols.

Like many of the disillusionments we've endured in the last fifteen years, the unmasking of the machinations of the Mills Commission provoked in me an outrage which was swiftly succeeded by self-righteous cynicism. I lost no opportunity to proclaim that baseball was really invented by Alexander Cartwright and first played in 1845 at the Elysian Fields in Hoboken, New Jersey. But when I described this setting as "appropriately oxymoronic," a reader from New Jersey wrote to complain that I was bad-mouthing Hoboken.

It may be that the 1980s are not a good time to go on debunking American institutions. It may be that The Strike has stripped away the few illusions we had left about baseball. In any case, my cynicism gave way to gratitude when I discovered earlier this summer that baseball has a fitting shrine in Cooperstown, a place well worth the pilgrimage to meditate on baseball's past.

Thanks to the understanding support of Macalester College, I spent a little more than a week on a busman's holiday at the National Baseball Hall of Fame and Museum in Cooperstown. Housed in a separate building of the late 1960s, and "dedicated to the communications of Baseball," the library is the unofficial repository of the crystalline statistics, player files, periodicals, and volumes of history, biography and fiction which baseball had to communicate with. This unique collection is attended by a very helpful staff, including Jack Reading, the librarian, and Cliff Kachline, the baseball historian, and is accessible to anyone who comes in search of information – from a batting average to the history of a player, a team, or the game itself. This great store of words, numbers the photographic images is also a compelling invitation to the exercise of the historical imagination in a way that the objects in the museum, and perhaps in baseball itself, are not.

My task was to survey and sample the library's unmatched holdings in baseball fiction – the bulk of them fiction for younger readers – but I found time to examine some of the player files and periodicals. If memory serves correctly, approximately 14,000 men have played major league baseball. Beginning in the

1950s, the library has been able to compile basic biographical data on about 9,000 of them by sending questionnaires to the players themselves or to their relatives. The files I examined were uneven but intriguing collections of clippings. Most contained the library's biographical questionnaire which ends with the question, "If you had it to do all over again, would you pursue a career in professional baseball." Of the eight "Black Sox" of 1919 who filled out the questionnaire, all answered a poignant "yes."

In search of some of the germs of Malamud's **The Natural** (1952) I also pored over the numbers of **Sport** magazine between 1949 and 1951, and had the uncanny experience of finding myself reading articles I remembered reading more avidly as a teen-age fan.

My experiences with the "communications" housed in the library thus were an encouraging reminder that memory and imagination can make baseball's past into "living history." It is therefore not surprising that memory and imagination have responded to The Strike by recreating games past and playing "fantasy baseball."

The library keeps human hours – 9 to 5 – leaving the researcher time to enjoy the visual pleasures of the charming village (and that is the right word) of Cooperstown, and the collection of the Hall of Fame and Museum, one of three museums in the area. Bearing in mind that one is stalking in the landscape of the mythic Natty Bumppo more so than that of the legendary Nap Lajoie, and temporarily resisting the call of the Tunnicliffe Hotel's wonderful combination of the English Pub and the Hot Stove League, it is possible to put in some hours each evening in the baseball museum.

The museum is an assemblage of mute objects – balls, bats, uniforms, photos – which try to reveal the history of an institution and of a human activity, which was and is largely unspoken but performed. Wandering through this collection, memory is not enough. It takes a more-than-historical imagination to pump life back into these inert objects on walls and in cases. For this reason, perhaps the best place for the fans is the section which deals with old ballparks. Most of the items in the museum document a profession which the fan has not practiced, but the old seats from Ebbets Field and the enlarged photos of the parks testify to the fan's real access to the lore and wonder of the game, and they speak more powerfully than the hundreds of artifacts of the game itself.

A pilgrim to the imaginative past of baseball may be permitted some literary reflections in this summer of The Strike. One remembers that Chaucer's Canter-bury-bound pilgrims included the venal Pardoner determined to profit from a a sacred institution. The spectres of Grebey, Miller, et. al. are inevitable compan-ions, but they cannot destroy the enchantment of Cooperstown. Together, the village, the museum and the library suggest that baseball is both continuous and timeless. When you try to imagine the past, the various eras of baseball seem as one, defying compartmentalization. At the same time, the objects, photos, records and written histories and stories all seem to exist — thanks to fittingly rural and inaccessible Cooperstown — in a Keatsian "silence and slow time," inviting the imagination to penetrate to a truer essence of baseball, a quality that survives strikes and seasons.

My favorite object in the museum was an enlarged-to-life-size photo of the then still living Hall of Fame "immortals" of 1939. Aging men, somewhat uncomfortable in their suits and ties, they seemed to express the paradoxical elements of the human figures who represent baseball's real history. They were at once legendary players – Alexander, Collins, Johnson, Lajoie, Mack, Ruth, Sisler, Speaker, Wagner and Young – whom one imagines as the lithe, cunning and powerful figures on a ball field, despite the fact that in the photo they really look like somebody's grandfather. (To the imagination, Cobb, who arrived too late for the photo, is off somewhere in search of a stolen base.) At the same time, they are the "immortals" whose faces and great accomplishments gleam from the memorial plaques in the hallowed Hall of Fame.

Yet in the photo, the Babe, flanked by the dapper Collins and the ministerial Mack, sits at his ease, the only figure disdaining a ceremonial still collar and tie, his casually crossed legs revealing his two-tone sport shoes and the indescribable gesture of fancy socks rolled jauntily down around his ankles.

Blodgett's Blotter

With me now it's a struggle of playing the game in the daytime instead of night. In the beginning it was a celebration, a game played to show the beauty of nature (Ceres), in the great outdoors in a land of all outdoors. But now it's a land of doors. And I know you struggled against that. And now it's turned into something even more Art Official. My student dictionary reads: of-fi' ci-ate, 1. Eccl. to conduct a service; act as celebrant of any rite or ceremony.

As this letter is being written on what used to be "Inauguration Day" but now is National Teacher's Day, I can only wonder as how the rules have changed. Now St. Louis' Coleman says he's going to steal 200 bases per year. That means 2 bags per at bat, or 200 base hits. Something has to swing back to favor the "Designated Pitcher" or the game is kerput.

The ballplayer is now a man of two hats. The hard hat worn at bat resembles the battlefield helmet of the Second World War. While the First World War helmet resembled the petasus of Mercury (Hermes). That was back when baseball was the national pastime, but now it's the national past bedtime.

And we wonder what tomorrow will bring –

E. Wright Blodgett

Report from Washington
(Or, A Washington Fan's Lament)

George R. Kaplan

The saga of baseball in the free world's capital is full of distant lasts: last World Series championship in 1924, last pennant winner in 1933, last major league team (to stretch a point) in 1971. Among Washington's other distinctive low points are losing two franchises, including an expansion team, and holding the American League record for last place finishes.

No laughing matters, these. The hurt is deep. It's almost as bad as the pain that comes from knowing that it may never end.

There is no state of the baseball art here at a time when Washington has finally arrived as a world-class capital. Only a small fraction of the population even remembers a procession of Presidents throwing out ceremonial first pitches at Senators' openers. Walter Johnson is the name of a high school in suburban Maryland. The excellent RFK Stadium, big league in every particular, has only the football Redskins as a permanent tenant.

Yet the habits and values of baseball are embedded in much of this town (Washington is always "this town" to insiders and lifers). Even the President allowed that greeting a contingent of Hall of Famers in the White House had been a transcendental experience. Pundits like James Reston, George Will, and Tom Wicker, among others, sprinkle their columns with strained references to their baseball-connected triumphs and simply aren't Washington's team. They belong to Baltimore, a marvelous, self-contained city with a distinctive style and without the slightest cultural or athletic affinity to Washington.

There is irony in our isolation. This town's principal commodities are supposed to be the clout and savvy its brokers of influence deploy in disposing of the affairs of a world power. Yet no one seems capable of putting a baseball team into a stadium that American tax-payers built a generation ago and that saw fewer than 30 days of use, none of them for baseball, in 1981. Even the city's beautiful people, the social trend-setters and power-wielders, are ready for big league ball and will throw a series of Embassy balls and pre-season galas when it returns. We don't want the Twin City Griffiths back. Minnesota got them fair and square by capitalizing on one American family's greed. Nor do the Arlington Rangers have even vestigial appeal. They will always come up Short in our book.

We face another long season in 1982. There will be late night drives back from

Bawlmer, the rare pleasures of spotting a comer in the Carolina League, and the questionable delights of Monday Night Baseball.

Why are we being punished? So what if we seem to squander your tax dollars and screw things up around the world. Everyone makes mistakes. We're human, too. Return major league baseball to Washington, and we promise instant restoration of all that's great and good in American life.

Daytona Beach

Seth Moskowitz

My first brush with the Florida Leagues came when I was working as a musician in Daytona Beach. Wandering home after a few too many free Budweisers at the Boot Hill Saloon, a local biker bar, I happened upon City Island Ball Park. Noting that the stadium lights were on, I went in to explore. As I came around the back of the stadium I found a wooden fence. When I got closer I realized that knotholes in it provided a perfect view of center field, so I stayed and watched a good six innings without anybody asking me to move. I had come upon my personal baseball fantasy.

And that's what "A" ball is, one of the last true remnants of the baseball days of old. All too often we are exposed to the tribulations of those who have made it, those six hundred who have reached the top. "A" ball gives us an opportunity to see those on the rise, and those in their decline, those who might only go as far as double or triple A, those who may go all the way, or those who are simply giving it one last shot. All of this at an admission price of $1.50, five for $5.00.

One night I went to City Island Park to see Brent Strom, a fair-to-middling pitcher for the Indians, Mets, but most notably the Padres, who developed arm trouble, had the same "Bionic arm" surgery as Tommy John, and was trying to make his comeback through the Astros organizations. That night, his pitching debut, he was facing the Lakeland Tigers.

I took my seat in the Herb Sussman Grandstand instead of the old stands for two reasons. Not only was it close enough to the plate to catch foul balls, but it also, to me, served as the ultimate monument to the fickle nature of the Major Leagues, having been built to appease the Montreal Expos. It seems that the Expos couldn't get enough people in the Daytona stadium to make their exhibition games profitable. Local entrepreneur Sussman responded by building his beautiful grandstand; the Expos responded by moving their Spring Training camp to West Palm Beach. So this "beautiful monstrosity" ended up strictly for the use of die-hard minor-league fans like me.

Strom was obviously not in major league form. Many of his pitches were high and wild, many were jumped on for base hits, but every once in a while he'd let go a real major league pitch. You could see the difference in the way the ball would give that extra curve, or drop just oh so much as it reached the plate.

Strom's wildness got the better of him and he was pulled after a few innings. He was replaced by a youngster who kept sending low fast-balls — one doesn't find control pitchers in the Florida Leagues — over the plate. Though the Tigers were unable to score another run off of this young whiz, the Astros' helplessness at the plate led to Strom's defeat, 4-0.

Strom didn't regain his form that summer, and, as I moved north shortly afterward, I never had the chance to fully chart his attempted road to recovery. For all I know, with minor league coverage the way it is, he might still be in Daytona today.

Though I never won any door prizes and my Astros wound up in last place both summer seasons, it didn't matter, for I *was* seeing baseball at its finest. It might not have been great – it might not even have been good – but it was played with spirit, and that's what counts.

A Poem Written While Breaking Curfew with Rhod 'Stork' Wallace in Corpus Christie, Texas after the Texas City Stars Won a Game

Paul Shuttleworth

– for Al Gallagher & for Bill Bryk, who owes me a bottle of vodka
for a slider of his I took relatively deep in Beeville, Texas.

When I had the catcher's gear on
during batting practice tonight
McKay's curve was a wolf, never
taking the same trail to the den,

yet, Stork, you practiced hitting
foul tips back at me with
precision of a king's son riding
a favorite horse.

What does it
mean in this derelict league when
a shortstop has his best game in
a whorehouse in Reynosa, Mexico?

I own the nothing of a swollen
left hand. It's the nothing of
an ant hill swarming over a knife
a child stabbed into the labyrinth.

Stork, you got two hits, and you've
a right to eat that Coors can in
your fist, but shit, stay off the
motel balcony; don't get Gallagher
down here to fine us.

Maybe it'll
rain on our hangovers tomorrow, but
what will it mean when a pitcher we
both know finds out Billy Graham
won't bring back the fastball?

And
thank you, Stork, for pulling me off
that car in the motel parking lot in
Harlingen the last time we were shit-
faced after curfew. Before I passed
out on it, I was sure I saw my orphan
self dead in the swimming pool.

This
drinking, Stork, is as nifty as the
hickey that girl in Refugio has. You
know her, the waitress in the all-night
cafe. It's a blue star rotating on her
neck, just about that gold-plated
necklace that has a lynched unicorn
dangling off it between her two chalk-
colored breasts.

You've got a right
to eat that motel light bulb, and I'm
sure you'll do it, but why spit out the
best part all over the Cadillac below
the balcony?

You got it all wrong
on the team bus yesterday. I have
no argument with the first baseman
who wants to fuck a cow. But why
spend two hundred miles talking it
over? The poor man's head is a coffin;
and it has nothing to do with the Mets
releasing him over the curve low and
away.

Driving across Texas the other
night, looking out the bus window at
the land between Beeville and Victoria,
my eyes filled with tears: it was the
train window I looked out of as I left
my Irish love in '71. Her pale blue
eyes were inches from mine. And it
has nothing to do with being O-for-July.
I used to look at her photo the way
Sty Verbam inspects balls he bobbles
at second base: carefully, as if he's
just found a bag of moonman shit.
No, that's not it . . .

It's loving
your wife and kids, yet wanting to
hold an hour you robbed in a place
where there are castles, where there
is waist-high grass some farmer will
cut to find a girl's azure panties –
still smelling of sex.

I've forgotten
the signals I need to know: hand to shirt
to cap, to ear, to belt buckle – the magic
of hit & run that denies the nothing of
my swollen left hand that's taken too
many of Brooksey's fastballs.

You've
got a right to eat that beer can, Stork,
and I hope it tastes okay, but why walk
out to Gallaghers' room to see if he'll
fine us for breaking curfew? That's
like the Galveston girl getting laid
by our relief ace and telling the guy's
roomie not to pay attention: "I'm only
a dream."

And thanks, Stork, for throwing
me the extra batting practice, though it
hasn't done me much good. Still, I enjoy
seeing my name on the bat as it passes
under a knuckle-curve. It makes me think
of my daughters trying some day to make
some
sense out of this.

Sure, let's mix in another
Coors and talk about what we know: if we're
true, we carry nothing but Red Man chewing
tobacco, knowing that good seasons are
followed by eyeglasses or orthopedic jock-
straps and pacemakers.

All we can do
is laugh, laugh the kind of laugh a
man laughs when he writes his own obituary
for **The Sporting News**, the kind of
laugh
I've taught my old wolfhound to laugh –
dry and without malice.

Stork, we don't
have big-league meal money, but there are
no brochures for tombstones in our
luggage. We don't sip tea with widows
as an insurance policy is placed on a
kitchen table like a butcher knife.
What I'm trying to say is there are
men who smell like sulphur, who take the
odor to the cribs of their children.

What I'm trying to say is I don't
think the cabbie hauling us back
from the whorehouses on the other
side of the storm-flooded river
gave a shit about our batting averages.
He only trembles and endures the bad
shock absorbers in his cab.

                              Stork,
it's been a long time since I've heard
rain bounce off a tin roof. But that's
not what I meant to tell you:

                         When I had
the catcher's gear on during batting
practice tonight, I'd beaten the nausea
of America, the hair dryers, queens for a
day, laundromats filled with fat district
attorneys waiting to indict some fool
who wants to steal a dime's worth of
detergent to commit suicide with.

Yes, I really do believe the woman with
massive tits at the Sheraton pool in
McAllen is a doctor, and no, I don't
think the Victoria third baseman is in
love with their left-handed starter, and
yes, the umpires are horseshit (especially
Bennett, who's a decent guy), and no, I
wouldn't keep Jim around if I were
Gallagher
just 'cause the guy plays a decent game of
spades on the all-night rides. What the
hell, the guy hasn't found the third
inning in weeks. And no, I ain't mad
because Jim put the slider off my leg in the
Victoria bullpen at nearly a hundred miles
a bruising hour.

No, my wife doesn't
mind "Hard Throwing Ink" living with
us. He's quiet and my daughters like
him, and it's no big deal when the
chewing gum falls out of his mouth
onto the living room rug when he falls
asleep.

What I meant to tell you is
this: we're beating the nothing we'll
have when this is a hundred years old
and no one remembers there was a Lone
Star League. I play baseball because
I'm the man in the Supervielle poem
who liked to pass his hand over a
candle flame to convince himself he
was alive. You're my friend, Stork,
because you carry, next to your glove,
a candle or two, which is as good as
chewing Red Man and hitting the longball.

Remembering the Soos

David A. Evans

The ball I threw while playing in the park
Has not yet reached the ground.
   – Dylan Thomas

1

I was a boy running at night, inside a yellow river of headlights, running
alongside the slow, bunched-up cars flowing out of the main parking lot of the
baseball park after a game. I was running and breathing easily. My light-footed
steps on the gravel shoulder blended with the kicked-up dust and reddish
exhaust and the ticking gravel that sounded like grasshoppers popping around
in dry weeds. I was in no hurry; I was saving up my energy. I was just going
home like everybody else. In my right hand was a baseball. Now and then a car
honked at the one in front of it, or at me.

The river of headlights divided, at 11th and Steuben, into two rivers: One kept following south toward the South Bottoms, a neighborhood near the packinghouses; the other – the one I took turned right and headed toward the Wall Street bluff and the west and north parts of town. The noise of the traffic was cut almost in half. I had to quicken my pace because now there were fewer cars to run with, and they were moving faster.

I ran past the gravel company, past the soybean mill with its odor of baking soybeans, over the four sets of railroad tracks east of the mill, past two empty boxcars under the bluff – the light from the headlights shooting through their open doors – then hurried up the steep, one-block hill that ended with a stop sign on the Wall Street, my street.

The river of traffic flowed on, car by car, through the stop sign, dividing again, this time in three ways: straight ahead toward Court Street and the West Side, left for downtown, and right, up Wall Street. I turned right, ran about 10 more yards, and stopped beside a telephone pole. I was not winded, even after the run up the hill. I had discovered a steady, untiring pace. But my heart was pounding anyway, through my hand held on my chest. I would wait a few minutes, settle down, before I started again. That was my habit.

Now I was on top of the bluff. I stepped up on the curb and looked back across the valley. Except for a few lights on utility poles, and the lights of the stadium, which lit only the ballpark itself and the sky over it, the valley was dark. There was no moon because of clouds – grey streaks – so I couldn't see the shiny railroad tracks running out to the end of the horizon and over it, south to Omaha.

But I knew where things were. The roundhouse with all its pigeons cooing or asleep inside the rafters of the fast, tarred roof. The pyramids of gravel and sand inside the high mesh fence of the gravel company. The small rat pond with those tensely-pinging powerlines above it. I tried to fix my sight on the exact places for all these things – even that lone boxcar just north of the roundhouse. It had to be there too, with its sides busted out like a bloated cow because it had stood too long in Missouri flood water.

I looked at the empty ballpark a mile away. A smoky haze, like a low cloud, hung over the brown infield and green outfield. Soon the line of cars from the parking lot would be gone. Then a few minutes later the stadium lights would go out, and the whole valley would be black. I watched until the last car was leaving. I wondered what the driver was thinking. Did he know he was both the beginning and the end of a river?

I had two blocks to go – one block downhill, one block uphill – mostly in the dark because very few cars were going up Wall Street now. I stepped off the curb onto the pavement, and leaned toward home like a runner poised under a starting pistol. It wasn't exactly fear that I felt. It was the *anticipation* of the fear that would be running with me when I got to the bottom of the hill. It was like being on a roller coaster at the top of the ride, above the trees and about to start down. You know your guts will drop and your breath will be sucked out as you fall. It would be like that, without the wild screaming of the girls and the clattering of steel wheels on steel tracks.

With springy steps I crossed the street to the sidewalk and broke into a half-sprint just as a car turned down the hill behind me. Running downhill was easy; all I had to do was lengthen my stride and relax. Yet if I relaxed too much my legs would jolt me as if I was running on stilts. The car coasted the first half-block, then as I leveled out down the brief straightaway its momentum carried it past me and the lights flashed by. A second car was gaining on me now, and as I shortened my stride into a full sprint, uphill now, suddenly fear was running with me. Fear was not a shape; it was the sound of footsteps, *my* footsteps, that I could speed up or slow down at will. The second car's headlights flashed past me just as I hit the incline at top speed. No headlights replaced the last ones so I was running in a gap of darkness. I knew by the sound of my steps on the brick sidewalk – the lightness, the intervals – exactly how fast I had run before and how fast I was going now, and I was surprised by my speed. I couldn't outrun the fear, but I could make it run faster than ever. My knees were pumping almost chest high, my gym shoes ticking over the smooth bricks. When I got to the alley I flew across it without glancing down its black throat, then reached the picket fence of my house, vaulted over it on one hand and leaped onto the cement porch.

The fear was gone. No lights were on. Everybody was in bed. Breathing hard, I steadied myself on one knee close to the porch swing, and felt my heart again. It was still flying up the sidewalk on light legs.

Upstairs in my bedroom, I tossed my new baseball on my bed. I opened my dresser drawer and reached in under the rolled-up socks and folded tee-shirts and pulled out the other balls, filled my stretched-out shirt with them, and dropped them all on the bed. I arranged them in a row from oldest to newest, smudgy to clean white. Twelve balls. I could almost count my birthdays with them. I jumbled them together on the bedspread to see if I could spot the new one. It was the shiniest. I picked it up and turned it over in my hands, feeling the hard seams and rubbing it down the way an umpire does. I smelled the white leather mixed with palm sweat.

I gathered all the balls in my shirt again and put them back in the drawer, and closed it. I undressed, switched off the light and got into bed. I watched the little pasted silver stars on my ceiling gradually appear. Now and then the headlights of a car flattened out and slid over the ceiling and down the wall. A few minutes later, facing the open window, I saw the faint glow in the sky over the Cardwell roof across the street and over the valley, go out. That was the ball park light. I wondered, as I often wondered: Do the lights make a noise when they go out?

2

Thirty years away, when I remember the Sioux City Soos' ballpark, it's the sounds that came back first. The spirited, piercing, two-tone whistle of the left fielder, immediately followed by "Come babe" – an exhortation to the pitcher. The call of the pop vender making his way through the grandstand and box seats: "Iiiiiice cold pop! . . . Iiiiiice cold pop! . . . – and sometimes, the smart-aleck, anonymous echo: "Tastes like slop!" The theme song on the P.A. system before the game, during warmups:

Sioux City Sue,
Sioux City Sue,
There ain't no gal as true
As my Sweet Sioux City Sue

And, from the roof over the grandstand, the lofty voice of the captain of the ball shaggers, after a ball has popped up over the stadium lights and is about to land with a chunky thud on a shiny car top in the parking lot: "Overrrr!" And then the chunky thud.

The taste of water from the men's restroom comes back too – the best water I've ever had. If you weren't careful when you turned the loose knob, the sudden blast could knock the little coneshaped dispenser cup out of your hand and soak your clothes. What worked best – and is still the way I prefer to drink water – was to stick your head in the sink and use one or both hands for a cup. The water was so cold it made my teeth ache. I couldn't get enough of it; I drank until my stomach hurt.

Several friends and I used to hang around that ballpark in our early teens, in the early '50s. The Soos were a class A farm club in the old Western League that included teams from such far-away places as Colorado Springs, Pueblo, Wichita, and Des Moines.

Just outside the right field fence was a line of trees along a creek. We could always sneak in. We usually waited until just before the game started; then, with a ball glove dangling on a wrist, we climbed a tree, dropped over the fence and scattered slick as rats into the moving crowd. Or if we were already in the park when the game started, as we often were, it didn't make sense to have to pay, so we didn't. As the season waned, the game cop gave up chasing us out when he saw us topping the fence. He would simply look the other way, knowing we had a dozen more entrances. Sometimes just to look respectable we'd buy tickets and walk through the front gate with honest faces. But that was rare.

A second group, which my friends and I were part of, not only watched the game but played catch behind the bleachers, got to know some of the players by running errands for them – getting them cokes, chewing tobacco or cigarettes from the concession stand – and moved freely around the park, both outside and inside the fence. We couldn't keep the game balls we retrieved, but we could take home a practice ball now and then, if it was watersoaked or too beat up to use for batting practice.

At the top of the pecking order were the shaggers, those hired to retrieve balls. Because they were the oldest, and usually the biggest and toughest, we made sure they could tolerate us. They didn't quite have the authority to kick us out if we acted up, but they could man-handle us if they needed to. We too wanted to be shaggers when we turned 16 and were eligible for work – and be paid for having all that prestige – and so we made their job easier by helping them chase balls. Up to a point, anyway.

The captain of the shaggers for a couple of seasons was a big, barrel-chested, awkward guy named Sam Hastings. Sam lived in my neighborhood on the Wall Street bluff and was in high school while I was still in Woodrow Wilson Junior High. He was dependable and commanded respect. His position during a game was on top of the long roof over the grandstand. From that height he had a panoramic view of the action and would shout down his instructions to the other shaggers. Though there were chairs on the roof, he never sat down. He kept shambling back and forth like a bear, always ready with each pitch to follow the ball wherever it might go.

Sam had several other shaggers under him: one or two in the bleachers, one in the front parking lot, one on the scoreboard, and often a "floater" who had to get the balls from the others and relay them up to the roof. The scoreboard shagger had the extra job of shoving the big slate numbers, usually zeros, into the slots after each half-inning. It was a privilege to be able to stand on the scoreboard catwalk with the shagger. With your head stuck through an empty square hole, you had an excellent view of the game, and might even start up a conversation with the right fielder, who always seemed bored because he was so far from the action.

But Hastings on the roof had the best view of the game, and he was in control. Any balls we got hold of had to go to him. Even though every shagger except the one in the parking lot could see the ball off the bat and respond to it on their own, Hastings made everything official with his shouting. When a ball went over the left-field fence, fair or foul, he shouted "Leffffft!" when a homerun ball was driven far enough over the left- or center-field fence to make the dump (Dick Stuart of Denver, who later starred for the Pittsburgh Pirates, had the habit of slugging the ball over the flag pole at the 402-foot mark in dead center); the word was Dummmmmmmp!" When a ball barely cleared the right-field fence, the the word was Creeeeek!" (We pronounced it "crick" but when you shouted it the "ee" sound carried better.) The shaggers knew where the ball was going, could see it with their own eyes. That's what they were being paid for. And yet Hastings kept shouting the obvious.

I resented him for it. He was, I suppose, one of the first non-adults in my life, not including my older brother, who could make me do something I didn't necessarily want to do. I resented him also — and envied him — because he was being paid to watch the game. How could a person get paid for having such a good time? And yet he always looked too serious and busy to be enjoying the game.

Sometimes I would sit alone on a tree limb outside the fence, leering up at Hastings. He wasn't looking at me; he had work to do, and who was I to him but another punk waiting for a chance to steal a ball? I shouted at him, not loud, from my safe perch.

"You bastard you!"

If I ever caught his eye, nothing came of it. Hastings got to know which batters hit the most foul balls and homeruns. When they were at the plate he tensed up with each pitch. When the batter swung and missed, his tension released itself in body English.

A shagger could never throw a ball back onto the playing field unless the umpire or a player called for it. Between innings, when he had accumulated four or five balls, Hastings rolled them one by one down the screen stretched over the grandstand to the bat boy – a clean kid named Denny in a clean white uniform – who gave them to the plate umpire, who inspected them, rubbed them down and, if they were still usable, dropped them into the ball bag slung from his waist like a sower's pocket.

Catching or chasing after foul balls or home runs was sheer joy. Getting your hands on a brand-new baseball was like suddenly finding a huge diamond. And it was a challenge, since all of us wanted to be the one who got to the ball first and then turned it over to a shagger. If you were fast enough and rough enough with your elbows and were able to retrieve several balls in one game, you might even be in line for a shagging job. Once, standing near the bleachers, I reached up to snag a towering foul ball, with everybody watching, and the ball grazed my glove and struck me in the left eye, knocking me out. When I came to, somebody was holding a chunk of ice on my left eye.

But there was another, hairier challenge: to be the first one to the ball and, with nobody watching, to nonchalantly kick it into a clump of weeds or under a board and hope that it wouldn't be found. Then you would try to lure the others to some other spot where you were sure you say the ball landed. After the game you would go back and find the ball and take it home. It didn't work often, but I managed to squirrel away my share of balls over several seasons. The excitement was in that moment when you had found a ball and then you had to decide, in a split second, whether to surrender it or ditch it. It never failed to start up a surge of adrenalin.

I remember well my first encounter with a shagger. By the age of 13 or 14 I had an ambivalent role at the park: too old to be a mere scrambler, a ball surrenderer, and too young to be a shagger. And I was no wimp, and shaggers knew it. One night I was sitting on a favorite limb, outside the right-field foul line, watching the game. The batter hit a high foul ball my way and I heard Hastings' "Creeeeek!" I lost the ball a moment, but then it crashed through the branches over my head, barely missing me, and splashed in the creek. I slid down the trunk, rolled up my pantlegs to my knees and waded in, scooped up the floating ball, scrambled up the far bank and started sprinting for the railroad tracks. I knew the scoreboard shagger saw it all; for the first time I was openly defying him. I wasn't looking back but I heard him on his side of the creek:

"Evans, I'll kick your ass!"

I kept running. Across the highway over the ditch into the weeds, onto the tracks. It was dusk. I could still see fairly well, so I was taking the shortcut home that would go around the rat pond and up the steps of the bluff onto Wall Street. When I had plenty of distance between myself and the park, I slowed down and looked back. A shagger was after me, Hastings' right-hand man, and then I saw Hastings on the roof, pointing at us, and others watching too.

By the time I got to the rat pond I could hear the guy behind me, since by then the noise of the ballpark had diminished. The long intervals of his steps, the hard huffing told me he was running all out. But all I had to do was keep running. I was fast enough. I slowed down on the narrow path that went around the pond; the path was muddy from a recent rain. Just as I was about to clear the pond by jumping up onto the next set of railroad tracks above it, I saw a rat. It was in the middle of the path, looking up at me, its teeth showing. It was one of the biggest rats I"d ever seen. I couldn't go around it because of the water on one side, and the mounds of rubbish which might have more rats in them, on the other side. Rats scared me, even when I was not alone. I'd seen people attacked when they tried to corner them, here and in the sewer under Wall Street, the rats charging with fierce squeaks. The fact that I had stolen a baseball – a brand new one at that – increased my fear by adding guilt to it. This rat, maybe had been laying for me? The Rat of Guilt?

So there I was, crouched, frozen, stopped by a staring rat, with a shagger bearing down on me. I cocked the ball, my only weapon, and aimed for the face. I brought it down as hard as I could into the rat's back just behind the neck. The ball struck like the apple in Gregor Samsa's side in Kafka's story. The rat squeaked once, and started to die. I looked closely at its eyes. Glass beads, crayfish eyes, bulging. The same eyes I had seen in the rat traps my father used to set in the basement of our acreage house many years before. The same hideous bubble of blood growing at the edge of the mouth.

I didn't want the ball now; I leaped over the rat onto the bank and headed for the steps. When I got to the first landing I stopped and looked back. The shagger had evidently found his ball because he was walking back to the park. I imagined him digging it out of the rat's back and wiping it off on his pantlegs to make it look new again for Hastings.

The incident changed my role at the ball park. I never again felt like I might be in line for a shagging job. The shagger didn't kick my ass. He had only been bluffing. But after all, Hastings had gotten his ball back, which was the main thing.

Now I had some leeway. I wouldn't from then on openly taunt the shaggers, and yet they knew I wouldn't hesitate to take game balls if I got the chance. The price of my relative freedom to disdain the shagger's authority was their lack of interest in me. No more sitting on the scoreboard. No more running the ball up to Hastings when the floating shagger was too busy. But it wasn't a bad price.

3

Watching the ball game and chasing after balls weren't the only recreations at the Soos' park. There were special nights, like Shrine Night sponsored by the Sioux City Shriners, with various contests and acts. I was in an ice-cream eating contest once, which took place near the pitcher's mount. Eight or ten of us kids were lined up and handed an ice-cream spoon and a quart of vanilla ice cream apiece. When the voice in the P.A. system said go, we were to see who could down the most in three minutes. The crowd laughed hysterically but we were gluttons in earnest. I won, and nearly froze my stomach.

The great pitcher Dizzy Dean was invited to town one day for a Shrine game. Dean had been drinking heavily all day. Obviously feeling loose, he stepped up to the plate before a packed-in crowd, somebody threw him a pitch at batting-practice speed and Dean clobbered the ball over the center field fence, a hell of a poke for anybody.

There was a man billed as "the clown prince of baseball," an ex-player evidently, who would put on a show before games. Dressed in a baseball suit, with a clown's face, he would shoot a ball almost straight up out of a cannon at home plate, get in his jeep and roar into center field where the ball – shot so high you could have taken a coffee break under it – was coming down. He would circle, do figure eights, zig zag, stand up in the seat, steer sitting backwards or with his feet and, at the last second drive under the ball and reach out and snag it in his oversized catcher's mitt. I never saw him miss. He was amazing.

We invented our own recreations too; for instance, peeking at the women. One way was to walk under the bleachers or grandstand pretending, official faced, to be looking for a dropped billfold or set of keys, and then simply look up under dresses and slips. There was a joke among us that always got raging laughs. Someone would say: "Ever read the book, **Under the Grandstand**, by Seymour Butt?" It wasn't until years later that I realized that "Seymour" was the name of a person; at the the time I thought it was spelled "See More," since that's what it sounded like. The joke was all the more delicious because we could raunch it up by changing the end of it.

"**Under the Grandstand**, by Seymour Pussy?"

"**Under the Grandstand**, by Seymour Ass?" And so on.

The other way of watching the women was even more interesting. Some clever boys, in the daytime when nobody was around, had drilled a couple of holes in the wall of the women's restroom. Usually the buses were parked just outside the back of the restroom, and the area was not well lighted, so we had a secret place for viewing. But we had to be careful. If we were caught we'd be kicked out, maybe for good. We took turns being a sentry, and took turns peering through the holes. The bigger you were the longer you got to look, and the better was the scene for your eyeball. Sometimes we'd make such a racket arguing over whose turn it was to look, that the woman inside heard us. She would either stuff the hole with tissue or leave and report us to the management, or both. Eventually there were so many complaints that the management boarded up the holes and alerted the bus drivers, some of whom had themselves been peekers, to report any funny business.

I have two unerasable images from that eyeballing. One is a woman struggling out of a girdle so tight I thought it was her skin. The other is a pair of white panties with blue stripes. They belonged to a player's wife, a beautiful woman I could never again look at without being both embarrassed and agitated.

4

The names. Thirty years away, the names are still an enchantment to me. To say out loud, to write down, Eddie Bressoud, Bill White, Ernie Yellen, Billy Pavlick, Mario Picone, Ray Johnson. Of all the names I once knew over the several summers of games I went to, so few come back to me, and yet those few blaze in my memory.

Bressoud, White, and Picone were the only ones on my remembered list who made it to the majors, and Bressoud and White distinguished themselves, especially White, one of the few blacks who played for the Soos. Maybe it's mostly because they made it big that I remember their names so readily. I have no image of White, though I'm sure I saw him play. He played one year with the Soos, and then was called up. One fact sticks: that he long-jumped 24 feet in high school. That may be legend, like being told once by old timers (as I have been) that a poor kid named Willie Mays once hitch-hiked to Sioux City, tried out for the team, and wasn't quite good enough. Only recently did I hear the real story, which is not what the legend says. During the 1949 or 1950 season somebody in the New York Giants' front office in New York (the Soos were a Giant farm club) called the brass in the Sioux City front office and asked if they wanted a kid still in high school in Alabama, a black kid destined to be a major leaguer. His name was Mays, they had already signed him up, and the Giants thought he was ready for class A. The only problems, as far as the Soos were concerned, was the color of his skin. Very few teams in the early '50s were ready to take black players, and Sioux City was not about to start anything.

Willie Mays then bypassed class A, went directly to the Minneapolis triple-A club, tore up the league with a .477 batting average, and soon was called up to New York City. The rest, as everybody knows, is baseball history.

I remember Bressoud, a true natural. He broke in with the Soos and quickly became a star shortstop at the age of 16 or 17. I can still see him moving, nifty as a cat, snagging hot grounders with unbelievable ease. In his floppy uniform, with his boyish face, he might have been mistaken for the bat boy.

For me, the name Billy Pavlick is magical. He too was young, an outfielder with a tremendous throwing arm, a good clutch hitter, and very popular with the crowd. Sometimes before a game several outfielders would get together in deep right center near the scoreboard and make bets on who could throw a ball the farthest. They took turns throwing toward the grandstand. I once saw

Pavlick actually throw a ball over the grandstand roof. His catapult arm was his main talent. You heard the name Pavlick so often around the ball park that you assumed he would one day be a big leaguer.

He did play briefly in double A, and was killed, young, in a car accident. His death reminds me of A. E. Housman's famous poem, *To an Athlete Dying Young*, in which the poet celebrates the death of a young runner, whom he calls a "smart lad, to slip betimes away / From fields where glory does not stay," and opposes him to those athletes who have sadly outlived their playing days, "Runners whom renown outran / And the name died before the man." For me and for hundreds of Soos' fans of the late '40s and early '50s, in the case of Billy Pavlick the man died before the name.

I have a clear memory of Ernie Yellen, a catcher. Tall, ghostly pale, reserved, one cheek packed with tobacco, Yellen had the peculiar habit of cocking and flicking his wrist once or twice before he released the ball. I imitated him as a catcher in my sophomore year in high school, but I could never get that sudden flick just before I released the ball. It was all show when I did it; it seemed natural for Yellen, though it must have cost him a split-second in his pegs on attempted steals. He was one of those "regulars" who stayed on year after year and was never good enough to play above class A.

Mario Picone. Black hair, handsome, a flashy pitcher with good speed. He was the kind that women – perfumed and high-heeled and lovely – not only came to watch but to seek out after the game for an autograph, a date, a diamond, a marriage, a family.

Ray Johnson was my favorite. He was a center fielder, extremely fast. He even looked fast. About five-ten, he had a piston-shaped body, a small, greyhound head with a thick jaw, a crewcut with a pronounced whorl in front, and legs that seemed too heavy for his body. His calves and thighs were immense. He hit first in the line-up because he was a good bunter and base stealer. He liked the ball high over the plate, almost eye-level. He rarely hit popups, often striking it near the top. Everybody loved to see him run. He could beat out routine grounders for singles if the ball was not sharply fielded and thrown. He could stretch singles into doubles, would hit the ball, say, deep into the right-center gap, and go flying around the bases, legs blurring, arms pumping wildly.

Johnson had one flaw that was to keep him from rising. He had stiff wrists, and so he couldn't get around well on the ball. He looked like a man swinging a board. The coaches worked with him constantly in batting practice, but he never found a natural swing.

His throwing arm was sometimes erratic too. Once I saw him field a high-bouncing single on one bounce, and with a man rounding third to try to score, he rocked into his throw with plausible grace and fired the ball almost directly into the ground! It wasn't that Johnson had trouble getting *to* the ball or catching it. I saw him make some wonderful back-handed grabs at full speed and some wonderful throws; but his arm, though strong, was inconsistent.

I've always thought it was Johnson's peculiar fate to have been blessed with so much speed that when it came to other talents he had to come up short somewhere. One great gift balanced by one great flaw. Yet if baseball was played like football – defense and offense – he might well have been a major league outfielder.

He was not one of the most accessible players on the team, but he was decent if somewhat standoffish. He did talk and joke with us boys. But one night everything changed, as far as he and I were concerned. What happened between us had a brief history.

In the spring of 1953, shortly after the Missouri River flood waters subsided, I was scrounging around the ballpark with a couple of friends, looking for anything useful. Outside the club house I found a lump of mud in the shape of a fielder's glove.

I took it home and over a period of several weeks fixed it pocket-down on a fence post in my backyard and pounded out the mud and water with a bat and the heel of my hand, and let the glove dry in the sun. I spent hours on it, squeezing the pocket, forcing it back into shape. It had a few cracks and was still soggy deep inside the fingers for weeks, but I had restored it pretty much to its original condition before the flood. Gradually, as the wrist band dried, I found a name on it: "Ray Johnson." I scratched out the name and wrote in my own. It was mine.

By the middle of the baseball season I had sold the glove for five dollars to a friend named Dale Nickolson. I loved that glove but felt slightly guilty keeping it, and money was too good to turn down. I had never had the nerve to take the glove to games because Johnson might see it and claim it. I might even be accused of stealing. But Nickolson had had no such fears. He of course could act innocent and say that he bought the glove from me which was true.

One night between games of a double header, Ray Johnson walked by Nickolson and me and noticed the glove. He stopped.

"Where'd you get that glove?" he said.

My legs went weak. Dale didn't hesitate. He pointed at me.

"From him," he said.

"Can I see it?" Johnson asked, and Nickolson handed it to him. He put it on, pounded the pocket a few times, then unbuttoned the wrist band and held the glove close to his eyes. He showed it to us.

"See this?" he said. There was a trace of hostility in his voice. I saw it: the name "Ray Johnson" printed neatly – secretly – in blue ink in a little circle around the steel wrist-band button. What could I say? I who had scratched out "Ray Johnson" and printed "Dave Evans" in its place; I who had sold the glove – whose glove? – to a friend who had scratched out "Dave Evans" and printed "Dale Nickolson" in bold letters on the thumb? Johnson asked me where I got it, and I told him about finding it after the flood, about restoring it on my fence post. He seemed surprised to see it in such good shape. He kept pounding the pocket, turning the glove over, pounding it, feeling it. I knew he wasn't pleased that I'd taken the glove in the first place, and yet he was happy to see it again.

He asked Nickolson if he could use it in the second game. Nickolson obliged, and he walked off, pounding the pocket. I watched him closely in the outfield. He was like a 10-year-old kid, pampering that glove as if it was a birthday gift. After the game he bought it back from Nickolson for ten dollars. From then on I more or less avoided Johnson's eye, and he treated me with what H. L. Mencken called a "freezing courtesy."

5

Why does one man, Ray Johnson, dominate my memories of the Soos? The ball glove incident is one reason, no doubt. But there is another, more fundamental reason, which I discovered only after I began to dig through my past: Johnson and I are alike. It's not simply that out of admiration I've unconsciously tried to emulate him. It's almost as if, through memory, which I now know is not static but dynamic and creative, Ray Johnson and I have melded into one person.

I too had powerful legs and the gift of speed. I too can be standoffish and arrogant, even when I seem friendly. One habit of the '50s, at least in Sioux City among those I grew up with, was to put all your fragile eggs in one fragile basket. Maybe it was a survival strategy we got from our fathers who had picked it up out of the Depression. The prescription: *take that one talent or skill or connection or label that says who you are, and apply it.*

By the age of 14 I had discovered a strategy that worked for me: speed, which my coaches used to say makes up for a lot of mistakes. I had run easily inside a river of headlights, had actually outrun cars on electric legs of fear up Wall Street. Later, in high school I stretched out for long, off-tackle touchdowns, and, like Ray Johnson, ran down fly balls, beat out bunts, stole bases. And when I graduated I was handed a football scholarship, a chance for an education on the promise of pure speed; but I found out after one season that speed wasn't everything. There were also blocking and tackling and guts. There were also others – including a kid with a butch haircut from Chicago who ran the hundred in 9.7 – who were faster or just as fast as I was.

I depended mainly on that one thing, but that one thing failed to sustain me. All I could do then, with that new knowledge, was fail all the more completely. So I did. Openly, honestly, deliberately, adamantly, wholesomely – I refused to perform, to attempt other strategies, until that moment when, coming home after a game on a team bus from Vermillion, South Dakota, to Sioux Falls, South Dakota, the words of the coach up front busted through the dark, words I knew would be coming sooner or later, like a baseball fired at my face: *Evans, you're through!*

And so I was, with the pure speed thing.

In the Bleachers

Richard Solly

We are surrounded by so great a cloud of witnesses.
   —Hebrews 12:1

A crack, a thud and dust.
The ball burns up the infield
and smokes as it spins past my glove
out into left field.
I hear someone calling, far beyond the grass,
beyond the fence. I can't see him.
                              That a boy, Ricky!

I kick third base, let the dust swirl:
maybe it's a genie, a leprechaun maybe.
Then crouch as Big Bomb steps up to homeplate:
the pounding of wood, spit and sweat.
I'm happy. I've quit dreaming of wings
as the blast rockets the ball over my head
blazing a path through the blue.
                              That a boy!

Some things belong up there. I love to watch now.
My elbow is cut and scratched,
only it isn't a wound
but a bubble of life's bleeding.
It happens here at third base.
Another ball is smacked, shot down the line.
I dive, stretching my body across the earth
in mid-air until I hear it kiss my glove.
                              And there it is:

a white orb, a stitched globe.
Fruit and ermine my father holds in his hand.
Everyone I've ever loved on this earth is applauding.
They've come back from the dead
and sit in the bleachers: There's Louise,
waving her yellow scarf, Greg, honking a horn,
Ted strumming a banjo. And my father:
                              that a boy!

Reminiscence from a Baseball Outsider

Kate Fuglei

Power Park. That was what it was called. I often answered the phone to a high, thin authoritative voice which squeaked, "Hey, Shrimp. Tell Buddy to get to ball practice at Power Park, diamond one, at 5:00." No one ever called it by the official name, which was the Omaha Public Power District Park. The **Omaha World-Herald** used the acronym O.P.P.D., but to hordes of little leaguers and their families it was simply Power Park. I suppose the Power company considered itself exceedingly generous in bestowing this land for that purpose. The chunk of pancake flat ground just above the Missouri River crossing of the Mormons some hundred years before was large enough for four diamonds. Backstops were provided. And one water fountain. This singular fountain was placed smack in the middle of the four diamonds. The courage needed to attempt a sip while all four fields were in use was more than I could ever muster. Those were long, thirsty summers.

To an eleven-year-old little leaguer the ride down wide, tree-shaded Florence Boulevard to Power Park, the prospect of upcoming competition looming ahead, must have had the feel of explorations by Captain Cook or Christopher Columbus. To me, that little leaguer's nine-year-old sister, Power Park was a vast expanse of grave nothingness. Little grass grew there and the blades that braved the Nebraskan sun were stubbly, bleached and chock full of cockleburs. To this day I marvel at Willa Cather's heroines, who seem to have navigated similar turf barefooted. The power company's open hand had balked at providing bleachers, so erstwhile fans had to provide their own campstools, lawn chairs or blankets. My mother, who faithfully attended every game, who rejoiced in victories, commiserated in losses, and who blithely refused to listen to pleas from her sons for less vociferous support during the games, had pale and delicate skin. Mother is from a generation that still considers this a beauty plus. To insure the protection of its alabaster quality she usually made a point of arriving early so as to claim a spot in the shade of the lone tree at Power Park. Johnny Appleseed obviously made a detour at this point in his trek or was at the bottom of his sack here. In any case, it was a tiny, spindly thing, so much so that its shade was only sufficient for one lucky recipient and her equally pale daughter. This is what my mother told me. The real reason was that if we arrived late, the precious space would be occupied by Mrs. Milhous and her red-hair, bovine daughter, Emily. Mr. Milhous was the Giants' coach. My father was the Dodgers' coach. Though no adult would admit it, and although polite "isn't-itboiling-out-heres?" were always exchanged, to actually sit with these people for the endurance of the game would be considered outright treason. So, laden with lawn chairs, coolers, jackets in case it ever got chilly (which it never did), books and dolls for me, Mother and I would trudge past the reclining and shaded Milhouses. Mother would curse silently, borrow a cap from one of my brothers and fish in her bag for Coppertone. In no time, she would be intent on the game, Old Sol and its freckling impact forgotten, yelling, "Atta way Keneeeee" or "Atta way Bruce-eeee" to the continued consternation of her sons.

I, on the other hand, was never able to work up more than a passing interest in either the sport or the observing thereof. Even when the grand finale of the season, the inevitable playoff between the Dodgers and the Giants, had everyone in a fever grip, I could be found lying on a blanket engrossed in a book, oblivious to the transpiring melees. I could put away a Nancy Drew mystery in one game if it went into extra innings. Same for a Mary Stewart romance. **Gone with the Wind** took a whole playoff series. I remember it well because "Frankly, my dear, I don't give a damn" coincided with a jubilant Dodger victory which to me meant root beer floats for all at Zesto.

I suppose I will always feel like a baseball outsider. However, the benefits of the game aren't lost on me. Whenever, as often happens in summer, the group I'm with becomes absorbed in a game, I take my cue. Adult deadlines and engagements are thrown out the window. I revert to the days of childhood. I find the nearest shade tree. I kick off my shoes. I snatch up the seedy novel I've been yearning to crack. At the end of it all, no matter who won, I dig into a root beer float.

Baseball With Steve Lyon

Bill Meissner

Steve and I could see chalk lines all the way to the majors.

For us, any long patch of grass
was a roaring stadium.
Day after day it was pitch, hit, field:
run for weeks to catch a long fly. Dive
for the tough fast ones just out of
reach, come up tasting dust and grass stains and white leather.

By mid season, the two of us were a whole team.
          (how could we know we'd end up
          swinging shovel in factories,
          pitching waste baskets, sipping
          slow beers in bars, ignoring
          the blaring ball game on the t.v.?)

Near the end of one summer
we sat winded on tin folding chairs at Kluge's Gas,
oceans of sweat gone from the bills of our caps.
We sipped strawberry sodas and stared
straight ahead beyond paint chips on the wall,
thinking only of the beautiful line drives of our futures.

Last Night at the Met

Ken LaZebnik

It came to this end: the lights of the Met
Reflect on wet blacktop an empty lot.
A rain delayed game inside. Who'll bet
This is the end, of season or of Met?
The infield tarp has pools, and kids come slide
And flop to third, where cops then wave them home.
An hour we wait: beer and dog hot by side.
Then play resumes; strike one, strike two, new poem.

It came to this end: The Twins lost at last
Jinxed to their end. Losing as always: thaw,
Melt, resolving into dew, no deep blast
To mourn their loss; just faint fan's calls and caw.
When it comes to my end, what will it be?
Will the end be as good for you or me?

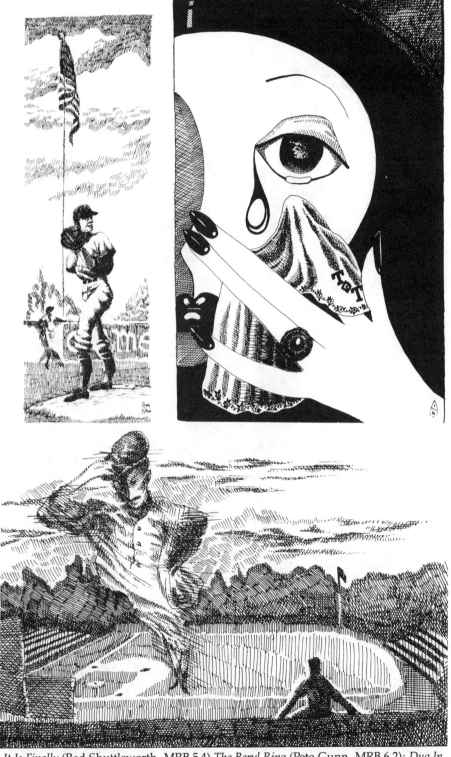

It Is Finally (Red Shuttleworth, MRB 5,4) *The Beryl Ring* (Pete Gunn, MRB 6,2); *Dug In* (Paul Weinman, MRB 6,3). Illustrations by Andy Nelson. *Base Paths: The Best of The Minneapolis Review of Baseball.*

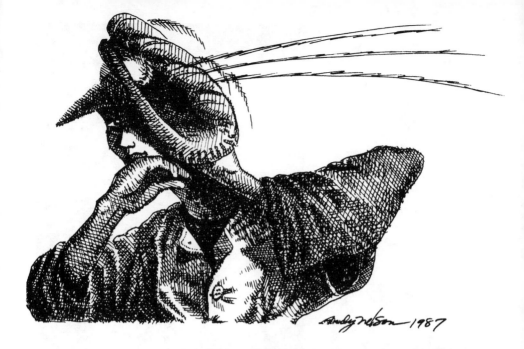

My Child (Paul Weinman, MRB 6,4); *Pappy was right!* (from *The Broken-Bat Single* by George Lausch, MRB 6,1); *Pennant Fever* (Scott G. Miller, MRB 5,4). Illustrations by Andy Nelson. *Base Paths: The Best of The Minneapolis Review of Baseball.*

"We are surrounded by so great a cloud of
witnesses."

Hebrews 12:1

A crack, a thud and dust.
The ball burns up the infield
and smokes as it spins past my glove
out into left field.
I hear someone calling, far beyond the grass,
beyond the fence. I can't see him.
That a boy, Ricky!
I kick third base, let the dust swirl:
maybe it's a genii, a leprechaun maybe.
Then crouch as Big Bomb steps up to homeplate:
the pounding of wood, spit and sweat.
I'm happy. I've quit dreaming of wings

as the blast rockets the ball over my head
blazing a path through the blue.
That a boy!
Some things belong up there. I love to watch now.
My elbow is cut and scratched,
only it isn't a wound
but a bubble of life's bleeding.
It happens here at third base.
Another ball is smacked, shot down the line.
I dive, stretching my body across the earth
in mid-air until I hear it kiss my glove.
And there it is:
a white orb, a stitched globe.
Fruit and ermine my father holds in his hand.
Everyone I've ever loved on this earth is applauding.
They've come back from the dead
and sit in the bleachers: There's Louise,
waving her yellow scarf, Greg, honking a horn,
Ted strumming a banjo. And my father:
that a boy!

We are surrounded by so great a cloud of witnesses (from *In the Bleachers* by Richard Solly, MRB 6,4; *The Resurrection of Johnny Callison* (Pete Gunn, MRB 6,1). Illustrations by Andy Nelson. *Base Paths: The Best of The Minneapolis Review of Baseball.*

God Knocking on the Twins' Door (cover art, MRB 7,1). Illustration by Andy Nelson. *Base Paths: The Best of The Minneapolis Review of Baseball.*

F A L L

The Whole World Was Rooting For the Cubs: A Personal Report on the Chicago Cubs of 1984

Barry Gifford

(The summer of 1984 was the first time the Chicago Cubs had won anything since 1945. Two Cub fans – Barry Gifford and Paul Schersten – and our faithful White Sox fan, Judy Aronson, wrote of their extraordinary season. —Eds.)

* * * * * * *

Back in the neighborhood of baseball, only this time the neighborhood looks different. The seats are filled. Wrigley Field is still the "Friendly Confines," but the team is winning. It's almost July and the Cubs are in a virtual tie for first place in the National League East with Philadelphia and New York. I missed 1969, when the Cubs almost won it, but I'm here to see the 1984 incarnation and believe. The Cubs are almost 300,000 ahead of their 1983 attendance.

It might actually be said that the Phillies are really tied with themselves for first place. There are so many ex-Phils in the Cubs lineup — thanks to general manager Dallas Green, the former Philadelphia field pilot, under whose direction the Phillies won the 1980 World Series — that it reminds me of the New York Yankees-Kansas City Athletics symbiosis of the '50s. Bob Dernier, Gary Matthews, Dickie Noles, Warren Brusstar, Larry Bowa, Keith Moreland, Richie Hebner, Ryne Sandberg, even Jay Johnstone, are all former Phillies doing their best to displace their erstwhile sponsor at the top of the heap.

Combined with other imports such as Bull Durham (St. Louis), Ron Cey (L.A.), Ron Hassey (Cleveland), and the practically homegrown Jody Davis (who in 1983 hit twenty-four homers, second only to Gabby Hartnett for a Cub catcher in one season), and a decent pitching staff, the Philly connection just might pull it off — if not this year then next.

The pitching staff, for the first time in recent memory, is worth talking about. Scott Sanderson, Rick Sutcliffe, Dennis Eckersley, Dick Ruthven (another ex-Phillie), Steve Trout and the Cub Comeback Kid, Rick Reuschel — if they're healthy — make up an acceptable group of starters and part-time starters. Rich Bordi, George Frazier (throwing a great spitter taught to him by Art Fowler when he was with the Yanks), Lee Smith and Tim Stoddard are an often more than adequate relief corps. It's not on a par with the Mets staff (which is reminiscent of the '69 miracle crew that aced out the Cubs at the wire), but it's a tough veteran bunch that should keep the Cubs in contention.

The Tribune Company owns the team now, they're willing to spend some money, and Dallas Green has proved that he is not afraid to stick his neck out on a deal. (Witness the trade of top prospects Mel Hall and Joe Carter to the Indians for Sutcliffe, Frazier and Hassey.) But I think the real reason I want the Cubs to win the pennant now is to see the National League home games all played during the day!

Today's eleven-inning, twelve to eleven Cub victory over St. Louis was certainly one of the most amazing games I've ever seen. At first it seemed that it was merely the Willie McGee and Ozzie Smith Show for national television (it was the NBC Game of the Week), with McGee hitting for the cycle and driving in six runs, including what appeared to be the winning tally. The Wizard of Oz, the redoubtable Mr. Smith, made one spectacular fielding play after another, single-handedly preventing the Cubs from scoring four more runs in the first four innings. But all this was before Ryne Sandberg, the should-be All-Star Cub second baseman, took over.

In a game the Cubs trailed seven to one after two innings and nine to three after five and a half, Sandberg had five hits in six trips to the plate, producing seven runs batted in, including the tying runs in both the bottom of the ninth and the bottom of the tenth. The story there, however, is exactly how Sandberg did it. In the bottom of the ninth, the Cubs down by one and Bruce Sutter (1.19 ERA) on the mound, Sandberg belted a split-fingered fastball over the left field fence to send the game into extra innings. The Cardinals scored two runs in the top of the tenth and it appeared to be the end of a long and interesting afternoon at Wrigley Field. It was to prove even more interesting.

After losing Cub leadoff man Bob Dernier on a three-two count, Sutter had to face Sandberg again. With his next swing, Ryno, as the fans call him, had twenty-four hits in his last forty-eight at bats, twelve in his last sixteen. In what seemed to be a superhuman, Joe Hardy/Roy Hobbs-like performance, Sandberg hit another home run that landed in almost the exact same spot as the previous inning's homer. Forty thousand (!) fans rose as one to cheer him and the Cubs; even the jaded, mostly cynical denizens of the press box, from which vantage point I observed the scene, stood as they marveled over this awesome feat. On the mound, Bruce Sutter, baseball's premier reliever, stamped around like a kid having a fit. Ryno had once more smitten a roundtripper off Sutter's best pitch.

In the eleventh, rookie infielder Dave Owen, the last position player available on the Cub bench, delivered a pinch-hit, bases loaded single to right to drive in Bull Durham with the winning run. After nearly four spine-tingling hours the game was finally, absolutely over. As erstwhile Cub broadcaster Jack Brickhouse was fond of saying, "Nothing beats fun at the old ballpark." All I can add to that at this point is that it may be an old ballpark, but it's definitely a new era.

Bob Dernier belted Eric Show's second pitch of the first game of the National League Championship Series into the left field bleacher seats to put the Cubs up one to nothing over the Padres. After Ryne Sandberg, the National League's Most Valuable Player of 1984, struck out, Gary Matthews later lined another one out, this time to the opposite field, and Ron Cey crushed the fifth of the day to center to establish a new record for the number of home runs by a team in one game of a league championship series. The Cubs were off and running.

Yes, Virginia, the Cubs won the National League East — almost handily, I should add — and for the first time in thirty-nine years the north side of Chicago had a representative in post-season play. On the eve of the playoffs all the major league umpires went out on strike and forced the use of amateur arbiters, but the Cubs figured they had the edge regardless of such unforeseen circumstances. Not only did the Las Vegas oddsmakers and Pete Rose install them as favorites over San Diego (Rose, writing a special column for **USA Today**, picked the Cubs over Kansas City in the Series, too!), but The Tribune Company invited Sam Sianis and his goat to the ballpark.

In 1945, when the Cubs last won a pennant, Chicago tavern owner William "Billy Goat" Sianis put a hex on the team — dooming them as losers from then on — when he was forbidden to bring his goat with him into a World Series game. The Cubs lost that Series to the Detroit Tigers, four games to three, and the curse held up for the ensuing four decades less a year. "Billy Goat" Sianis died in 1970 and his heir, Sam Sianis, lifted the hex in 1981 after the Cubs invited him — and his goat — to a game at Wrigley Field, which proved to be a fortuitous rapprochement. It might not be as good as having God on one's side, but with the Vegas bookies, Charlie Hustle, and the Sianis capricorn behind them, the Cubs were looking good.

As stated above, this version of the Cubs is really Dallas Green's team. If next season they played in Memphis or Tampa it really wouldn't matter in terms of their Chicago origins. But most every major league team these days is a carpetbagged group, so there's no particular reason why the Cubs should be any different. My friend Steve Fagin makes a good case for the Cleveland Indians as the new Cubs. "They've got four Cubs in their starting lineup," says Fagin, "in Mel Hall, Joe Carter, Pat Tabler, and Andre Thornton. The Indians have some power, a few exciting players, only one good pitcher (Bert Blyleven), and they're consistent losers. Plus, they play in an empty ballpark. Just like the old Cubs. Remember all those articles in past years about how one team or another wouldn't win because of their "ex-Cub factor", the number of former Cubs on the Team? Well, one reason the Cubs won this year is that they have the fewest ex-Cubs in their lineup!"

As a gesture of public relations good will, and to establish a respectable link with Cub teams of the previous, decidedly less distinguished era, The Tribune Company, which earlier in the year had severed him from their payroll, invited Ernie Banks back to Chicago to sit on the Cub bench — wearing number fourteen, his old (retired) numerals — during the playoffs. Banks, now a representative for a Los Angeles bank, gladly accepted the offer to participate, albeit in honorary form, in an event he'd never had the opportunity to view from such a perspective during his nineteen year career as a player.

The Cubs won the first game of the National League playoffs by an astounding score of thirteen to nothing, the most lopsided contest in the history of post-season play, including the World Series. In addition to setting a new record for most home runs in one playoff game, the Cubs established new National League marks for hits (sixteen), runs in an inning (six), runs in a game and, in a more esoteric vein, the number of men facing a pitcher in one inning (twelve). Perhaps the most remarkable statistic is that each Cub player in the starting lineup had at least one hit and one run batted in; the combined Cub batting average for the game was .421 (also a National League record).

This auspicious debut was followed by a second Cub victory, this time by a more modest count of four to two. All they needed was one more win to do away with thirty-nine years of failure. It would have to be done, however, in San Diego.

In his final *Newsletter* of the season, a supplement to the *Baseball Abstract*, Bill James wrote — three weeks or so prior to the National League playoffs — that the Padres seemed to have the edge over the Cubs should they meet in the championship series, but that the Cubs were a "heck of a team." The Pads, James said, would have to beat Rick Sutcliffe at least once in order to take the pennant in what was likely to be one of the best league playoffs of all time. My hat, if I wore one, would at this moment be off to Mr. James.

For a while it looked like San Diego wouldn't have another shot at Sutcliffe, but they knocked off the Cubs in style, seven to one, in the first game back at Jack Murphy Stadium. My daughter Phoebe and I went down to San Diego for game four, certain that the Padres had had their brief flurry of success, that Scott Sanderson would administer the coup de grace, saving Sutcliffe for the opening World Series game against Detroit, which had wiped out Kansas City in three straight. (So much for Pete Rose as prognosticator.)

We got much more — and much less — than we'd bargained for. Game Four turned out to be Steve "Call Me Senator" Garvey's Impossible Dream. In the battle of "our" ex-Dodger versus "their" ex-Dodger, Garvey stroked two singles, a double and the game winning two-run homer in the bottom of the ninth, driving in five of San Diego's seven runs; Garvey's counterpart, Ron Cey, who had piled up a club leading ninety-seven RBI during the regular season, stranded seven baserunners during an oh-for-five that included four pop-ups and a weak ground-out to second with the bases loaded in the ninth. It was a great game and the greatest post-season single game performance by a player since Reggie Jackson's three homer show that put LA away for keeps in 1977. Now the Cubs were forced to shoot the works with Sutcliffe.

Phoebe and I watched Game Five on television. She was confident the Cubs would come through; after all, she'd been born and raised in California, land of sunshine and optimism, the New World. I wasn't so sure; I had that Old Cub feeling and I couldn't' shake it. I kept seeing in my mind a sign a Padre fan had held up the night before in Illinois Governor Jim Thompson's face: 39 MORE YEARS.

What happened in game five is public knowledge: After staking Sutcliffe to a three to nothing lead after two innings, the Cubs blew it. Manager Jim Frey left Sutcliffe in too long but that wasn't the only crucial factor. Durham made a critical error on a ground ball, Sandberg had a sure double play hopper off the bat of Tony Gwynn take a crazy leap over his head that went for two bases, Cey went oh-for-four and stranded four more runners; and Steve Garvey, named Most Valuable Player of the series, knocked in the final nail with a single up the middle to lock up the game for the Padres, six to three. It was their first title in the sixteen years of their existence, and they deserved it. Bill James was right: San Diego beat Rick Sutcliffe when they had to and it had been a great series, one of the best.

Walking out of Jack Murphy Stadium on Saturday night, after Garvey's off-field blast had guaranteed tomorrow for the Pads, I took a close look at Padre fans celebrating around me. They were mostly well-groomed, tanned, healthy looking people, Southern Californians. If the Padres lost the playoffs they could say, "Okay, it's too bad, but its been a great season," and look forward to a "winter" of windsurfing and sailboats. But what about the Cub fans? If the Cubs lost, all they had to look forward to was wearing galoshes and parkas and hats with flaps over their ears to ward off "The Hawk," the bitter Chicago winter wind, while they waited at snow-swept streetcorners for busses that never arrive. Without that inner warmth, the glow that comes from knowing the Cubs had finally come home a winner, the wait could be unbearable.

"You spend thirty years in this game, and you get good and damn disappointed,' said Dallas Green. "But this ranks the hell up there with any of 'em." Goose Gossage, the San Diego relief pitcher who had saved the pennant-winning game, understood. "The whole world is shocked right now," Gossage said in the victor's clubhouse. "The whole world was rooting for the Cubs."

— *October 8, 1984*

As the Sparks Fly

Paul Schersten

Man is born to trouble as the sparks fly upward.
— The Book of Job

Christ.

I've been getting a lot of understanding smiles lately, and compassionate shakes of the head and empathetic chuckles. I'm not complaining, but as reactions go, they don't measure up. The only word for games 3-4-5 is pain, vicious pain, and even I was shocked at how bad it hurt.

The tangle — the Cubs, their fans, the relationship — endures. It crosses the generations, and 1984 only kicked it onto a larger stage, with greater possibilities for tragedy. "Believe it or not, it's true," reads a T-shirt the club started selling in August. I have one; it was a gift. I'm afraid to wear it.

Yet it was a good year for Cub fans, a year of stories that will go well with the fated legends of the past. The world watched Sandberg's two impossible home runs off Sutter, tying one contest in the ninth and again in the tenth, but for a favorite I'll go with the game in August that ended with Peter Rose's last at bat as an Expo. With one out, two runners on and the Cubs up by one, Rose's line drive up the middle caromed high off Lee Smith's shoulder and floated down gently to the shortstop, Dave Owen, who doubled the runner off first. Old Harry Caray couldn't contain himself: "God *does* want the Cubs to win!" he cried, as if he'd been arguing about it the night before.

Call it sentiment, or a peculiar aesthetic sense, but I swear Cub fans crave these stories more than other fans do. Give us tales of awesome accident, of unreasonable, unrepeatable heroics. We'll grow silent with wonder, and give the stories names, and fill the decades with things that just could not have happened. And it isn't just baseball. In life, too, we notice coincidence and treasure little unplanned wonders, taking them as evidence of given order, of truth beyond logic: something we're always on the lookout for, and hardly ever find.

So as it began to appear that the Cubs might do it and pull that sword from the stone, I allowed myself thoughts of larger meaning: Would they still be the Cubs, in victory? Were we thoughtlessly engaged in celebration of an ending?

I was ignoring some things.

Such as the fact that all year, like every year, and even on television, they felt like little kids. Steve Trout had psychological problems. Lee Smith, 6'6" and hugely talented, always looked worried on the mound and terrified — near tears — when batting. "In his heart, every Cub fan knows they'll find a way to mess it up," wrote Mike Royko in early August of 1969. The end, when it came this year, hit like an ice pick at this dark heart of the team's fans.

It's awful trying to explain the collapse in San Diego — why the offense became perverse, reduced to occasional illogical home runs, or why a drag bunt and a funny bounce were enough to expose Sutcliffe's mortality. Maybe the problem was the oft-mentioned finiteness of the playoffs, but to me it looked like they froze, convinced by their fans' overwhelming adoration and rickety world view of the rightness of their cause more than the sufficiency of their talents.

"It's a hard thing to find out," sang Gram Parsons, "that trouble is real, in a faraway city, with a faraway feel."

Up against mundane ability, they crumbled. The bad hops of game 5 — under Durham, over Sandberg — only completed the sense of inevitability and the weird thrill that goes with it.

Some have seen good and evil in the playoff, but I'm not sure instinctive fury justifies that analysis. For me, the rage was directed at Steve Garvey. Ineffectiveness and a silly pose disqualify Eric Show and his friends from really serious hatred; Ray Kroc is dead, and he never played baseball. Only Garvey — so self-assured, so reliable in his banality — was a perfect mannequin foil for our love. He has perspective and sees his chances; he'll soon leave baseball and enter politics.

Evil, though? Who knows. It's in this old tension between dreamers and realists that evil hides, and chooses, with a taste for the bland, its proxies.

Names of the Game

Rory Rebecca Metcalf and Gael Montgomery

Mickey Mantle. Say it. *Mic-key Man-tle.*

He's no fool, Mickey. When asked why, on a team of so many talented players, he was especially popular, he gave credit to his name. It sounds good, he said.

Michael Mantle. Mike Mantle. Nah.

Baseball is, as Bill James fans know, a game of science: measurements, formulas, statistics. And baseball is, as Roger Angell fans know, a game of poetry and elusive wonder. Baseball is also, as all fans know, a game of crackpot theories. Which are what you get when you attempt to apply science to poetry. Which we are about to do.

It is a certified fact that only in the world of sport is "Wally" a cool name. Put a Wally in a high school, an office, or on the *Hollywood Squares*, and you have at best an eccentric, and at worst, a genetically determined nerd. But put a Wally in a baseball uniform, and you have thousands of people screaming their lungs out.

Wal-*ly!* Wal-*ly!*, Wal-*ly!*

Yeah. It sounds good. It *feels* good. Even at home — it's quiet, you're reading this — and don't you wanna, well, *yell*? Imagine, then, a summer day, a diamond, and a double, or maybe a double play. And: Wal-*ly!* Wal-*ly!* Wal-*ly!*

Yankee fans know who we mean; Wally Joyner, the Angels' rookie slugger, aka "that punk who beat out Don Mattingly for the All-Star team." And Mets fans know who we mean: Wally Backman. A hitter from the start, and a man who has worked a slow alchemy on his glove, turning lead into...who knows? The name probably hasn't helped their popularity, just made it easier for fans to shout their appreciation.

But what of Howard Johnson? Howard Michael Johnson, to be exact. he's the only player we've ever seen take a curtain call for his fielding. He's also the player whose string of errors inspired a fan to yell, "Hey, what flavor was *that?*" One time at the plate he can look like Reggie Jackson, smashing the ball over the wall for a game-tying three-run homer. The next time up, he can look like, well, Reggie Jackson striking out. This year he's caught between a rock (Ray Knight) and a hard place (shortstop), and there's a hole in the lineup. Knight's got the bat, and Rafael Santana's got the glove, but neither's got the name: "HoJo! HoJo!"

If this man had called himself Mike Johnson, he'd be a nobody.

Any talk of baseball names focuses on the odd and exotic: Urban Shocker, Elroy Face, Vida Blue, Razor Shines. What lore-mongers have missed, though, is the importance of the prosaic. Sometimes, in baseball, the ordinary is transformed. Even the most unassuming name can take on the power of incantation.

It is obvious that some names trip blithely off the tongue while others trip *over* it and fall into a heap, especially in the late innings after much beer has been consumed. However, that mysterious and vital quality which makes a name satisfying to shout — the chant Factor — has remained unexplained. Until now.

The answer lies in poetic meter, or poetic *feet*, the different combinations of accented and unaccented syllables.

Dave Righetti, Greg Luzinski, Phil Rizzuto, Carl Yastrzemski, Keith Hernandez.

These names consist of a monosyllable followed by an amphibrach. In their entirety they sound good. Phil Rizzuto. Amphibrachic feet have a satisfying rhythm when spoken. But try to chant them and the arches fall.

Jim Morrison. Dave Anderson. Paul Molitor. Don Mattingly.

Less common, a monosyllable followed by a dactyl. Like names in the first category, sounds good in toto; try chanting either "Don" or "Mattingly" and you'll understand why Yankee fans just yell "MVP".

Bill White. Jack Clark. George Brett. Pete Rose.

The spondaic foot — two accented syllables — has a real kick. Terse. Tight. Spondees lack the Chant Factor, though Jack Clark sounds great swith all those "K" sounds. *Tough.* Try to chant it and you sound like a clock.

One syllable names generally fizzle unless they have a long "ee" sound:

Pete! Pete!

Keith! Keith!

Heep! Heep!

Gary Carter. Yogi Berra. Eddie Murray. Roger Clemens.

As Mickey Mantle instinctively recognized, trochaic dimeter produces a name of perfect balance.. NO-lan RY-an. The trochaic foot — an accented followed by an unaccented syllable — naturally lends itself to the chant. *Wal-ly, Ga-ry, Oz-*zie. As the chant intensifies, it becomes an iambus with the accented shifted to the last syllable: Ric-*key,* Reg-*gie.*

Reggie. Reginald Martinez Jackson; if this man were called Marty Jackson, he would be exactly three-fifths as famous as he is today. Reggie Jackson, with that repeating "J", sounds *right.* And this: Reg-GIE. Reg-GIE. Reg-GIE.

It's the best hook in baseball.

Some names are just clunkers. George, for instance. Despite the "J" sound, which works such magic with Reggie Jackson, it falls flat. Try to chant for a George, and what do you get?" Jor-Jor." Uh-uh. This, we suspect, accounts for at least some of George Foster's unpopularity. *(But wait a minute, you say. What about George Brett!* That's just it. Only a god like Brett can overcome the handicap of a name like George).

Carlton Fisk. Totally impossible. What's this aristocratic name, which should have "The Third' tacked on the end, doing in baseball?

Kent Hrbek. Not only does this name make an awkward cheer, in print it looks like a creation of the box score typesetter, like Sabrhgn or Krnche. Or his own teammate, Brnnsky. Small wonder that to Minnesota fans, Hrbek and Tom Brunansky are "Herbie" and "Bruno".

Dwight Gooden has overcome his doubly damning name through sheer talent. The name that triggers fits of terminal whimsy in headline writers ("Gooden Plenty." "Dwight is Gooden Ready," "Goodenough") is hell to chant.

Goo-den. Goo-den. Goo-den.

Mushy.

Dwight. Dwight. Dwight.

Worse.

But so what? We would find a way to cheer him even if his name was Toy Boat or Rubber Baby Buggy Bumper.

Some fans will go to extremes to cheer a favorite player. Mets outfielder Leonard Dykstra appears on the roster as Len, but whether he likes it or not, it's already "Lenny" to most fans. Over yells of "Lenny" at one game, however, we heard a deviant cry of "Come on, Dyksie!" Dyksie. Will not catch on.

What has caught on everywhere is the magical "ooo". Fans love to moo. American or National, they all do it. The Brewers have Cecil Cooooooper. The Expos have Hyooo-bie Brooks. The Mets have Moooookie Wilson. The Yankees, of course, have manger Looooo Piniella and the undiscovered Paul Zooooovella. It's the siren song of baseball. Ooooooooo-ee!

* * * * * * *

This simple chart demonstrates the relationship between the meter of a name and the greatness of a player: (Note: Multiple winners of MVP or Cy Young Awards are counted once for each time they were so honored. Example: Joe DiMaggio accounts for all three incidents of an MVP with a monosyllabic first name and a last name consisting of an iambus followed by a pyrrhic.) All statistics supplied by SOBR, the Society of Occult Baseball Research.

METER (Ballplayer Example)	MVPs ('31-'85)	CY YOUNG ('56-'85)
Monosyllable and Trochee (Don Drysdale)	29	24
Trochee Dimeter (Mickey Mantle)	18	7
Trochee and Monosyllable (Lefty Grove)	18	6
Monosyllable and Dactyl (Don Mattingly)	10	2
Spondee (Pete Rose)	8	3
Monosyllable and Amphibrach (Carl Yastrzemski)	6	1
Trochee and Dactyl (Harmon Killebrew)	4	0
Trochee and Amphibrach (Willie Hernandez)	4	1
Monosyllable and Trochiac Dimeter (Roy Campanella)	4	0
Monosyllable and Iambus/Pyrrhic (Joe DiMaggio)	3	0
Monosyllable and Iambus (Rod Carew)	2	0
Trochee and Iambus (Denny McLain)	2	3
Amphibrachic Dimeter (Roberto Clemente)	2	0
Dactyl and Trochee (Ferguson Jenkins)	0	1
Iambus and Monosyllable (LeMarr Hoyt)	0	1
Amphibrach and Trochaic Dimeter (Fernando Valenzuela)	0	1
Monosyllable and Trochee/Pyrrhic (Bret Saberhagen)	0	1

A Poem to Tell You
Why I Named My Son Luke Appling
After the White Sox Hall of Fame Shortstop

Red Shuttleworth

I guess you don't know I was
Dirty Al Gallagher's bullpen coach
In Durham in nineteen-eighty,
that I was Bob Veale's home roomie,
or that Luke Appling was there
as hitting instructor, saying
every time he came into the clubhouse,
"Come on, what's it to you;
hey, what's it to you ... ah ...
go shit in your hat."
I guess you've never warmed up
Big Joe Cowley and had him
cross you up with a slider
that went into the dugout
at a hundred miles an hour
after going off your throwing
hand, and you haven't tossed
batting practice to Brett Butler
and dodged a liner back
to the mound.

                    But that's not
the reason, pal. And the reason
isn't the time Leo Mazzone
("Just tits," Leo says),
drunkenly said, "Fuck
peace, love, an' nutrition,"
after a night game we lost.

And the reason isn't the time
Gallagher, Hank Aaron, Appling
and I ate at a Chinese restaurant.

And it isn't because Appling
homered in that Old Timers Classic
in Washington, although he did
get every piece of Spahn's fastball,
and Luke did make it into **Sports
Illustrated** in color (and even
my mother-in-law sent me a picture
of Luke out of **People** magazine.)

It has more to do with Miles Wolff
giving me a contract to be bullpen coach
and seeing my name on the program,
being able to put on a Bulls uniform
every day for a season and sweat in it.

It has more to do with Luke Appling
working with my swing until I hit
one 325 to the wall, and then
another and another. And Luke doesn't
talk about Luke until you ask him to.

My son has big hands. That's a
good start. I hope he has Appling's
spirit, Appling's love for the game.
One day, after the morning workout,
we were walking up the runway
behind the bleachers in Durham.
Pal, it was hot. Appling ran past us
up that steep cinder runway, clicking
his heels together, laughing, and I said,
"Hey Luke, ain't you worried you're gonna
have a heart attack? Man, you're over
seventy." He said, "Shit, Red, I've
had three heart attacks. None of 'em
came while I was running, fucking,
or playing ball."

When I called Luke
to tell him the boy was born, named
for him, Luke said, "I'm thrilled."
I told him, sheepishly, I was still
teaching English at a junior college,
and he said,"I'm glad somebody's smart,"
taking some of the sting out of my
not being part of the game.
Gallagher came to baptize the boy
and we drank some beer to get it done
after he restrained me from a few brawls
I could have started for the laughs.
We took some pictures to send to Appling,
maybe both of us thinking of that fine man
who at seventy-five took Spahn deep.
Gallagher came to baptize the boy
and neither of us chewed tobacco
in church, although I thought we
should have, for God made tobacco
as well as he made anything
except Luke Appling.

Baseball-Nica, 1986

Joel Millman

(Joel Millman led several Baseball for Peace visits to Nicaragua, bringing baseball equipment and working on ballparks. He wrote of baseball Nicaragua-style. —Eds.)

* * * * * * *

Lunch — rice, black beans, barbecued beef and fried banana chips — costs thirty-five cents in Nicaragua. They serve it on a rolled-up banana leaf. It's the kind of country where a mother duck and her brood of downy offspring peek out from behind a washtub filled with ice and chilled "gaseosas," which are what Nicas call soda pop. The mamasita who sells the sticky nectar pours the bottle out into a plastic baggie, then hands the startled North American the baggie and a straw. But since the Revolution you can't always get a straw so the streets of Managua are dotted with Nicas, their necks craned like calves to udders, straining to suck out the dark Coca Colas and ruby-red *Rositas.*

The country is full of Revolutionary passion. Last summer thirty thousand Sandinista militiamen and their supporters tramped fifty kilometers from Managua to Masaya in a reenactment of 1979's *Repliegue.* Repliegue means retreat, and it's the name of the Sandinistas' daring evacuation of barrios they controlled in Managua. They did it at night, after learning that Somoza was about to quit the country after first bombing the homes of his enemies.

On both marches Nicas hiked past a curious item, a terra cotta Rotary wheel, sitting at eye level on a weedy traffic island just outside Masaya. The wheel is badly pockmarked from the bullets fired in the 1979 war, but it's still standing.

The Rotary Club? In Nicaragua Libre? Masaya hosted the final game of this year's Campeonata Nacional de Beisbol, too, so to settle an argument that launched a thousand undergraduate debates, if you're reading this Ted, the answer is: Yes, after the Revolution, there will be baseball.

Not baseball at its best, mind you. During the seven game set-to between los equipos (the teams) from Leon and La Costa Atlantica, Leon made twenty-two errors (nine by el paracorto, shortstop, Arnolda Munoz), but it was baseball just the same. The see-saw battle was played out against a backdrop of anti-Reagan rhetoric, a war-economy, and the enduring legacy of Agusto C. Sandino.

Sandino is the George Washington, the Abraham Lincoln and the Martin Luther King of Nicaragua Libre. He is not, however, the Babe Ruth, and while billboard, leaflets and graffiti everywhere affirm " A 50 Anos . . . Sandino Vive! (For 50 Years . . . Sandino Lives!)," Nicas still love baseball as much as they love their Revolution. The lead story in **Barricada**, the Sandinista newspaper, is an assault by armed *contras* on the port of El Bluff. The account is six days old by the time it reaches Managua. In **La Prensa**, the principle opposition paper, there is an item from Scottsdale, Arizona, where Al Oliver, "un de mas consistences bateadores de Las Grandes Ligas," has reported to Los Gigantes' training camp. That story is only a day old.

In the days before the Sandinistas, Nicaragua's eight-team First Division was the property of seven Managua capitalists, with one team belonging to Somoza's army, the National Guard. Today, the First Division fields seven teams sponsored by state-owned collectives, with one team made up of the best players in the Sandinista army. It gives the cream of Nicaragua's horsehide establishment an almost semi-professional, even corporate-softball, status, which suits most Nicas just fine since all the real talent is up in North America playing in Las Grandes Ligas.

Dennis Martinez of Los Orioles, and Alberto Williams of Los Gemenos (the Twins) are national heroes. **La Prensa** ran "El Drama de David" a series on the preseason progress of St. Louis's David Green (now with San Francisco). And Nicaraguans and Philadelphians eagerly await the first full season of the majors' newest Nica-star, relief pitcher Porfiro Altamirano.

Los Leones (the Lions) were the favorite to repeat as this year's Campeon Nacional. Costa Atlantica, or The Bluefields Boys, were treated in the nation's dailies much the same way the **Daily News** dismissed the 1970s Kansas City Royals: hayseed in the big city, perennial also-rans. But when Bluefields took Game One behind the four-hit pitching of Rodolfo Taylor, even blase Managuans took notice.

Bluefields was settled in the 18th Century by English sugar planters, who brought black slaves in from Jamaica and Trinidad. Most of Costa Atlantica's players have names like Walters, Humphries and Ellis, while Leon's players are descendants of the original Spanish conquistadors. It gave the Series a *West Side Story* flavor.

"Moya Siempre Moya!" cheered **Barricada** after Julio Moya, the country's most celebrated *tirador* pitched a complete game, thirteen inning performance to even the Series. But when Bluefields rallied to take Game 3 (*Double Play Mortal* was **La Prensa's** analysis) the sportswriters started to get nasty. One dubbed Leon's Parque Metropolitan to which the series returned "el abismo negro (the black hole)." Without a Steinbrenner to dump on, fans vented their anger on Noel Areas, Leon's manager.

"Que Planea Noel? (What's Noel Planning?)" demanded the headline in **Barricada**. It was the same question on the lips of fans from Managua to Matagalpa (even, perhaps of fans in the ruling Sandinista junta) after Noel announced his intention to bench Moya in Game 4, and start *el curvista* Andres Torres: Torres prevailed, and with Moya's second Series victory in Game 5, even **Barricada** toned down its attack. It began anew when Bluefields evened the series in Game 6, and Moya dropped a bombshell of his own.

"No Soy Robot," said Moya in a headline stretching across the **Barricada** sports paper. Moya, after his thirteen-inning stint on Monday and his win on Thursday said he would not start the final game for Leon. A North American, remembering Lonborg-Gibson in 1967, and Lolich-Gibson the following season, could only wonder at Moya's motivation. Was his stand the final act in the drama that began in Game 4? Or was Moya simply heeding Karl Marx and "seizing the means of production?" **Barricada**, it is noted here, came down squarely on the side of labor in the dispute, while both **La Prensa** and the centrist **El Nuevo Diario** stayed neutral.

The scene set, both equipos repaired to Masaya, followed by their fans in buses, cars, oxcarts and Army trucks. Outside the ballpark (official capacity of ten thousand is official optimism) scalpers scalped, chickens scratched and mamasitas grilled beef on braziers made of old auto-parts. Kids hawked gaseosas under the blazing sun.

Inside early birds and latecomers alike got the same comb's eye view of the action as thousands of Nicas, and one North American, crammed the rickety grandstand. The game was more felt than seen, with heaves and sighs signaling all the close calls, and thunderous cheers welcoming scoring bateadores across the plate. Leon took an early lead, Bluefields tied, then went ahead, then Leon tied, then . . . then. Well, even in a Revolutionary Society there has to be a winner and a loser. Final Score: 4-3. Leon.

Minneapolis: City of Protests

Stew Thornley

When the Minneapolis Millers packed up their spikes and shin guards for the final time following the 1960 American Association season, they had racked up 4,800 wins against 4,366 losses since the formation of the league in 1902, good for a .524 winning percentage, best by far of all the teams which had ever played in the Association.

The Millers held the top spot in the league with 37 first-division finishes over the years, and shared the lead for pennants won — nine — with the St. Paul Saints. Minneapolis hosted the American Association All-Star game four times, more than any other city. In addition, the Millers held the distinction of being the only Association team to never finish in the cellar.

However, there is one category — protested games — for which no official statistics are kept. Had they been, the Millers may have found themselves number one in this department as well.

Over the years, the Millers displayed an uncanny knack for winding up in the middle of games which had been formally protested. By the mid-1950s, they had even found a partner, the Omaha Cardinals, in what almost seemed a determined effort to make league president Ed Doherty's job as difficult as possible.

The teams' first encounter in this activity came in a game August 23, 1955. Trailing by five entering the top of the ninth, the Millers rallied for eight runs for an apparent 16-13 victory. But, during the ninth-inning uprising, Omaha skipper Johnny Keane had lodge a protest when Minneapolis player-manager Bill Rigney entered the game as a pinch-hitter.

According to the National Association of Minor Leagues rule book, "A player-manager cannot be placed on the active list more than once during a season." Rigney had been activated as a spare infielder and pinch hitter by the Millers on three separate occasions in 1955. President Doherty, while acknowledging his part in allowing Rigney's name on the active roster when it was illegal, declared Rigney ineligible and ordered the game replayed from the point of protest.

(Had the Toledo Sox been as familiar with the National Association rules as

Keane was, they might have avoided a loss two weeks earlier when Rigney beat them with a pinch-homer in the ninth, knocking the Sox 4-1/2 games out of first and giving the Millers their eighth victory in what was to become a 15-game winning streak that vaulted Minneapolis into first place to stay.)

But even Keane's rule-book acumen was not enough to save the Cardinals, for when the protested game resumed two nights later, Don Bollweg's three-run homer game the Millers a 16-14 win.

This protest, however, turned out to be only a warm-up for what was to come a month later. After capturing the American Association pennant, the Millers swept the Denver Bears in the opening playoff round, then faced Omaha to determine who would advance to the Junior World Series against the champions of the International League.

After the Millers took the first two games at Nicollet Park in Minneapolis, the Series shifted to Omaha for a Saturday night game. In contrast to the slugfests of the opening contests, game three was a tight pitching duel. The game was scoreless after six innings, and Cardinal starter Stu Miller had yet to allow a hit when he faced Monte Irvin, leading off the Minneapolis seventh. Irvin took a half-swing at an 0-1 pitch, and third base umpire Bob Stewart, without waiting for a request for help from the plate umpire, Eddie Taylor, signaled that Irvin had gone far enough with his swing for the pitch to be called a strike. Taylor, however, stuck to his guns and ruled the pitch a ball, bringing Stu Miller off the mound to ask why he refused to accept Stewart's call. Invoking a league rule calling for the automatic ejection of any pitcher protesting a ball or strike decision, Taylor threw Miller out of the game.

The Omaha fans, seeing their pitcher ejected while working on a no-hitter, began hurling seat cushions and other debris on the field; it took three policemen to pack off one large, unsteady fan who charged onto the diamond, and even General Manager Bill Bergesch (now a New York Yankee Vice President) got into the act, asking the arbiters to consult with Doherty, who was in the box seats. The umpires consented, and Doherty, overruling Taylor, allowed Miller to stay in the game. This brought Rigney out of the Minneapolis dugout to announce his intent to protest the game should the Millers lose.

When the game resumed, Stu Miller retired Irvin and Rance Pless, but lost his no-hitter and shutout when Bob Lennon, who had his 64 home runs for Nashville in the Southern Association the previous year, sent a towering fly over the 380-foot mark in left-center.

The Millers' Whitey Konikowski, also pitching well, had given up only two hits until Omaha catcher Dick Rand homered with one out in the eighth to tie the game. One out later, Wally Lammers singled and Don Blasingame homered to right. The scoring ended there, Omaha coming away a 3-1 victor to pull within one game of the Millers in the series.

With Minneapolis' protest still pending, President Doherty called the opposing managers and the four umpires together for a midnight conference at a downtown hotel, at which time Doherty overturned his earlier decision and upheld the protest, ordering the game replayed from the seventh inning on, with a one ball-one strike count on Irvin and Stu Miller ejected from the game. Ironically, this meant that Miller's no-hitter was once again intact, although he would not be allowed the chance to complete it.

Omaha immediately protested Doherty's action, appealing the ruling to the directors of the other Association clubs, but the directors backed Doherty. The Cardinals protested again, just before the start of the game that afternoon, on the grounds that "not sufficient time was taken in arriving at a decision on Rigney's original protest." This final challenge did not worry the Millers as it would require a meeting of the executive board of the minor league, which was not scheduled to convene for several months, to rule on Omaha's latest appeal.

This bizarre series of protests sparked memories for old-timers of the grand-daddy protest of them all — the infamous Play of Six Decisions — which occurred in the 1932 Junior World Series between the Millers and Newark Bears, the only time up to that point that Minneapolis had represented the American Association in the inter-league series.

The fifth game of that deadlocked series was tied 8-8, in the top of the ninth at Nicollet Park. With two out and runners at the corners, Newark's Johnny Neun laced a low liner into short left-center. Center fielder Harry Rice seemingly captured the drive with a diving, back-handed stab and slid on the ground for a considerable distance before coming up with the ball. Both the second and third base umpires signaled out, bringing a group of protesting Bears, led by manager Al Mamaux, out of the Newark dugout. After listening to the Newark arguments, the umpires huddled and reversed their decision, ruling that Rice had dropped the ball, which allowed the go-ahead run to score. Out charged Miller skipper Donie Bush, demanding an explanation. Again, the umpires called an impromptu conference, and, again, they came out with a different decision, ruling once more that Rice had caught the ball, which, of course, brought a return of Mamaux to the field. This scene continued — the arbiters listening to the remonstrations of the offended manager, huddling, and emerging from the convocation with a ruling opposite of their previous call — until a total of six decisions had been made and the game had been delayed 40 minutes. Bush finally ended the rhubarb by announcing his intent to formally protest the ruling, rather than trying to persuade the men in blue to reverse their decision one more time. A pursuit of the latter option may have proven more productive as a vote of the league executives, composed of an equal number of representatives from the American Association and International League, ended in a partisan deadlock, allowing the Bears 12-9 win to stand. The next night a three-run, ninth inning rally gave the game, 8-7, and the Series, four games to two, to the Bears.

The 1955 Millers, receiving a more agreeable ruling on their protest, took advantage of it. When the protested game in Omaha resumed, Bob Tiefenauer took Stu Miller's place on the mound and got Irvin to ground his first pitch to shortstop Dick Schofield. But Schofield booted the ball for an error and Irvin was safe at first. Pless followed with a sacrifice, bringing up Bob Lennon, whose home run the night before (which was erased from the official records by the protest) had been the first hit for the Millers. This time he tripled off the center-field fence 400 feet away — narrowly missing another home run — to score Irvin and give himself the possible distinction of being the first player to ever break up a no-hitter twice in the same game. Lennon was squeezed home by Dave Garcia, and the Millers added five runs in the eighth en route to a 7-2 win. Minneapolis took the regularly scheduled game 7-3, to sweep the four-game series and move on to the Junior World Series for the first time since their 1932 encounter with Newark.

Aided by the protest, the Millers became the first team in American Association history to win eight straight playoff games. They made it nine in a row with an opening victory in the Junior Series versus the International League champion Rochester Red Wings. The Series went the limit with the Millers winning the decisive seventh game, a game which also marked the last hurrah for 60-year-old Nicollet Park, slated for the wrecking ball at season's end.

In 1959, with the Millers then playing at spacious Metropolitan Stadium in suburban Bloomington, Minneapolis and Omaha decided to give Ed Doherty one last headache before departing.

Meeting in the opening round of the American Association playoffs, the teams split the first four games. In game five, September 15th at the Met, a young second baseman, activated by the Millers just before game time to replace service-bound Lee Howell, hustled home with the winning run in the last of the tenth, sparking a rhubarb in which Omaha pitcher Frank Barnes had to be restrained from attacking umpire Tom Bartos, who had made the call on the close play at the plate.

The arbiters decision on the play stood, but, after the game, Omaha General Manager Bergesch announced he was protesting the game for another reason, questioning the eligibility of the new second baseman. Ruling that the player had not been certified for eligibility until Sept. 18th, President Doherty upheld another Minneapolis-Omaha protest and ordered the entire game replayed.

The next night the Millers won the replayed game, as well as the regularly scheduled contest, to capture the league semi-final series without the services of their new second baseman, Carl Yastrzemski.

With Yaz officially eligible two days later, the Millers went on to defeat the Fort Worth Cats for the league championship before bowing to the Havana Sugar Kings in seven games in the Junior World Series.

Omaha dropped out of the American Association following the 1959 season. Thirteen months later, Calvin Griffith's announcement that he would transfer the Washington Senators franchise to Minnesota signaled the end of the Minneapolis Millers. Ed Doherty was one man who would not miss them.

Fare Thee Well, Bombo

Ken LaZebnik

Bombo Rivera was a player dear to the heart of Minnesota fans. Blessed with a great baseball name, he had an instant popularity. Much to his surprise, he was an unsolicited, but successful candidate for the presidency of the student body at the University of Minnesota. Garrison Keillor wrote a ballad about him for his Prairie Home Companion radio show. He accepted this spontaneous enthusiasm for a classic baseball name with grace and modesty. And now he is gone. Released. Picked up by the Royals and sent to their Omaha farm team.

The Twins, however, have chosen a poetic successor to Bombo Rivera. Up from Toledo comes catcher Sal Butera. I composed the song below, and recorded it on the "cassette" label with Steve Yoakam doing vocals, Dave Carlson on mandolin, and Michael Kissin on violin, myself filling in on piano. We dedicate it to Bombo and his kinsman in baseball monikers, Sal Butera.

FARE THEE WELL, BOMBO   Words & Music © Ken LaZebnik, 1981

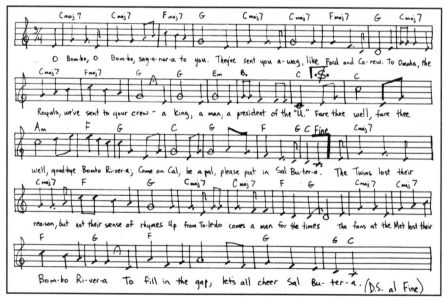

Left-handed Catchers

Robert Warde

My favorite defensive play. Late in the game, medium-fast runner on first, one out, middle of the batting order, tie score. Picture a sharp ground ball toward the hole on the right. First baseman has been holding, but he breaks with the runner, stretches out as if to lean on the left-centerfield wall, and spears this harvest from a green sea on the webbing of his lobster claw. Almost stumbles in the act of transfer, brakes sharply even as his cocked elbow whips the forearm toward thin air above a bag occupied by no one. And then, pellet flying on a line toward the three dollar seats, he turns away (an exhibition of trust that breaks my heart) and moves back, supple boomerang, to the spot where he began, wheels once more, echoing in now static fashion his former fluid extension, to squeeze the ball again as it returns from nowhere to its home, his legs a compass, set to inscribe the largest of circles, his dark claw now sweeping down to skim the ocean floor, his body hardly conscious of the streak that flashes past the blank indifference of his left heel. The 3-6-3 double play. Watch it and weep.

It seems unlikely I suppose — this compass-legged, lobster-clawed boomerang, dashing right, dashing left, pivoting right again. Frantic indecision, we conclude, until an egg drops into place for the top half of the eighth, and we realize that the base paths have been swept clean for yet another beginning.

There are poets who favor a one-bounce throw from right to third, cutting down the man from first; he tried to take two on a single. I have seen, at twilight, on an unkempt high school diamond, a ghost runner act out that folly; while like a wraith descended from a dark silver bird, Roberto Clemente fires a flame across the day turning to night. But nothing touched the 3-6-3 double play.

"Touched." Yes, touched, because it now goes like this. Late in the game, medium-to-fast runner on first, one out, middle of the batting order, tie score. A sharp ground ball toward the hole on the right. First baseman has been holding, but he breaks with the runner, stretches out as if to lean on the left-centerfield wall, and grabs an elastic, invisible mixture of gases. Jerk up your head, watch the puff of cotton blow across the synthetic product that covers right field (how sweetly nostalgic, how pathetic, they colored it green ... in memory of ... something), and hope, sad dreamer, that Roberto Clemente is out there to get it, for otherwise any decent fly ball will bring home the tie-breaking run.

We can explain this easily. He missed the ball by one inch (it's a game of inches, never over 'til it's over, and there's no tomorrow). By one inch because he had to reach across his body to find the ball. His mitt (and I think we'll just call it a mitt now) was on his left hand. What other choice, save to barehand it?

Don't tell me about all of the excellent right-handed first basemen. Don't tick them off for me. I don't want to hear about it, because they have turned the primary sack into an old grey pillow for dead-legged catchers and broken-kneed outfielders, and that is all there is to it. The 3-6-3 is dead.

So where does that leave the southpaws? I'll tell you, friend, it leaves them huddled in a damp corner of the outfield unless they can pitch. Can you imagine a lefty at third? at short? at second? Of course not. Nor can you imagine a right-hander at first, but there he is, fucking up the 3-6-3 double play.

That's not all though. There's another position. Let me just put it on the line with no nonsense. The old Brownies used a midget. We've seen one-armed outfielders. There's a woman ump in Triple-A who may be coming up soon. They even let black men manage. So I think it's about time for a left-handed catcher.

Straight up the middle you go either way. Center field, pitcher, catcher — reaching out both ways to the six on the sides, three and three (unless Ted Williams is batting). Either way in the center, either way on the mound, and, by god, either way beneath the tools of ignorance. Clears the throw more easily with a left-hander up. Better shot to first on the bunt. Has the pill on the proper side with a runner coming in from third. Same mitt, same target. On the mirror side he's worse off, but everything behind the plate splits down the middle. Plus, lefthanders are better people.

There are two simple reasons for the present situation. First, Spaulding and the rest don't make catchers' mitts for the right hand. A typical example of the manner in which supply bullies demand in a hopelessly corrupt capitalistic society. Lefthanders are socialists. Second, the whole grim planet is a plot against left-handers. How often has it happened? Chunky ten-year-old kid wanders into the rec center for a Little League tryout. We're somewhere out in the mountains of Iowa, or the deserts of Rhode Island, or in any other impossible place. Maybe we're in Japan. The coach (somebody's dad) says, "Hi, son. can ya hit? (Kid nods) Can ya run? (nods) Can ya throw? (nods) Can ya catch? (nods) Why's yer mitt on that hand? Oh yeah? Well then kid, first lesson, ya can't catch. Get out there and shag flies. " As Virginia Woolf would put it, that kid was Yogi Berra's sister. And I wonder how many of Yogi's sisters have been lost to the game. A few lucky ones may still be shagging flies. But our chunky ten-year-old, now middle aged, can probably be found on the end stool in some lonely bar and grill near a blacktop highway off the coast of Kansas, sipping beer with one hand, and flashing forlorn signs with the other, as it droops over his crotch.

Try this one. Seventh game of the World Series, tied in the ninth, two down, runner on third, fast "lefty" power hitter up, infield way back, and he drags one down the right side. Catcher springs up and out simultaneously, drives straight along the chalk line, scoops the apple niftily with his entirely naked, beautiful-beyond-description left hand, and guns it to first ... and on into right field ... because to miss the runner, he had to come in with his throw on the second base side, and the righty first sacker, once again, failed to come across fast enough.

People even praise right-handed first basemen. Kent Hrbek, best blah, blah in the blah, blah. They can do that; they can take a portsider's position from him and drive him out to pasture. But they won't let him catch. Everything. He can do everything! Pluck the foul pop off the screen. Drop the mask straight down so it won't be in his way. Knock down the knuckler. Pull the inside fastball over the plate to get a call. Hit a glove three inches off the ground on his peg to second. Everything. So it's gotta be a capitalistic plot, because you cannot give me a reason. You cannot give me a reason. The 3-6-3 is dead, and you *cannot* give me a reason.

Robert Frost and Baseball

Jack LaZebnik

Robert Frost, the poet-laureate of America, loved baseball. In 1886, when he was twelve in New Hampshire, he had a "fast drop, a roundhouse, and a jump ball." His dream was to become a Major League pitcher. In those days, school boys played "scrub," a pick-up game; Frost could run the bases "faster than any other boy in school."

In 1888, he could think of nothing but baseball. His school team was winning everything in sight, so it challenged the best in a nearby town. Rob (Frost) was knocked out of the box and his team faced a shut-out. Well, if he got on base he'd steal around to home. So the opposing team walked him on purpose. He stole second: safe. A big lead, the jump, the grand slide: out. What a humiliation for him. For months after, he had to suffer the taunts of his classmates, so he quit the team — and his fantasy of the big leagues.

But he kept track, through the papers, of the standings, batting averages, pitching records. When he entered Harvard in 1898, the Boston papers were full of Edward "Parson" Lewis, a 25-game winner for the Boston Nationals (later the Braves). Lewis' parents, strict Calvinists, forbade him to play baseball, but, in college, he found his talents as a pitcher. When Boston signed him, he included in his contract the stipulation that he would not play on Sunday — so he became "Parson" Lewis. He ended his baseball career (after five years) with the Boston Americans (later the Red Sox) and taught speech at Columbia University, then literature at Massachusetts Agricultural College. Frost met him, learned that when Lewis was a boy his father — to the boy's astonishment — won a poetry prize. "So," Frost said, "poetry to him was prowess from that time on, just as baseball was prowess, as running was prowess. And it was our common ground. I have always thought of poetry as prowess — something to achieve, something to win or lose."

In 1927, Lewis became president of the University of New Hampshire; in 1930, he gave Frost an honorary degree there. Before that event, the two men played catch in the president's back yard; Frost wanted to know how Lewis threw his famous curve. "He let me onto the secret," Frost said, "of how he could make a ball behave when his arm was just right. It may sound superstitious to the uninitiated, but he could push a cushion of air ahead of it for it to slide off from, any way it pleased."

In 1932, both men received honorary degrees in Williamstown, Massachusetts; Frost wrote Lewis then. "The last time we played an exhibition game you pitched and I caught. This time we'll both be on the receiving end and it will remain to see who catches it the worse. You can show your freedom from professional jealousy by bringing your wife up to visit us at our farm if only for a night." And so Lewis did, and they played catch once again.

[Information from Lawrence Thompson's three-volume biography of Frost.]

THE VIEW FROM LEFT FIELD

Ueberroth's "Thing Called Baseball'

Steve Lehman

So many important issues confront the national pastime that we couldn't decide which cause to espouse in this space. Should we urge you to vote against the DH in any upcoming referendum on the issue? Should we suggest that you write the new commissioner urging the re-instatement of Mantle and Mays and discouraging forcing lights on Wrigley Field? Perhaps, like a latter-day St. George, we should raise our swords against the dragon of interleague play, which has returned to terrorize the countryside, and recruit you to battle alongside. Well, you should do all of those things. They are all issues about which new commissioner Peter Ueberroth wishes the owners to be on the offensive.

"I've been baffled by our lack of offense...we seem to be a defensive unit...So many people have been offering ideas about getting some speed in this thing called baseball. I'm not thinking about the game. I'm thinking about everything around the game, an offensive plan with some goals."

What is this "thing called baseball?" Well, unlike football, there are no separate offensive and defensive players in baseball. And unlike big business, success is not measured in perpetual expansion and change. Baseball has no "goals" situated at the far end of a linear territory to be conquered. Rather, mandala-like in shape, baseball bids you return to the point at which you began.

We are suspicious of any commissioner who talks about baseball in football metaphors, suspicious that perhaps he, too, has no concept of how important it is that baseball maintain a close connection with and respect for its own history as it moves into the future.

Yankee Stadium, October 3, 1985:
A Meditation on Hope

Ken LaZebnik

It rained last night, a misty seacoast sort of rain. Yankee Stadium, approached by 155th Street, loomed brightly on a dark horizon, like the great ocean liner in *Amarcord*. It was ablaze with light in the dark Bronx sea. There were no lines, the ticket takers seemed happy and sleepy, and Seth and I passed easily to our general admission seats.

We were in Section 6, with a splendid view. There were perhaps 3,000 people there — the announced attendance of 15,000 drew hearty guffaws. Here were the diehards, here were the true faithful, here were baseball fans at their best — the standard bearers of hope eternal. "It's never over 'til it's over" — not true of other sports, not even true of life, but Yogi thus pricked the heart of baseball.

It was a night peculiar to hope. The bright outfield lights seemed to hang as a beam of light. Particles and waves: Light possesses this duality, and if quantum mechanics can bear the metaphor, baseball does, too. Particles: Rickey Henderson hitting a first inning home run, Don Mattingly blooping a hit into left and driving in two runs. Waves: the ball leaving the pitcher's hand, being struck by the bat, rolling to the shortstop, thrown to the second baseman, relayed to first — a wave of action rolls over the game and changes its course. Particles: Henderson's 79 stolen bases, Mattingly's 144 RBI. Waves: 11 game winning streaks. Particles and waves: Ron Guidry throwing a strike, then another and another, and, with a man on second and nobody out last night, striking out the side. Particles and waves create the season's image, as a sunbeam creates a pattern through the windows of Grand Central Station that we read on the floor. At the end of a rich season such as this, the beam glows through the haze fully, maturely, at sunset.

Light. Faith. Belief. Hope. A meditation arises in this night in which a trinity of games floats about us: the game before us, Guidry pitching with such assurance that we have faith he will win; the scoreboard telling us the Blue Jays lost, giving us belief; the score from St. Louis bringing (to this life-long Cardinal fan) hope. (The tension from watching the first two Cards-Mets games on television had become unbearable. When Seth, whose faith in the Yankees gave him hope that bordered on belief, proposed attending tonight's game, I accepted: inning by inning scores could not be as excruciating as play by play.)

Hope. Light. There is in human nature a potential joyfulness in the hope that our lives will be bathed in sunshine, that amidst dark nights in the rain, miracles are possible.

There was, in the cry of the fan down the aisle last night, pleading with Bobby Meacham (bottom of the eighth, crucial insurance run on first base, Meacham trying to get down a bunt) — "For once in your life, do something right!" — the joyous possibility of hope. Under an ashen Manhattan facade, what ebullience would erupt if Meacham got that man to second! (He didn't, bunting foul three times.)

The night of baseball unfolded in Aristotelian fashion. The game moved swiftly. In our deserted rows we cheered each strikeout and raised our umbrellas high for Mattingly. The climax was the eighth inning. Hero Mattingly, rising above an injured foot, drove in two runs, creating an irreversible turn in the action. A swift ninth inning denouement. Cheers for the Yanks and Billy, who looked Oedipally gaunt and broken. Music in the orchestra, sung by choric leader Sinatra, as guards lined the sacred ground. Then, a unity of time and place: driving home, the Mets and Cardinals fulfill their destiny. Particle: Cox a better third starter for the Cards than Aguilera for the Mets. Wave: Mets tide recedes.

Prometheus was the bearer of fire, and in an extended sense, hope. No longer were men bounded by the immediate stimulus of the senses. One could create light in the darkness, bring light into a cave and begin to create an alternative world to the one nature provides. Judy Aronson describes her baseball fanaticism as looking bleakly at the real world of the '80s and choosing an alternative reality.

In this soaking night, the few thousand banded together in Yankee Stadium seemed like prehistoric men and women huddled in a cave. Darkness about us, we roared at the action below, and pounded our hands for the figures in the light. Lights of the scoreboard told us of distant news. Like residents of Plato's cave what care we if it be real or not? Tonight, we echoed Plato's student. Aristotle says: "Hope is a waking dream."

The Aerodynamics of An Irishman

Barry Gifford

There was a man on our block named Rooney Sullavan who'd come walking down the street while the kids would be playing ball in front of my house or Johnny McLaughlin's house and he'd always stop and ask if he'd ever shown us how he used to throw the knuckleball back when he pitched for Kankakee in 1930.

"Plenty of times, Rooney," Billy Cunningham would say. "No knuckles about it, right?" Tommy Ryan would say. "No knuckles about it, right!" Rooney Sullavan would say. "Give it here and I'll show you." One of us would reluctantly toss Rooney the ball and we'd step up so he could demonstrate for the fortieth or fiftieth time how he held the ball by his fingertips only, no knuckles about it.

"Don't know how it ever got the name knuckler," Rooney'd say. "I call mine The Rooneyball." Then he'd tell one of us, usually Billy because he had the catcher's glove, the old fat-heeled kind that didn't bend unless somebody stepped on it, a black mitt that Billy's dad had handed down to him from his days at Kankakee or Rock Island or someplace, to get sixty feet away so Rooney could see if he could "still make it wrinkle."

Billy would pace off twelve squares of sidewalk, each square being approximately five feet long, the length of one nine year old boy's body stretched head to toe lying flat, squat down and stick his big black glove out in front of his face. With his right hand he'd cover his crotch in case the pitch got away and short-hopped off the cement where he couldn't block it with the mitt. The knuckleball was unpredictable; not even Rooney could tell what would happen to it once he let it go.

"It's the air makes it hop," Rooney claimed. His leather jacket creaked as he bent, wound up, rotated his right arm like nobody'd done since Chief Bender, crossed his runny grey eyes and released the ball from the tips of his fingers. We watched as it sailed straight up at first then sort of floated on an invisible wave before plunging the last ten feet like a balloon that had been pierced by a dart.

Billy always went down on his knees, the back of his right hand stiffened over his crotch, and stuck out his gloved hand at the slowly whirling Rooney-ball. Just before it got to Billy's mitt the ball would give out entirely and sink rapidly, inducing Billy to lean forward in order to catch it, only he couldn't because at the last instant it would make a final, sneaky hop before bouncing surprisingly hard off Billy's unprotected chest.

"Just like I told you," Rooney Sullavan would exclaim. "All it takes is plain old air."

Billy would come up with the ball in his upturned glove, his right hand rubbing the place on his chest where the pitch had hit. "You all right, son?" Rooney would ask, and Billy would nod. "Tough kid," Rooney'd say. "I'd like to stay out with you fellas all day, but I got responsibilities." Rooney would muss up Billy's hair with the hand that held the secret to The Rooneyball and walk away whistling "When Irish Eyes Are Smiling" or "My Wild Irish Rose." Rooney was about forty-five or fifty years old and lived with his mother in a bungalow at the corner. He worked nights for Wanzer dairy, washing out returned milk bottles.

Tommy Ryan would grab the ball out of Billy's mitt and hold it by the tips of his fingers like Rooney Sullavan did, and Billy would go sit on the stoop in front of the closest house and rub his chest. "No way," Tommy would say, considering the prospect of his ever duplicating Rooney's feat. "There must be something he's not telling us."

THE VIEW FROM LEFT FIELD

The Curse of the Designated Hitter

Steve Lehman

Soon after his ascendancy to the commissioner's throne, Peter Ueberroth promised to poll baseball fans on their feelings about The Great American League Experiment, the designated hitter. He even was so bold as to suggest that he would attempt to foist it upon the NL or pry it away from the AL depending on the results of the poll. He never, to our knowledge, has given specifics on just where and when and to whom this wondrous gathering of fandom's deepest desires on the issue was to occur, however, and the whole issue has apparently faded into the mist with other political grandstanding efforts, never to be heard from again.

Unless, of course, Howie Newman has his way.

Ueberroth's empty pledge may have gone nowhere fast, but it was around long enough to stir the blood of a small town sportswriter/songwriter in Massachusetts. Spurred on by the hope of a return to what he calls "real baseball," Howie Newman has started a groundswell campaign to convince PU that the DH should be retired — permanently. His organization, Dump the DH, is a grassroots lobbying effort designed to, in Newman's words, "alert Americans to the inherent evils of the DH — and convince them to cast their votes accordingly." Although the **MRB** is cynical enough about the PU's motives to doubt that any such vote will ever occur, we applaud and whole-heartedly support Howie's efforts to rid the Grand Old Game of one of it's three Demons. We'll discuss ballpark roofs and plastic grass in future issues.

Newman makes the following points in support of his anti-DH thesis: (1) baseball is intended to be a nine player game wherein the players exhibit all-around skills both defensively and offensively. The creation of two part-time positions is a case of over-specialization which discourages the development of complementary skills at all levels. This is especially damaging at the Little League level, but equally absurd on a AAA team with an American League affiliation where the player, struggling to make the bigs, works only on his hitting. (2) The absence of managerial strategy in DH cursed games is an oft cited but certainly valid point. Just about all that's left for AL managers to do is bring in lefties to pitch to lefties and righties to righties. No pitchers bunting, no defensive moves to put the pitcher's batting spot as far back as possible when a reliever comes in, very little move/counter move activity between benches. Sometimes watching Whitey Herzog work can be as much fun as checking out Ozzie Smith. (3) DH burnout is an argument put forth by Tony Kubek about the career shortening effects of overpitching American league starters, letting them pitch tired in the late innings when they might have been removed for a pinch hitter. Did Catfish Hunter's career end prematurely? Were Nolan Ryan's and Steve Carlton's extended? (4) The DH distorts statistics. If Roger Maris has to live with an asterisk to his 61 homer season because he had a few more games than the Babe to hit them, then what should go beside the career records for Reggie's home runs or Yastrzemski's games played? And how about the pitchers' complete games stat?

Perhaps the biggest argument against the DH, however, is that it eliminates an aspect of baseball that has enriched and enlivened the game since it's inception: the hitting pitcher. What about Guy Hecker who won a batting title with a .342 average while going 27-23 on the mound (see "The Blond Guy" in our Winter 1985 issue)? What about Babe Ruth, Bill Terry, George Sisler, Ted Williams, and Stan Musial, all of whom began their careers as pitchers? There are also countless special moments where a pitcher rose to the occasion at the plate, made all the more special by their relative rarity. Newman points out that Dave McNally was the last American Leaguer to hit a grand slam in the World Series.* Tony Cloninger is the only NL player to hit two grand slams in a single game. How about Ken Holtzman's .571 battering average and 1.429 slugging percentage in the '73 and '74 Series? And Rick Wise's feat of hitting two round trippers — one of two times he did it that season — to win his own no-hitter on June 23, 1973. The list goes on and on: Ken Brett homering in four consecutive starts. Joaquin Andujar's called shot grand slam two years ago. (We're talking *surprise* here.) Already this year Jim Gott, fresh over to the Giants from the DH-cursed Blue Jays, hit two homers to beat the Cards. And then there's Bob Gibson and Bob Lemon and . . .

We hope you get the point. Sure, there are more hits with the DH. But the game is about much more than just hits. We hope you've noticed.

* Written prior to the 1987 World Series grand slam by Minnesota Twin Kent Hrbek in the Metrodome against the St. Louis Cardinals.

The Beryl Ring (Oct. 10, 1926)

Pete Gunn

Nora woke up shivering. She jerked the blanket up over her head, but it was no use. It was just too cold to sleep. She kicked off the bedding, boosted herself up with her elbows, draped a wrinkled corduroy robe around her shoulders, plunged both feet into a pair of yellow slippers and padded across the floor. She turned on the radiator, warming her hands when it began hissing.

She yawned and lit a cigarette and pushed back a wisp of hair dangling over an eye. Then she heated up the coffee and poured herself a cup. Pulling back a chair, she sat down at the table and took a sip, staring at the beryl ring on her index finger. Suddenly she remembered about Tommy. She snuffed out the cigarette and removed her robe and negligee, wriggled into a corset and slipped on a gingham dress. She rubbed her eyelids and stretched her arms and plumped down on the edge of the bed, sliding her slender legs into a pair of long black stockings and then strapping her shoes to her feet.

Got to hurry. Tommy's waiting for me.

Still shivering, she went over to the bureau mirror and looked at her pale blue eyes and short up-turned nose and dimpled chin. With a hairbrush she raked the buttery hair cropped closely over her ears. She powdered her face, then picked up a tube of lipstick and painted her lips bright red. After dabbing perfume behind each ear she fit her feathered hat snugly over her head and put on her suede velour coat and silk gloves. She slung a woolen scarf around her neck, buttoned up her galoshes, and grabbed her umbrella and beaded handbag. Fully dressed, she stepped into the cold air outside.

A cable car clanged down the street. A horse-drawn cart creaked behind the cars and trucks and buses motoring by. A snowy-maned old man with shrunken cheeks, a rolled-up cigarette hanging from his withered lips, knelt in front of a shoeshine stand with a whisk broom in his bony hand. Not far away, a portly man in a zoot suit bought a paper at a newsstand.

Nora threaded her way through the traffic of pedestrians on the sidewalk, her umbrella rat-a-tatting on the pavement. She walked past the well-dressed mannequins standing in department store windows, trying to ignore the noises of the city, the honking horns and loud voices. She passed a marquee advertising a Rudolph Valentino movie. Across the street Douglas Fairbanks and Clara Bow flicks were showing.

Nora stopped at a curb, watching a Stutz Bearcat speed down the asphalt. Spotting a cab, she leaned over and waved a thumb. The tires skidded up to a stop in front of a parked Pepsi-Cola truck. "Where ya headin'?" boomed a voice from behind the cab's steering wheel.

She got in the back seat, not looking at the driver, a beefy, red-faced man with a half-smoked stogie sticking out of the side of his mouth.

"Yankee Stadium, " she said crisply.

The driver doffed cigar ashes onto the floor.,

"Goin' to the ballgame, huh?" He glimpsed out the windows, at the fat gray clouds quilting the sky. "Look at them clouds. They ain't gonna play."

"Just take me to the Stadium, please."

The driver shrugged. "It's your money." He switched on the ignition and steered the cab down the street. "Ya ain't from around here, are ya?"

"No. Why?"

"Don't sound like no New Yorker, that's all. Where ya from?"

"St. Louis."

"Ah, I see. Here for the Series. Must be some kinda fan, I'll say that much for ya. Hell, I love baseball as much as the next guy, but I ain't gonna travel across the country just to see a game. Not even a World Series."

"You don't know Tommy," she whispered.

"Huh?"

"Nothing."

The cab screeched to a halt in front of a scrawny little boy darting across the street. "Goddam kid," the driver growled. "Oughta be home where he belongs." He lifted his foot off the brake and continued driving. "Yep, no use goin' to the game today. Even if they do play — which I doubt — ya know the Yanks are going win."

"I wouldn't be so sure about that. We're throwing Haines, and remember what his knuckler did to your Yankees in the third game. A five-hit shutout."

"Just luck. He can't do it again. Not against Ruth and Gehrig."

"I think he can. And he's got the hitting to back him up, what with Thevenow and Bottomley and Hornsby."

"Ya ain't serious, lady."

"I most certainly am."

They stopped at an intersection. The driver glanced into the back seat. "For a dame, ya sure know a lot about baseball. How come?"

She smiled and felt the ring beneath her glove. "My fiancee plays for the Cardinals."

"That right? What's his name?"

"Tommy Thevenow."

"Tommy who?"

"Thevenow. He's leading the Series in hitting, that's all. Everyone brags about Alexander, but Tommy's the real hero. He is. He really is."

"Never heard of him."

"Figures. He's so underrated. But you'll hear about him, mark my words. He's only a rookie now, but wait till he gets some experience. He'll be another Honus Wagner. He will. He will."

"Yeah, yeah, here we are." The cab parked outside Yankee Stadium. Nora got out and paid the driver. He flipped his stogie out the window and put the money away. "Good luck to Tommy what's his name," he said.

"Thevenow," she replied curtly. "Tommy Thevenow." She turned and headed for the Stadium, zigzagging past the roadsters in the parking lot, past the Model T Fords and Buicks and Maxwells and Chevrolets. To her pleasant surprise, there wasn't a long line waiting outside the ballpark, amazing for a 7th Game of the World Series; maybe the bad weather kept most people home. Those in the line must have been expecting rain, for a number of raincoats and galoshes and umbrellas could be seen.

She stood in the back of the line, her foggy breath reminding her of the nippy air. She tugged at her scarf. At work in St. Louis — she was a department store clerk — she liked to guess the occupation of a customer by his or her appearance. Now she did the same with the people in the line — that is, when she saw more than the backs of their heads. That young man right in front of me, with a raccoon coat and slicked-down hair parted in the middle, turning the pages of an F. Scott Fitzgerald novel: must be a graduate student at an Ivy League university. Over there, that beetle-browed man in a yellow raincoat, cigarette smoke flowing from his nose; now that's a welder if ever I've seen one. Up there, that middle-aged woman clad in a rain-proofed leatherette jacket and beige rain hat, her umbrella up as if it's already raining; a schoolteacher for sure. That old man who just limped up behind me, chewing on a toothpick while humming to himself; a retired security guard, I bet. Or that bearded man with a derby hat and velvet-collared overcoat and a pince-nez, sprinkling tobacco into the bowl of his pipe; a college professor, no doubt.

Soon Nora was at the head of the line. She showed the ticket taker her ticket, oozed her tiny frame past the turnstiles and made her way to the box seats behind home plate. Cigar smoke made her cough as she seated herself and riveted her eyes on the playing field. The scoreboard said that two innings had been played with no score. Yankee righthander Waite Hoyt was finishing off his warmup pitches. Catcher Hank Severeid fired a shot to second, the infield whipped the ball around the horn, and Tommy Thevenow's name was announced over the loudspeaker.

Nora bit her lip and gaped at Thevenow crouching over the plate. "Come on, Tommy," she trilled.

Hoyt twiddled with the top of his cap, hitched at his belt, and peered down at the catcher. He shook off a sign, nodded. His first pitch was a ball, high and outside. Thevenow stepped out of the batter's box and rubbed his hands with dirt. He got right back in, drumming the bat on the plate, goggling at Hoyt, waiting for the next pitch.

"Good eye," Nora yelled. "Make him pitch to you."

He lunged at a low and outside fastball and lashed a foul down the first base line, past Gehrig and rolling all the way to the Yankee bullpen in right field.

"Straighten it out," Nora screamed. "You can hit this guy."

"Strike the bum out," shouted a man beside her, an olive-skinned man with flinty eyes, wearing a checkered golf cap and horsehide jacket. "He can't hit," he added with a grin.

Nora glared at the man but said nothing.

Hoyt broke a curve over the plate. Thevenow lined a single to left. Nora jumped up as Bob Meusel relayed the ball back to the infield. She sneered at the man next to her. "Not bad hitting for a bum," she crowed.

The man laughed. "Luck. Pure luck. I saw him swinging with his eyes closed."

"Lay off, Gus," said a slack-jawed man wrapped in a heavy maroon sweater, a thatch of rusty hair mussed up by the wind. "She isn't hurting you."

"Just havin' fun, Vince," Gus said. "No harm in that."

Nora looked at the man named Vince. "That insect isn't bothering me, thank you. Not unless he bites."

Gus laughed again. "That's a good one, lady. You oughta be on radio."

"I came here to watch a ballgame," Vince said. "Not to hear you two squabble."

Thevenow, they noticed, was now on second with two out. Billy Southworth lofted a high fly to left. Meusel circled under the ball and easily caught it for out number three.

The brittle wind smacked Nora in the face; she was glad she brought her scarf along. She breathed deeply as the Cardinals took the field. She watched Thevenow cleanly fielding first baseman Jim Bottomley's practice grounders.

"He's got a great glove, too," she said to Gus and Vince.

"You say somethin'?" Gus asked; he'd just bought a hot dog, and was busy splashing on mustard.

"I said he's a great fielder, too."

"Who you talkin' about?"

"Tommy. The shortstop."

"Oh. That guy again." He finished off the hot dog in a few large gulps, washing it down with a cup of black coffee. "What is it with you and this Tommy guy? You related?"

She smiled broadly and removed her glove and held up the beryl ring. "We're engaged."

"Really?" He stared at the bluish green stone on her finger. "That there's a beaut. Must've cost your Tommy a pretty penny. May I?" Beaming, she let him hold her hand to see the ring better. "Yesiree," he went on, "your Tommy must've paid a fortune for this here thing." He winked at her. "Just think of all the Crackerjacks he had to eat." He laughed, a big, boisterous laugh that exposed a jagged row of yellow teeth.

Her nostrils flared and her lips curled as she pulled her hand back and slid the glove back on.

A deafening roar caught her attention. A roly-poly man waddled up to the plate with two out and no one on base. She recognized Ruth at once.

"Strike him out," she shrilled.

"Just hope they got the guts to pitch to him," Gus said. "Been walkin' him every time he comes up."

A knuckleball floated past Ruth's shouldertips for ball one. The next pitch was another knuckler, this one chest-high, and the Bambino drilled it into the rightfield bleachers for his fourth roundtripper of the Series. The fans — especially Gus and Vince — went wild, whistling and screaming and tossing their hats in the air and stamping their feet. The next hitter, Meusel, made the final out, a routine fly to Chick Hafey in left, but the damage had been done.

Nora was quiet, her shoulders sagging. She cast a glum glance at the cloudy sky and hoped for rain; only three innings had been played, so the game wouldn't count if it were canceled now.

Craggy-faced Rogers Hornsby led off the top of the 4th, tamping a slow roller back to the mound for an easy out. Bottomley followed with a base hit to left. Then Les Bell, after fouling the first two pitches off, bounded a grounder to short. Mark Koenig booted the ball, sending Bottomley to second.

"Damn Koenig shouldn't be out there." Gus mumbled. "He don't know how to field."

Hafey gouged his cleats into the batter's box with two on and one out. He took an inside slider, then sent a popup to shallow left that fell between Meusel and Koenig.

"Whatcha doin'?" Gus croaked. "Tryin' to throw the game?" He clenched a fist. "Get Koenig outta there."

The bases were now jammed. Figures stirred in the Yankee bullpen. Thevenow was kneeling in the on-deck circle; Nora's heart throbbed. Bob O'Farrell, the Cardinal backstop, was batting. He pounced on the first pitch and cracked a flyball to leftfield. The ball landed in Meusel's glove, then popped right out, trickling across the grass. He scampered over and returned the ball to the cutoff man, but not before Bottomley had crossed home with the tying run. The bases were still loaded. Severeid went out to talk to Hoyt as Thevenow came up.

Gus rested his head in his palms. "Aw, come off it, Guys. Playin' like bush leaguers."

Nora wrung her hands, massaged her ring, pursed her lips. "Come on, Tommy," she murmured, as though in prayer. "Get a hit. Get a hit. Please." She turned to Gus and Vince. "Tommy's a great clutch hitter. He really is. You watch and see. He's going to get a hit. I know he is. I know it. I know it."

Gus lit an Old Gold. "Five bucks says lover boy fans."

Ignoring Gus, she steadied her gaze on the field. Severeid was back behind the plate. Hoyt blew on his fingers, checked the baserunners, and then blazed a fastball past Thevenow's swinging bat.

Nora groaned.

"Told you he's gonna fan." Gus said.

"Oh, shut-up," she snapped. He snickered.

"Lay off, Gus," Vince said again. Gus made no reply. He just sat there grinning, examining the burning embers of his cigarette.

The next pitch would have been a ball — it was clearly outside — but Thevenow reached out and poked it over Gehrig's head. The burly first sacker leaped up, but the ball sailed over his outstretched glove into right field for a single. Bell and Hafey scored, giving the Cardinals a 3-1 lead, while O'Farrell stopped at second.

Nora was on her feet, clapping and whistling.

"Way to go, Tommy. I knew you could do it." She squatted back down, her teeth flashing. "I told you guys he was a clutch hitter, didn't I? Huh? Didn't I? Didn't I?"

"Yeah, you were right," Gus admitted. "Lover boy did good."

Her smile widened. She caught a whiff of her own perfume as she gawked at Tommy's lead off first; she didn't even notice Jesse Haines striking out on three pitches.

Then Wattie Holm knocked a ground ball to short.

"Oh no," Gus lamented.

Koenig scooped up the ball and tagged second for an unassisted forceout.

"About time." Gus said.

Thevenow was cheered by a handful of St. Louis partisans when he returned to the dugout to get his glove. Nora was louder than anyone. "Way to hit," she squealed. Head down, he scurried back to his position.

"He's so shy," she said.

Gehrig started the New York 4th with a walk. Tony Lazzeri belted a long drive to right center field. Holm ran hard and hauled the ball in. He wheeled around and gunned a one-hopper to second, keeping Gehrig on first. Joe Dugan was the new batter. After taking a low curve, he fouled two off, one in the dirt and one back in the stands. Then he tapped a squiggler back to the mound. Haines glanced at second, but took the sure out at first. Two down with the trying run at the plate.

Hank Severeid took a practice swing in the batter's box. He attacked the first pitch and dribbled a grounder down the third base line. Les Bell let it roll foul. Haines came back with a knuckleball, and Severeid clubbed a shot over the shortstop's head. Thevenow jumped high, high ... and made a brilliant one-handed catch. Even some Yankee fans stood and clapped.

Nora was bouncing up and down on her feet, her arms waving, her voice shrieking. She sat back down to catch her breath. She blinked at Gus and Vince, simpering from ear to ear. "Didn't I tell you about his glove? Huh?" Another Honus Wagner, that's what he is. A great fielder and a great hitter."

"If lover boy's such a great fielder," Gus said, "then how come he made that bonehead play the other day?"

Nora lit a cigarette. "You don't know what you're talking about."

"I heard it on the radio, lady. They had this here guy in a rundown, but lover boy, he goes and drops the ball. Would've been the third out, too. The runner, he scored later that inning. And it turned out to be the winning run. So you see, lady, your Cards'd be World Champs right now if it wasn't for lover boy."

She scowled. "You're a liar."

He smirked. "Whatever you say, lady."

She twisted the strap of her handbag. "Why do you make up such vicious lies?"

"I ain't lyin', lady. I heard it on the radio. With my very own ears."

"I don't believe you."

"Don't care if you do. I know what I heard." He lit another cigarette. "So lover boy makes an error. Big deal. He ain't no god, you know."

"Oh yes he is."

"Lady, you're loony."

For the Cardinals in the 5th, it was three up and three down. The Yankees didn't do much better in their half of the inning: Ruth's walk was their only baserunner.

After St. Louis failed to score in the 6th, Gehrig opened things for the Bronx Bombers, ripping a sharp bouncer up the middle. Nora held her breath. Thevenow sped to his left and stuck out his glove and sizzled the ball to first, nailing Gehrig by several steps.

Nora stomped her feet. "And you said he once made an error," she said to

Gus. "He never has. He's perfect. Absolutely perfect."

"You really believe that, don't you?"

"I don't believe it, I know it."

"You belong in a straitjacket, lady. That's all I can say."

"You're just jealous."

Gus cracked up laughing. "Jealous? What of?"

"Of Tommy. He's going to be one of the greatest of all time, and you're jealous."

He wiped his lips on his coatsleeve, a streak of mustard smearing the horsehide. "If you say so, lady."

After Lazzeri struck out, Dugan drubbed a base hit between Hafey and Holm. Then Severeid, on a full count, slammed a sinking liner to shallow left. Hafey charged in and tried unsuccessfully to make a shoestring catch. By the time the ball came back to the infield, Dugan was touching the plate to cut the St. Louis lead to 3-2, while the slow-footed Severeid was on second with a stand-up double. Spence Adams was called in to pinch run for Severeid. The Cards bullpen came to life, along with the New York fans.

"Now we gotta game," Gus said.

Ben Paschal, pinch hitting for Hoyt, ended the inning by bouncing weakly to Haines.

"That bastard Paschal," Gus sputtered. "Why the hell did they put him in? He can't hit."

The Yankees had a new battery in the 7th: Herb Pennock and Pat Collins. Pennock took his last warmup pitch. The tall and skinny lefty blew on a hand and kicked the rubber and placed his glove on his knee and looked down for the sign. The first hitter he faced was Tommy Thevenow.

"Here he is, here he is," Nora gasped. "He's going to get another hit. I know he is. I know it, I know it." She cupped her hands over her mouth. "Come on, Tommy dear. Another hit."

Thevenow fouled off the first pitch, let two balls go by, and punched a hot smash right at the third baseman. On pure reflex Dugan webbed the ball and threw to first for a quick out.

Nora moaned. "Of all the rotten luck. Right at the stupid third baseman." She blew a smoke ring into the air. "But Tommy hit it hard. He did. He did." She shrugged. "Oh well. Can't get a hit every time. Not even Honus Wagner did that."

Jesse Haines followed with a single, but that was all the Cardinals could do in the inning.

Earl Coombs led off the Yankee 7th with a blistering pellet over Thevenow's outstretched mitt.

"How come lover boy never caught that?" Gus taunted. "Losin' his touch?"

"Shut-up."

Gus chuckled. His cigarette was almost burned down to this fingertips, so he dropped it, squashed it beneath a heel. Reaching into a shirt pocket, he pulled out the package of Old Golds. It was empty. He crinkled the cellophane and tossed it away.

"Gotta smoke?" he asked Vince.

"Just these," Vince said, holding out a pack of Lucky Strikes.

Gus made a face. "You know I hate Luckies."

"Sorry. All I got."

Gus turned to Nora. "Got any more cigs, lady?"

She rummaged through her handbag and brought out a package of Philip Morris.

"Never mind," he sighed. "Them are as bad as Luckies." Out of the corner of an eye he noticed a cigarette vendor trudging up and down the aisles. He called him over and purchased some Old Golds. "Now this here is a real smoke," he cooed after lighting up. "Not like them damn Luckies."

On the field, Koenig pushed a bunt down the third base line. Bell dashed in and pegged him out at first, sending Coombs to second. Ruth came up with the tying run in scoring position and the leading run at the plate. The crowd jeered as the Babe received an intentional pass.

"Cowards," Gus bellowed. He looked at Nora. "Hey lady, your team ain't got no guts."

"That's just smart baseball," she answered.

"More like gutless baseball."

"Can't blame them," Vince said. "He homers every time he bats."

"Yeah, well, if they had guts they would've pitched to him."

The wind picked up as Meusel grounded to third. Bell flipped to Hornsby at second, forcing Ruth. Coombs scooted to third. Gehrig, blowing on his knuckles, lumbered up.

Haines fondled his belt buckle, spied the baserunners, and tempted Gehrig with a slow knuckler. A swing and a miss.

"Thataway, Jesse," Nora cried.

A belly-high fastball nibbled the corner for strike two.

"Get the bat off your shoulder," Gus roared.

Haines glided in a high knuckleball. Gehrig didn't bite. Another ball, this one an outside curve, evened the count at two and two. Haines examined his index finger, then brushed Gehrig back with an inside fastball. The crowd booed. On a full count the Cardinal hurler let go of a knuckleball that soared over Gehrig's head. O'Farrell sprang up and stopped the ball from sailing into the backstop. From second base player-manager Rogers Hornsby trotted up to the mound. Haines held up his pitching hand, and Hornsby studied the forefinger.

"No, no," Nora repeated to herself. "I don't believe it."

"Believe what?" Gus asked.

"That." She pointed to the two relievers in the St. Louis bullpen.

"So?"

"Don't you recognize the righthander?"

He squinted his eyes. "That Alexander? Probably drunk. Usually is."

"Even if he's sober," she said, "he's in no shape to pitch. Not today. He just threw nine innings yesterday. If you ask me, Hornsby must be drunk." She hung a cigarette form her mouth, struck a match. "Just hope he brings Sherdell in. He can stop the Yankees. Wish Tommy was managing. He'd know what to do. He would. He really would.

"Bring Sherdell in." she squalled.

Hornsby motioned to the bullpen. Alexander plodded out to the mound. He took the ball from Haines, exchanged words with Hornsby, and began his warmup pitches. Haines, head lowered, slumped back to the locker room amid scattered applause.

Nora was shaking her head. "I don't believe it. I just don't believe it. Throwing a has-been drunk who just pitched yesterday. Can you imagine that? Tommy, he wouldn't manage like that."

She peeped up at the gray sky and prayed for a cloudburst.

The ever dangerous Tony Lazzeri was in the batter's box. He sank his cleats into the earth, thudded the bat against the plate, and took his stance.

On the mound, Alexander spat on the grass and rubbed up the baseball. His eyes flickered at the runners on base, at the batter, at the fans, at the clouds. He shook his fingers to keep the chill away. Then he read the catcher's signs. He came in with a curve that broke below Lazzeri's knees.

"What'd I tell you?" Nora said. "He shouldn't be pitching."

"C'mon, Laz," Gus yelled out.

Alexander was working fast. He whizzed a fastball past Lazzeri, nipping the plate.

"Well, that's better," Nora conceded. "Still, he shouldn't be out there."

Lazzeri was ready for the next pitch. He sliced a drive down the leftfield line. Going... Going...

"I knew it, I knew it," Nora wailed. "He shouldn't be pitching. Not in the biggest game of the season."

At the last second the ball swerved foul. Nora breathed easier. "Boy, did we luck out on that. Might not be so lucky next time. If only Tommy was managing. He'd bring in Sherdell."

Alexander reared back and snapped a low curve. Lazzeri swished the bat and missed. "Way to go, Alex," Nora cheered. "Way to go. Way to go."

"You were right," Gus said. "They should've kept that ol' drunk on the bench."

"You crazy? He's the best pitcher we've got. It was a stroke of genius to bring him in. Tommy must've told Hornsby to do it. Sure glad he didn't bring Sherdell in."

Gus shook his head. "You're something else, lady."

The top of the 8th began with a single by Hornsby. Bottomley dropped a bunt down third. Dugan surged in and sidearmed the ball to first, throwing out the runner. Hornsby advanced to second. Les Bell, tapping dirt from his cleats, was now the batsman. He bopped a long fly that Coombs outgalloped in center. That brought up Hafey. He bounded a foul past first and then clouted a liner between short and third. Dugan dove and deflected the ball with his glove. An infield hit. Hornsby took third. O'Farrell ended the inning with a forceout.

Dugan opened the Yankee 8th with a slow bouncer to Thevenow. Tommy hustled in and one-handed the ball and made a near-perfect throw to first.

"Way to go, Tommy honey," Nora cackled. She gloated at Gus and Vince. "Now do you believe me? Huh? He's the greatest. And he's only a rookie."

The next two Yankees went down in order, making it a one-two-three inning.

With his team leading by a run, Thevenow was the first hitter in the top of the 9th. Nora gripped her umbrella, her knuckle grazing the beryl ring. She wet her lips. The wind pelted her face. She tightened the scarf around her neck. "Come on, Tommy. Start it off."

"Strike him out," Gus hollered.

"Lay off, Gus," Vince said.

Thevenow, on a checked swing, topped a roller into the Cardinal dugout. He let the next pitch go by, a change-up that caught the inside corner.

"Just one more strike," Gus said, "and lover boys fans."

"Got to hell."

Gus slapped his knee, howling with laughter. Pennock baited Thevenow with two outside curves. Tommy took them both and then fouled a sinkerball into the dirt, just barely missing his ankle. Nora squeezed her hands, panting. Her knees shook. "Come on, Tommy dear," she said lowly.

Pennock brushed a pinstriped pantleg, got the sign flashed by Collins, and released the pitch. Low for ball three.

Nora heaved a deep sigh. She dug her fingernails into her kneecaps. She could hear herself breathing.

"That last pitch was knee-high." Gus said. "Should've been a strike."

"Oh, be quiet."

"Lay off, Gus," Vince said.

"Just havin' fun. Lighten up."

The wind spouted dirt off the mound. Pennock, his back to the batter, pounded the ball into the webbing of his glove. He turned around.

Thevenow banged a fly to right. "It's a homer!" It's a homer!" Nora wheezed. Ruth moved to his left and made an easy catch. Nora thumped her umbrella on the floor. "That stupid wind. That thing was gone. That is, until the wind got hold of it." She puckered her lips in a pout. "That stupid wind."

The next two Redbirds were easy outs.

For the Yankees in the 9th, Coombs and Koenig each grounded out to Bell at third. Then an earsplitting noise reverberated throughout the Stadium: Ruth shambled up to the plate.

"Pitch to him," Gus thundered.

"Come on, Pete," Nora screamed. "Strike him out."

Alexander fidgeted with his red and white striped cap. After glancing at Hornsby, who was slowly nodding his head, the Roman-nosed righthander licked his lips and inspected Ruth. He took a chance and fired it down the center of the plate. Ruth swung and failed to connect. A loud "ooh" arose from the crowd. Alexander sighed. He ran the back of his hand across his forehead and set himself for another pitch. This one was high and outside. He fingered the seams of the ball, stroked his bristly jaw, and toed the rubber. Ball two, low and away.

"Pitch to him, you coward," Gus yelled.

Alexander knew the next pitch was a mistake as soon as he released it. But it was too late. Ruth pummeled the ball down the rightfield line into the Upper Deck – but foul. Hornsby immediately went up to the mound.

"Aw shit," Gus said. "You know they're gonna walk him. They got no guts." He joined the chant spreading across the Stadium: Pitch to him. Pitch to him.

Nora stared at Tommy at short. "Isn't he handsome out there?"

Gus wrinkled his brow. "Huh?"

"Tommy. Don't you think he looks handsome in his uniform?"

"I don't believe it. Here we are, in the last inning of the last game of the Series, and you're worried about how lover boy looks. Jeez."

"You're just jealous."

"Let's watch the game, " Vince said.

Hornsby returned to second. They were pitching to Ruth: The catcher was squatting with his target behind the plate. A high fastball made it a full count. Alexander scratched his elbow and took a long and heavy breath. He curved one near the outside corner. Ruth didn't swing.

Alexander walked off the mound before the call was made. He was called back; the umpire had called the pitch a ball. Ruth wiggled his hips to first. Alexander argued the call, but it didn't do any good.

"Gutless wonders," Gus said to Nora. "That how your team won the pennant, lady, playin' chicken baseball?"

"What do you mean? That was a strike."

"Bull."

Alexander was now facing Meusel. Without checking the runner on first, he slipped a fastball past the Yankee leftfielder for a strike. On the next pitch Ruth shocked the entire stadium by attempting to steal second. "What the hell's he tryin' to do?" Gus snorted as O'Farrell rocketed the ball to Hornsby for an easy putout.

"We won! We won!" Nora chirped, dancing in the aisles. She embraced Gus and Vince. "And Tommy's the hero. He knocked in the winning run."

"Don't rub it in," Gus muttered. "You got that stupid Ruth to thank. Hell, a fat slob like that tryin' to steal."

"I don't think it was such a dumb play," Vince said.

"You gotta be kiddin'."

"No, I'm serious. The element of surprise that's what he was counting on. If it'd worked, you'd be calling him a genius right now."

"Yeah, but it didn't work — and Ruth is a jerk."

A jubilant Nora clutched her ring to her breast and watched the Cardinals mob each other on the diamond. She saw Thevenow pat Alexander on the back and then hug Hornsby. "I'm going to join Tommy," she said. "He wants to share his joy with his fiancee, I'm sure. You two want to come? I'll introduce you to him."

"Huh? Naw, that's okay."

"No, I insist. You'll like him, wait and see."

"Might as well," Vince said.

They left their box seats and hopped onto the field, needling their way past the fans streaming onto the infield grass, past the security guards trying to cordon off the diamond. Nora hurried up to Tommy, threw her arms around him, and planted a kiss on his lips. "You played great, dear," she whispered.

He shoved her back. "Who the hell are you, lady?"

"Tommy," she piped. "It's me, your love."

"Keep this crazy woman away from me," he ordered one of the security guards.

A barrel-chested guard stepped in front of her. "Come, Miss," he said, grasping her by the shoulder. "Leave him alone."

"That's okay," Gus told the guard. "I'll take her now." The guard shuffled way.

Nora and Gus traded blank looks. "I told you he's so shy," she said. "He doesn't like showing his love in public."

"I-I'm sorry, lady," he said softly.

She felt a blast of wind against her cheeks. "Did I show you the engagement ring he got me? Huh? Did I? Did I? She pulled off her glove and raised her ring finger to her eyes, a tiny raindrop spattering the tip of her nose.

Blodgett's Blotter:
Memories of the 1968 World Serious

Dear Editor,

The 1968 World Series, Deter-oit and St. Louis. Can you remember the depression years and that other Series and the outstanding performance of Pepper Martin in Philadelphia against Cochrane and then the Deans against the Tigers in 1934? The Tigers owed them one!

Well, that's not quite all the story. All year long Dennis, the Menace, McClain had been winning and winning, so much so that managers declined to send their best against him and used rookies or trial-horses on the mound. The upshot of it was that Mickey Lolich faced the better pitchers and, too, the Tigers had a bad habit of not hitting behind him. "Mack" was getting all the print. And even the great "Dean of Men" Dizzy came again to Detroit when McClain pitch'd his thirty-first win, and as I remember, a pennant clincher.

Came the Series and it was the Tigers against the Cards and they were stacked with Gibson and Brock and Flood, pitching and running and more running. The "Detryuts" had only an ace on the mound and Mgr. Mayo Smith's change of line-up, Stanley at short, and a shift in the outfield of Kaline and Northrup. And so it began. McClain against Gibson the first two times. The Series went even as the season had been play'd, with Lolich, "pitching from behind," one game down each time he took the mound. Well, Lolich won those games. And so it came to the Series final, with the total 3 to 3.

Lolich had some things going for him too! A darn good catcher in Bill Freehan, the last of the 'two-hand' catchers. And a strike-out pitch that could consistently hit the zone low and away from the swing, for a "cauld strike." And he kept the runner near the bag. Brock had been thrown out regularly in the Lolich games, and Flood too. And later a play in the field distroy'd Flood's confidence. There was a wet spot in right center that Flood slipped on and, missed trying to field and it was all over; the Detroits had finally broken the ice and won their CHAMPIONSHIP.

And did you know that Tom Yawkey's uncle brought the great Cobb to Deter-oit: And that Grandma and Grandpa Blodgett boarded the telegraphers of the Austin Lake Station on the old G.R. and I.? Holy Moses! that was a long time ago.

It even hurts to think about it,

E. Wright Blodgett

Blodgett's Blotter

Dear Editor:

As Webster's reply to Hayne was "to preserve the Union," so is needed a reply to "Why the designated hitter?" If all the other players are batters, why is he a hitter?

John Heydler, player, umpire, and league president, suggested a DH rule in 1928. In his proposal the DH was to hit for the starting pitcher only: the DH would leave with the removal of the starting pitcher. Thus a move by the manager to replace his starter taxes him with the loss of a hitter. This, plus a possible practice of having the DHs on the coaching lines when not to bat (to make them more a part of the game) could be an acceptable compromise to the National League — which voted *for* the DH in 1928.

Lastly, the editors and printers of the MRB need not worry if the issue seems to come off late. After all, it is a review and all review needs time for reflection. So give it time.

And Wrightly Field was built in 1914
When baseball was more important than war,

E. Wright Blodgett

Ted the Chimp (from *Winnipeg Baseball* by Paul Gertsen, MRB 6,4); *Under the Lights* (cover art, MRB 5,1); *Calvinisms* (Ken LaZebnick, MRB 6,4). Illustrations by Andy Nelson. *Base Paths: The Best of The Minneapolis Review of Baseball.*

But I want to memorize this grassy field in May sunlight (Red Shuttleworth, MRB 5,3); *Santa Ruth* (cover art, MRB 4,4); *Deal* (Gary T. Brown, MRB 5,3). Illustrations by Andy Nelson. *Base Paths: The Best of The Minneapolis Review of Baseball.*

My Friend Richard (Mike Shannon, MRB 6,3); *Babe Ruth* (from *The Beryl Ring* by Pete Gunn, MRB 6,2); *After Twenty Eight Years at Triple G Tool* (Tom Blessing, MRB 6,3); *Down to the Baseball Republic* (Linda Adler, 6,1). Illustrations by Andy Nelson.

Baseball Buddha (from *The Baseball Player as Bodhisattva: An Inquiry Into the National Pastime* by Matthew Goodman, MRB 6,1). Illustration by Andy Nelson. *Base Paths: The Best of The Minneapolis Review of Baseball.*

WINTER

Change of Pace

Jack LaZebnik

After the second hard strike shoots by:
the same full windup pause and
whirl, the body turning like a wheel,
the same shoulder down, armfling,
wristsnap and followthrough, the pounce
and wait for the judgment call, or the miss
or the foul or the hit, but now, now,
the ball hangs on the air, floats,
slides out of time, as if on a string
of balls forever coming, and now,
forever now, we step to swing, the bat
behind our head, and we learn to crack
in the thick of it, to clear the bases
as we knew we always could and will,
but the ball clings to the shining air
and we can't wait – from the top
of the throw to now we've gone stiff
and our chance has come, is coming,
drifting, easing along – the change is ours,
the aching try ever before its time
and we swing with all the rest
of our life into the sighing silence.

The Portsider

Staff Writer

(Staff Writer occasionally escapes his little box below the editorial to write a full column. His reading seems unusally broad for a broken-down lefty, but that's the sort of columnist we try to find. —Eds.)

* * * * * * *

Winter's coming slowly in Minnesota this year – no snow on the ground, and it's hardly been cold enough to fog your glasses when you step inside the St. Clair Broiler. But I hear a hollow whistle in the wind: Like an old sailor in a strip joint, it's darkly hinting of a set-up. I dropped a log on the fire here in the **MRB** library, poured a glass of brandy from the oak panelled Phil Douglas Memorial bar, and eased into one of our padded Chippendales. It's the time to luxuriate in fat stored from the month of holidays.

I was hibernating like an old bear my age deserves to do, when Lehman stuck an article in my hand. It was in the magazine with all the great cartoons and, every now and then (about as often as the **MRB** comes out), the best baseball story you ever read. The guy who wrote this was named Jonathan Schell, and he quoted a pole named Czeslaw Milosz. With a name like that he should have been a back-up catcher to Ernie Lombardi, but he was a writer instead. Milosz wrote: "A country or a state should endure longer than an individual. At least this seems to be in keeping with the order of things. Today, however, one is constantly running across survivors of various Atlantises." He was writing about countries that had sunk during the wars in Europe this century. Schell said he sensed a way of life in America, very vibrant just thirty years ago, has slipped away, too.

We have our own Atlantis – a life that many of us remember, a neighborhood life, a life of routine, yes, but continuity and community. Community – that's what's changed. We've changed from a community life to individuals' lives. And, to bring the point around to baseball, why, the same's true there. Teams had continuity and a communal personality. Nowadays, each individual – player and owner – is out for himself (or for Marge Schott). Now it seems to make just as much sense for the Cubs to win a pennant as for the Yankees to lose one.

Since free agency it's easy to say the ballplayers are out for numero uno, but now it's completely clear the owners are, too. Gone are the men of community like Phil Wrigley. With their refusal to sign free agents everyone knows the owner's sole interest is in profit. The only reassuring continuity is management's stupidity; they prove collusion by their actions.

That's why there's more baseball writing than ever. Writers imply community – a book is an identical object shared by a group. Writers are always trying to achieve community; the bigger the better as far as they're concerned.

Of course, me, I'm just an old ballplayer. I'm just trying to get a winter's nap. Got to rest up for the Hot Stove League Banquet. Winter will be upon us. No time to be alone.

THE VIEW FROM LEFT FIELD

In Memorium: The Winter of 1985

Remembering Burleigh Grimes, Bill Wambsganss, Roger Maris, and Bill Veeck

All these were honored in their generation.
And were the glory of their times.
  — Ecclesiastics 44:7

On December 6, Burleigh Grimes, 92, died in his hometown, Clear Lake, Wisconsin. The same weekend, Bill Wambsganss, 91, died in Lakewood, Ohio. These contemporary baseball greats played against each other in the 1920 World Series. Grimes was the losing Dodger pitcher in the famous 5th game in which "Wamby' made his unassisted triple play for the Cleveland Indians.

Grimes and Wambsganss were honored in their generation. Roger Maris, at least two baseball generations removed from them at the age of 51, died a week later, and may (and probably will) find honor posthumously. The player who broke the most famous single season record (set in the era of Grimes and Wambsganss) is the same player whose birthplace is listed as either Fargo, ND, or Hibbing, MN. The cavalier attitude about tracking down his birthplace (it was Hibbing) is an indication of how much he was not honored in his generation. He was, however, the glory of 1961, capping his second straight MVP season with the record-breaking homer. Six years later he anchored the Cardinals in the '67 Series with his .385 average and series-leading seven RBI.

The death of a long-ago baseball player makes us reflect on athletic abilities that "died" decades ago. What we mourn, apart from the man himself, if anything can be apart from that, is the living memory of the player, as in Grimes' case, who pitched to Wagner, the Waners, Ruth and Frisch. It is that memory we tap when we have the opportunity, and more often than not, we ask not about the personal life of the ball player, which he may be reticent to give, but about those famous events that the player witnessed – like the Wambsganss triple play, the Stengel bird-under-the-cap, and the Ruth called shot – or the players and managers he knew, like Zack Wheat, Wilbert Robinson and John McGraw.

Maris' abilities were still warm in reality as well as memory – we should have been seeing a facsimile, at least, of his home run swing, as we do with Aaron, Mays and Killebrew, in old-timers games - but of course, after retiring from baseball in 1968, Maris wasn't a participant. Most of the players he knew are still around (Yastrzemski was in the Yankee Stadium outfield on October 1, 1961 and played against Maris in the '67 Series) and they will continue to recall for us, for our children, the Roger Maris story well into the 21st century. The 1961 trial by the baseball establishment (press, fans and officials) and the subsequent recognition (by some at least) of the injustice of it all, made it a little bit easier for Hank Aaron and Pete Rose in their pursuits of Ruth, Keeler and Cobb. Roger Maris was the first great record breaker, the first to take away a Ruthian batting record, the first to successfully challenge a "Golden Twenties" milestone.

The living memory of the first three decades of 1900s baseball is now in its final innings, and with the passing of Grimes and Wambsganss we are two outs closer to the time when those decades, like the 1800s, will be found only in the history books and museums. That is where you can find Burleigh and Wamby now: Read the chapter on the minister's son and seminarian Bill Wambsganss in Lawrence Ritter's **The Glory of Their Times**: "By the time I got to the bench it was bedlam, straw hats flying onto the field, people yelling themselves hoarse, my teammates pounding me on the back." Go to the Burleigh Grimes room in Clear Lake, Wisconsin.

Maris (I can't just call him Roger, like I've called Grimes Burleigh or Wambsganss Wamby; I don't believe he would have wanted that sort of familiarity) has a monument on the outfield wall in the "new" Yankee Stadium. It took them twenty years to put that up. It was also a number of years after Maris left the Yankees that they decided to "re-do" the House that Ruth built. The germination of that remodeling really began when Roger Maris, on October 1, 1961, rocketed a Tracy Stallard 2-0 4th inning pitch into the right-field stands. And it wasn't just the Yankees who were forced to take notice. Maris's 61st home run forced all of baseball to take another look at its blueprints.

  - Jim Lee

Bill Veeck is dead at age 71 and no one in Chicago will believe it. He was the son of a local sportswriter whose careful analyses of the Cubs so impressed Mr. Wrigley that he was hired to run that club in 1917, and so young Bill grew up in Wrigley Field. In 1940, the 26-year-old Veeck bought the Triple A Milwaukee Brewers and tried out (out of town) the promotional acts that in the majors so beautifully entertained fans and outraged the baseball establishment. He ran the St. Louis Browns to the bottom and both the Cleveland Indians and the Chicago White Sox to the top, and brought millions of people to their ballparks. And when he died, flags in Chicago flew at half-mast, and radio, television and newspapers forgot for a few days that the Bears were heading for the Super Bowl. You could open the phone book, find his number, and up until two days ago, call and talk to him about anything. And if you were so inclined, you could go to Miller's Pub at Adams and Wabash downtown and find him on his stool at the end of the bar, stein in hand. "I would still be remembered, in the end, as the man who sent a midget up to bat," said Bill Veeck at the end of Chapter One, *Veeck As in Wreck* (G.P. Putnam's Sons, 1962). But in Chicago, we remember the end of the book: "Sometime, somewhere there will be a club no one really wants. And then Ole Will will come wandering along to laugh some more. Look for me under the arc-lights, boys. I'll be back."

And he came riding back to Chicago on his white charger in 1976 and kept the Sox from being moved to Seattle. And, just maybe, in a year or so, we'll wish he was here, as the Sox get shipped to Denver or New Orleans.

- Judy Aronson

Seems like all I do is go to funerals these days. I see my old friends gathered for death. They come grouped together like flowers in a vase, or pallbearers around a coffin; and the next time we meet it's one of the old friends we're gathered around and it's his body we're hoisting down some slippery church steps. My old friend Burleigh. Bill Veeck. Roger Maris was too young for me to know well, and doesn't that seem a damn shame.

When a ballplayer dies, a strange thing happens.

They shed their earthly bodies, but an image settles into the public's mind, as big as those Easter Island statues. A ballplayer's career is a process of constructing a graven image of himself. He doesn't always have control of the sculpting. He does what he does on the green ball field. The media can chip and hack at this work and try to shape him as they see fit. The size of his image is often dependent on where he plays, and whose steps he's following. When he dies, we all have a sudden shock. This baseball card, this graven statue in right field we booed at and cheered, was just a guy, a human being, and he lived and died as we all do. But the funny thing is, his image remains behind, just as large and solid as if he were still alive. The human being behind it seems as insubstantial as a shadow – it disappears in a cloud, and we hardly notice the difference.

Bill Veeck, though not a player, left us a happy monument, one that he sculpted as he saw fit. He made an art of his life. Roger Maris was chiseled by other's hands. His art was on the field. What others wanted him to be and what he was were at odds, and the friction of that contrast gave him some pain, I'm afraid.

People left Veeck's funeral feeling happy about baseball and life; people left Maris' sensing the damage that a game can do. Hey, folks, I ain't a philosopher, and like some wiseguy says, I should maybe block this metaphor, but it seems to me that the lesson of the winter, of all those funerals in the cold, is that we should be a little kinder to those guys down on the field. We made their images; they didn't. And they may not like the one they got stuck with anymore than we do.

- Staff Writer

The Master of the Spitter:
A Remembrance of Burleigh Grimes

Jon Kerr

There was a local hardball team playing across the street when we arrived. The scene couldn't have been much different than some eighty years before, when young Burleigh Grimes was mowing down western Wisconsin farmboys.

Now the ballfield is named after him, Clear Lake's most famous son — surpassing even U.S. Senator Gaylord Nelson. His plaque sits in the Cooperstown's Hall of Fame as testimony to 270 Major League wins between 1916-34 and appearances in four World Series. But Burleigh Grimes himself sat in his own personal museum, connected to the town school, amidst the photos, newspaper clippings, autographed baseballs and other memorabilia of a by-gone era.

But the 92-year-old, bespeckled man wearing an upside-down Hall of Fame pin on his jacket was hardly a relic, as a rock-hard handshake demonstrated. The grip used for the last legal spitballs seen in baseball apparently hadn't left him despite recent cancer treatment. And while a ready smile belied the competitive drive for which he was equally famed as a player, his quick wit remained.

"Why is it there are so many nice guys interested in baseball?" he joked, after becoming familiar with his visitors from the Twin Cities. "Not me. I was a real bastard when I played."

Indeed, as he described at least one famous incident he observed as a member of the 1932 Cubs, Babe Ruth's "called" World Series homerun ("I've been listening to that bullshit so long. If he'd a done that our pitcher would have had him in the dirt."), his bench-jockeying, umpire-baiting spirit comes out. Several of the museum's framed warnings from league officials confirm that even in later years as a minor-league and Dodger manager, Burleigh Grimes was a fiery competitor.

But most of his recollections had obviously become more pleasant with the passing of time. As he exchanged stories with Dave Moore and several of the other older members of the SABR group, it was apparent that playing with or against stars such as Ruth, Gehrig, Dizzy Dean, Bill Terry, Babe Herman, Pepper Martin, Casey Stengel, Hack Wilson and Branch Rickey remains fresh in his memory.

Who were some of the toughest outs he faced? "All of them," Grimes laughed. "But I used to break the backs of some of those big-swingers."

The wicked spitter he learned as a youthful spectator at St. Paul's Lexington Field and later perfected with the help of a batch of slippery elm wadded in his cheek, baffled batters to the point where baseball changed the rules. "Somedays that's all I threw. It got 'em real upset."

Like many oldtimers, Grimes felt little connection to the modern game. ("Too many teams and players moving around.") After retiring as a major league scout in the early '70s he briefly ran a farm in Missouri but yearned for the Wisconsin fishing and hunting grounds of his youth.

So Burleigh returned to live with his third wife in a ranchstyle home, incredibly only 100 yards from the schoolyard where he played his first sandlot games. Most residents knew the treasure in their midst only as the elderly man who contentedly smoked a pipe while riding a lawnmower around the yard.

But a friend recounts how the drive that made Burleigh one of baseball's fiercest competitors still came out on occasion. Speaking at a local high school banquet several years ago, Grimes stopped his speech in mid-sentence after noticing a banner that read "Humble in Victory, Gracious in Defeat." "Folks," he laughed, "that's a great motto – when you're playing for free."

Bus Crash Memories

(Poet Paul "Red" Shuttleworth responded to a reader request for information about a fatal baseball bus crash with a reminiscence of his own. —Eds.)

* * * * * * *

Although I don't have any information for Lowell Johnson as per the 1948 Duluth Dukes bus crash (surely a nasty saga), that letter to the editor from Johnson amused me.

In 1977 the Texas City Stars, an independent Class A Lone Star League team owned by L.A. educational TV producer Van Schley, had Tommy Martin driving the bus. "Bussy" Martin had driven previously for Elvis Presley and Waylon Jennings and had been a recorded gospel singer in his own right. Bussy measured distance by how many cans of Coors he needed to consume enroute:

"Harlington? That'll be four more Coors." To compound things, all road trips began after midnight on game nights (to save team owners the $5 per day meal money they would have had to pay players for leaving before midnight.) So the players, naturally, had a few beers between showering around eleven o'clock and the one a.m. departure, and I imagine Bussy did too.

Although several of the players played spades at the front of the bus all night, most slept fitfully, either in their seats or – here's the potential for suicide if the bus ever rolled – in the overhead luggage racks.

One anecdote before I get to the core: On our last trip, on our way back from south Texas, I got to drinking canned drinks and a variety of liquor out of small bottles. I passed out in a luggage rack, but the spades game woke me up. Dirty Al Gallagher, as was usual when he was losing, was cursing his spades partner soundly in a gravelly, yet booming manner. I jumped down and ran up the aisle and kicked a suitcase, which was between the seat rows as a card table, off the windshield as we were passing through downtown Refugio. Since we'd all been drinking heavily, I feel I must take credit for waking up Bussy Martin and preventing any potential accident. Gallagher and I rolled around in the aisle trading ineffectual punches until one of us passed out (they say it was me) ... it's truly hard to remember because I've spent a good portion of my life trading punches with the Dirty Man.

The core: actually Tommy Martin was an excellent driver and once prevented loss of life at the end of a road trip. We were coming into Texas City from Beeville at four in the morning. A carload of drunk teenagers crossed the center line and entered our lane. Tommy Martin had the reactions to evade a front end collision by going into the other lane and back into ours, nearly hitting another oncoming car.

Three years later found me half asleep in the front seat of a team bus on its way from Durham to somewhere in Virginia. Bob Veale was sleeping next to me in the aisle seat, taking up part of my seat as well (the man is about 6'7" and 260 pounds), so I struggled up to stretch and glanced over the bussy's shoulder and notice we were cruising at 80 miles per hour. Shit. I got over big Bob and went back a few seats and told Gallagher, our manager. Gallagher told the bussy to slow down, which the bussy did for a while, but then we were balling down the highway again over 80. Because the Durham Bulls were an Atlanta Braves minor league club (with an alleged total player value over $3,000,000), the driver was summarily fired when we reached our destination. Among the people on that bus were Gerald Perry, Joe Cowley, Rick Behenna, Paul Zuvella, and Albert Hall; I suppose that's valuable cargo. Yeah, and Brett Butler was with us too.

Oh well, I guess all that is useless to Lowell Johnson. Sorry, its the only bus carry-on that comes to mind now.

All the best,
Paul Shuttleworth

The Blond Guy

Phillip Von Borries

A solid-hitting pitcher who coupled a lifetime 177-150 mound record with a career .284 batting average, Guy Jackson Hecker today still remains the only pitcher in major-league history ever to win a batting title. Given the specialization of pitchers within modern times, notably the short-and long-reliever, along with the advent of the designated hitter in the mid-1970s, it is unlikely that this feat will ever be duplicated.

Born on April 3, 1856 in Youngsville, Pa., Hecker began his baseball career in 1879 as a first baseman on an Oil City, Pa. team that included the ambidextrous pitcher Tony Mullane, whose good looks indirectly led to the establishment of "Ladies Day" as a standard baseball promotion later in that same decade. In 1882, Hecker joined Mullane at Louisville, which had just entered the newly-formed American Association. Originally a charter member of the august National League which had been founded in 1876, Louisville had left that fold after the 1877 campaign when evidence was uncovered that four of its star players had conspired to throw that year's pennant to Boston. Staying in the American Association until the league's collapse at the end of the 1891 season, Louisville then returned to the National League and competed there through 1899 when the franchise was abruptly shifted to Pittsburgh, bringing the curtain down on the city's mercurial 20-year major league history.

Despite a modest 6-6 record with the Louisville Eclipse as a rookie, "The Blond Guy" as he was nicknamed because of the color of his hair, gave early signs of his greatness. On September 19, 1882, just eight days after teammate Mullane pitched the American Association's first no-hitter, Hecker followed with the league's second, a 3-1 triumph over Pittsburgh marred by six errors, including two by that year's batting champion, the legendary Pete Browning.

While Mullane stayed only one season, however, chalking up a solid 30-24 slate for Louisville during the inaugural 1882 American Association campaign, Hecker worked there through 1889, racking up 175 victories for a Louisville entry that was a perennial non-contender. Twice a 20-game winner and once a 30-game winner, Louisville's ace had his best season in 1884 when he compiled a gargantuan 52-20 slate and predictably led the league in nearly every major pitching category.

But that was only a warmup for the 1886 season, Hecker's personal masterpiece and his finest *all-round* year. Besides posting a 27-23 record for a fourth-place Louisville squad, Hecker that year also become the only pitcher in major league history ever to cop a batting crown when he led the American Association with a .342 average that just nipped Browning's .340 mark and denied the latter a chance at consecutive titles as well as his third championship in five years. In addition, Hecker that same season set the all-time major league record for runs scored in a game when he crossed the plate seven times against Baltimore on August 15 off a phenomenal six-for-seven performance that saw him hit three home runs, bang out three singles and get on base a seventh time via an error. Completing the scenario, Hecker also picked up the win in the wild 22-5 rout!

The next year, 1887, Hecker's last productive season with Louisville when he batted .319 and tallied a 19-12 pitching ledger, marked the last of his major-league records when Hecker became the first man in professional baseball history to play an entire game at first base without registering a putout.

Dragged down in 1888 by a terrible Louisville squad that finished next to last, Hecker posted an 8-17 slate, dipping below the .500 mark for the first time in his career. Hoping to improve things, Hecker the next year sought the managership of the Louisville entry, only to be denied it because of the enmity of several players still with the club over a wild pitch Hecker had uncorked during the closing days of the 1883 season in a game against the Philadelphia A's. The errant pitch enabled the A's to just nose out the St. Louis Browns, whose eccentric owner, Chris von der Ahe, had promised all the Louisville players a new suit of clothes if they won the game.

In retrospect though, Hecker's failure to get the managerial reins for the 1889 season proved to be a blessing in disguise as that year the team set the all-time record for consecutive losses (26) enroute to an abysmal 27-111 mark and a .190 winning percentage, a pair of marks in futility exceeded only by the 1899 Cleveland Spiders, whose atrocious 20-134 ledger translated to a pitiful .129 wining percentage. Caught up in the slaughter and trapped by a cellar-dweller that scarcely knew any equal, Hecker fell even further, to a 5-11 mark.

Closing out his nine-year career in 1890 with Pittsburgh in the National League as a player-manager, posting a 2-12 mark for the senior circuit's counterpart to Louisville, Hecker then managed several minor league clubs for a few years before finally returning to Oil City, Pa., where he entered the oil business. Later opening up a grocery store there, Hecker in 1931 was involved in an automobile accident that left the fine right-hander's pitching arm so damaged he could not write except with a typewriter.

Issued a lifetime pass by the game in his final retirement years, Hecker died in Wooster, Ohio on December 4, 1938 at the age of 82, his death causing a brief ripple of attention from the press who for the last time recounted the unique records and deeds of this great and versatile pre-modern player.

Baseball's First World Champions:
The Providence Grays

Thomas Carson

Few baseball fans know that Providence once had a major league baseball team and fewer still know anything about this team. However, one of the most interesting chapters in the history of baseball was written by the Providence Grays who were part of the National League from 1878 until 1885. In eight years the Grays fielded two pennant winning teams. Five members of baseball's Hall of Fame played for the Grays, two of whom managed the team. In 1884 the Grays won the National League pennant and went on to win the first interleague, post-season playoff (the first equivalent of the World Series) sweeping all three games from the New York Metropolitans of the American Association (then a major league). That year the Grays were led by pitcher Charles (Hoss) Radbourn who posted what is probably the greatest single season record in the history of baseball – 60 victories.

1878: The First Season

The Grays joined the National League in the third year of its existence, 1878. The team finished in third place with a record of 33 wins and 27 losses. Centerfielder Paul Hines was the batting star of the team. He led the National League in batting average (.358), runs batted in (50), and home runs (4). Hines was the first "triple-crown" winner in major league history. That year he also gained the distinction of being the first major league player to make an unassisted triple-play. Hines is the only player who was a member of the Grays during all eight years of the team's existence. The pitching star of the team was Hall of Famer John Montgomery Ward who posted a record of 22 wins and 13 losses and led the league with an earned run average of 1.58. The eighteen year old Ward set a record that he shares with several other pitchers by pitching shutouts in his first two major league starts with the Grays in 1878. Ward's lifetime earned run average of 2.10 is the fourth lowest for all major league pitchers. Ward pitched for the Grays in the early part of his career; he later played for many years as a shortstop and outfielder for the New York Giants. He earned a law degree in the off-season and organized the Players' Brotherhood, the first professional baseball players union. Ward was the main leader of the short-lived Players' League, organized by the Player's Brotherhood in 1890. Although the Players' League collapsed after only one season (due to poor financial backing), the league succeeded in signing most of the top players of the day and enjoyed better attendance than the National League during the 1890 season.

1879: The First Pennant

The Grays added two members to its roster in 1879: rightfielder "Orator Jim" O'Rourke and shortstop George Wright, who replaced George Ware as manager of the team. (O'Rourke left the Boston team in a huff over a financial dispute with owner Arthur Soden, a notorious skinflint who demanded that O'Rourke pay $20 for his baseball uniform.) O'Rourke added offensive punch to the Grays and hit a splendid .348. In addition the Grays acquired star firstbaseman "Old Reliable" Joe Start from Chicago. The 37-year-old Start hit .319 for the Grays in 1879 and stayed with them for the rest of their history. Start ended his career with a lifetime batting average of .301. Hines hit .357 and Ward posted the best record of any pitcher in the league: 47 wins and 19 losses. Manager Wright led the team to its first pennant. The Grays finished with a record of 59 wins and 25 losses, 5 games ahead of the Boston Red Caps managed by George Wright's brother, Harry. The excitement of the close pennant race was enhanced by the fierce sibling rivalry. The Grays clinched the pennant in the last week of the season by winning a game against Boston, with George Wright scoring the winning run. The Providence fans erupted in what was described as the biggest demonstration "since Lee's surrender." In spite of an outpouring of interest and enthusiasm for the games with Boston and Chicago, the Grays drew poorly in this and other years. Total attendance for 1879 was only 43,000; total receipts were about $12,000 – considerably short of the team's expenses.

The Wrights were among the most important figures in early professional baseball both as players and managers. Harry Wright was the owner and founder of the Cincinnati Red Stockings, the first professional baseball team. He introduced "knickers" or the "knickerbocker" style of uniform still used in baseball to this day. Brother George was the team's star player. In 1869 the Red Stockings toured the country playing local teams and taking on all comers; they won 68 of the 69 games in which they played, the other game ending in a tie. George Wright is generally considered to be one of the greatest players in early professional baseball. In 1937 he became one of the first 11 men elected to baseball's Hall of Fame. Brother Harry was elected in 1953. After the 1879 season, George Wright entered into a partnership to found the Wright-Ditson Sporting Emporium on Dorrance Street in Providence; Wright-Ditson later became an important manufacturer of sporting goods.

1880: Second Place

In 1880 the Grays lost both right fielder O'Rourke and manager shortstop George Wright to Harry Wright's Boston team. Jim Bullock (who was replaced later in the season by Bob Morrow) became the team's manager. In spite of these losses, the Grays posted a record of 52 wins and 32 losses – a won-lost percentage of .619 – good enough for first place in most years. But 1880 was the year that Cap Anson built his Chicago White Stockings (later to become known as the Cubs) into the dominant team of their era and the Grays finished in second place 15 games behind Chicago who won with 67 wins and 17 losses. The highlight of the season was Ward's perfect game (the second in major league history) on June 17 against Buffalo.

1881: Radbourn Arrives

In 1881 the Grays finished second to Anson's White Stockings for the second consecutive season. The most important development of the year was the arrival of pitcher Charles Radbourn. Radbourn quickly supplanted Ward as the team's best pitcher. He posted a record of 25 and 13 and also played 38 games as an outfielder and shortstop when not pitching.

1882: The Wright Brothers Make a Run For It

In 1882 the Wright brothers joined the Grays; Harry as manager and George at shortstop where he hit a very disappointing .162 in what was to be his last season as a player. The Grays finished second to Chicago for the third season in a row; but they came close to taking it all, finishing only three games behind Anson's team in a very exciting and bitterly fought pennant race. Radbourn was quickly emerging as the top pitcher in the game and posted 33 wins and 19 losses. Ward had 19 wins and 12 losses in his last season with the Grays. On August 17 he threw the longest shutout ever pitched by one pitcher (18 innings). Radbourn, who played the game in the outfield, hit a home run to win the game 1-0. At the end of the season the financially troubled Buffalo team received permission to play its last three home games against Chicago in Chicago in the hope of making more money. This gave Chicago a home field advantage and Anson's team swept all three games – the margin of difference in the pennant race. The Wrights protested bitterly and league officials scheduled a post-season play-off between Chicago and Providence. Chicago swept the series.

1883: A Fall to Third Place

The Grays slipped to third place but still finished only 5 games behind first place Boston and 1 game behind second place Chicago. In 1883 George Wright retired and Ward was sold to the New York Giants where he ended his career as a pitcher and began a long and illustrious career as a shortstop and outfielder. Charlie Sweeney, a very talented and hot-tempered pitcher, joined the team to replace Ward. Radbourn established himself as the best pitcher in baseball with a record of 49 wins and 25 losses. Radbourn threw the only no-hitter of his career against Cleveland on July 25. The Grays won the most lopsided shutout in baseball history on August 21 beating the Philadelphia Phillies 28-0. Another noteworthy event of 1883 was the invention of the baseball glove by the Grays' shortstop Arthur Irwin who broke two fingers in his left hand and had a buckskin driving glove modified to protect his hand. When the expected jeers of the fans failed to materialize, other players quickly acquired their own gloves. The attitude of early professional ballplayers towards baseball gloves is called to mind in the poem about the Cincinnati Red Stockings by George Ellard:

> We used no mattress on our hands,
> No cage upon our face,
> We stood right up and caught the ball,
> With courage and with grace.

Irwin is also credited by some baseball historians with the invention of the hit-and-run play.

1884: The Great Year

Frank Bancroft became manager of the team as Harry Wright left to manage the Philadelphia team. Radbourn began the season with a very sore arm and the team's chances seemed to depend on fireballer Charlie Sweeney, the fastest pitcher in the game at that time. The Grays were locked in a tight pennant race with Chicago in the first part of the season. Radbourn and Sweeney were the best pitchers in baseball that year finishing with the two best earned-run averages in the league. On June 7 Sweeney struck out 19 batters in 9 innings against Boston – a feat matched only by Steve Carlton in 1969 and Tom Seaver in 1970. [Ed. Note: Written prior to 1986 when Roger Clemens struck out 20 Seattle Mariners at Fenway Park.] During a game on July 16 Radbourn became disgusted with the poor play of his fielders and with what he thought to be unfair calls by the umpire. He began lobbing the ball up to the plate without making any effort to get the batters out. He lost the game and was immediately suspended without pay by manager Bancroft. During Radbourn's suspension Sweeney got drunk and was also suspended by Bancroft. Angrily, Sweeney quit the team and signed with the St. Louis team of the short-lived Union Association thus leaving the Grays without any pitchers. (Sweeney was noted for his terrible temper and later served time in San Quentin prison after he killed a man in a brawl.) Bancroft was compelled to lift Radbourn's suspension and offer him a bonus to pitch all of the Gray's remaining games. Radbourn rejoined the team on July 23 and began what is arguably the greatest single season performance in the history of baseball. Radbourn started 37 games in a row and completed all of them, winning 32 out of the 37. During the period from August 7 until September 18 he won 26 out of 27 decisions putting together winning streaks of 18 and 8 consecutive victories. Radbourn posted a final won-lost record of 60(!) victories (an all-time major league record) and 12 losses. He completed all 73 of the games that he started (two short of the major-league record), struck out 441 batters (an all time National League record) and posted an earned run average of 1.38. "Hoss" also pitched 679 innings (1 short of the all-time major league record). Since the rules of the National League in 1884 required 6 balls for a walk and 4 strikes for a strikeout, Radbourn presumably was required to throw considerably more pitches per inning than present day pitchers. The team finished with a record of 84 wins and 28 losses, 10 games ahead of second place Chicago. (To post a comparable winning percentage under today's longer schedule a team would have to win more than 120 games.) At the end of the season the Grays participated in the first post season championship. They played against the New York Metropolitans led by Tim Keefe, Hall of Fame pitcher. Radbourn completed his heroics by pitching and winning all three games. Each member of the Grays received a $65 share of the gate receipts and the team was presented with a large silk pennant bearing the inscription *World Champions*. Radbourn's achievements during 1884 are even more impressive when one remembers that the Grays were a weak hitting team; Hines was the team's only real batting star and four of the other seven teams in the National League scored more runs than the Grays in 1884. Further, Radbourn began the season with a sore arm, which became worse during the season. By the end of the year his arm was so sore that he couldn't raise it to comb his hair. Radbourn threw underhanded (overhand pitching was prohibited before 1884) and took a running start (cricket style) before each pitch, which was permitted by the rules of the time. In 1883 a rule change limited pitchers to only one step before throwing the ball. Pitchers threw the ball from a rectangular 4' x 6' box, rather than a pitching rubber.

1885: A Sorry End

1885 was the last year of the Grays' existence and the team's only losing season; they finished with a record of 53-57. The Providence fans never turned out in large enough numbers to support the team adequately. The Grays had a winning record for the first half of the season. But then the team's financial problems came to a head. Owner Henry Root was compelled to suspend without pay Radbourn and some of the other star players for the rest of the season. The team played badly and at one point lost 18 games in a row. At the end of the season, Root sold the Grays to the Boston Beaneaters (formerly the Red Caps, later to be the Boston Bees, The Boston Braves, The Milwaukee Braves, and, finally, the Atlanta Braves) for $6,000. The Beaneaters kept the Grays' battery of Radbourn and catcher Con Daily. The other players were sold to other teams. Hines, Start, secondbaseman Farrell, left fielder Carroll, catcher Gilligan, and pitcher Shaw were all sold to the Washington club of the National League, and Irwin was sold to the Phillies. Providence never fielded a major league baseball team after 1885. However, there was later a team in the International League also known as the Providence Grays; Babe Ruth played for them in 1914. The Grays' home field, Messer Street Park, has long since disappeared. The park was located in the vicinity of the present Bridgham Middle School at 1655 Westminister Street in Providence. A bronze plaque in the school cafeteria is all that remains to acknowledge the fact that a great baseball team once played there.

Charles Radbourn played with the Beaneaters for four seasons; in 1890 he pitched for the Boston team of the Players' League and in 1891 he played his final season for the Cincinnati Reds. Radbourn ended his career with a record of of 308 wins and 191 losses. The final years of Radbourn's life were very unhappy. He retired from baseball to his hometown of Bloomington, Illinois where he opened a pool hall. Several years before his death he had most of face shot off in a gun accident. He refused to be seen in public after this and spent the last years of his life hiding in the back room of his pool hall. He died of syphilis in December 1897 just a few days short of his 43rd birthday.

References

Appel, Martin and Goldblatt, Burt, **Baseball's Best,** (New York, McGraw-Hill, 1977).

Danzig, Allison and Reichler, Joseph, *The History of Baseball,* (Englewood Cliffs, Prentice-Hall, 1959).

Einstein, Charles, (ed.), *The Fireside Book of Baseball.* (New York, Simon and Schuster, 1956).

Joyce, William L., *Never a Wild Pitch, Yankee Magazine,* October 1973, pp. 223-224.

Leitner, Irving, *Baseball: Diamond in the Rough,* (New York, Criterion Books, 1972).

Reichler, Joseph, ed., **The Baseball Encyclopedia,** (New York, Macmillan, 1982),

Reichler, Joseph, *The Great All Time Baseball Record Book,* (New York, Macmillan, 1981).

Reidenbaugh, Lowell, *100 Years of National League Baseball,* (St. Louis, The Sporting News Publishing Company, 1976).

Richter, Francis C., *Richter's History and Records of Baseball,* (Philadelphia, Richter Publishing Company, 1914).

Seymour, Harold, **Baseball: The Early Years,** (New York, Oxford University Press, 1960).

Smith, Robert, **Baseball in America,** (New York, Holt Reinhart and Wilson, 1961).

Voight, David, **American Baseball,** (Norman, Oklahoma, University of Oklahoma Press, 1966).

A Poem for Dirty Al Gallagher's Fortieth Birthday

Red Shuttleworth

When I gave up chewing tobacco, I gained nightmares:
rats slobbering on chest protectors, showers pouring
slime on my arthritic throwing arm, pitcher's mounds
swelling like infected prostate glands, and each time
I stride into a fastball, my bat becomes as porous
as a sponge.

             You're turning forty, Dirty Man,
and maybe some doctor will tell you to narrow the habits
down before you sicken, as I've been told. But they're
the guys who heckled and booed from the safety
of the ass end of home plate, a dozen rows back behind
the screen, their pallid faces more at home in clinics.

Secretly I pluck fresh snuff out of a round can
once a week, remember the taste of baseball, the feel
of running foul line to foul line with Rick Behenna,
Big Ike Pettaway, and Joe Cowley, our spikes spraying
new cut grass behind us.

                                   We can't transfer the past
to the present. Leo Mazzone's coaching for Atlanta
and Bob Veale for Salt Lake City. Cowley's playing
for the Yankees, I'm playing cowboy in Nebraska,
and you're playing softball in Fresno.

                                      Do you remember
the day in Golden Gate Park twenty-five years ago
that I batted my wristwatch into the outfield? I never
liked the steadiness of time.

                                 When we lived in Durham,
my belly was flat and I hunched down only to catch
flashy sliders. Now the ballpark spins in my dreams
like a stripper's firm tits.

                                   As we left that yard
after a nightgame one July midnight, someone switched
off the lights pole to pole, saving the sickly green
around third base until last. You mumbled something
about the clubhouse boy leaving your spikes unshined
that morning. No. I was the mumbling one, "Did you know
spikes or cowboy boots can be polished with the inside
of banana peels? You're right it wasn't like this
when you played for the Giants."

                                 When my plane
landed in Durham, you and Mazzone met me. An hour later
I scattered a half dozen batting practice balls around
the infield. Mazzone said, "At least Red brought
a bottle of Old Crow." The same Mazzone who believes
the invention of the breaking ball was the dawn
of civilization.

                                 You're turning forty, Dirty Man,
and maybe tonight you're sitting with Terry and the kids,
a bat in your hands because someone is taking a snap shot
for yet another nostalgia article. Perhaps your fingers
are tracing your burned-on autograph on the bat.

Suddenly, in the first good dream I've had in weeks,
you snap the bat into a cockshot fastball and it
rises into a darkness full of cheering, going
as deep as any pennant clinching homer.

The Baseball Player as *Bodhisattva:*
An Inquiry Into the National Pastime

Matthew Goodman

The fascination of what's difficult
Has dried the sap out of my veins, and rent
Spontaneous joy and natural content
Out of my heart.
                    - William Butler Yeats

But just this line ye grave for me:
"He played the game."
                    - Robert Service

Baseball seems to touch a chord deep within us. The game offers us an escape from our day-to-day realities, and yet it simultaneously brings us back to what is important and what is real. Our existence is out there on the baseball diamond: chance and necessity, individual struggle and common effort, lost opportunities and the luck of the bounce. Baseball shows us what we might not otherwise see, and thus refers us back to our lives.

In this way, baseball acts in much the same way as other vehicles human beings have created to amplify and make sense of reality; thus it acts as a form of poetry, and may serve some of the same purposes as religion. And of all the major religions, the one it seems to most closely resemble in its forms and rhythms is Buddhism. Although baseball is a home-grown American game, it often takes on an appearance decidedly Eastern in nature. (Might this help explain the popularity of baseball in the Orient?) Buddhists commonly refer to life as a game, and perhaps it might be possible to experience the Buddhist view of life through this particular game. Willie Stargell of the Pittsburgh Pirates has claimed that "The purpose of this game is to be your natural self,"[1] and though he was speaking of baseball, the Buddhists would surely agree; the purpose of the game, the larger Game, is indeed to be your natural self.

Baseball is a spontaneous game. It is not a game of militaristic machinations, like football, or the severely delimited restraints of basketball or hockey. "Wisdom is the outcome of creative spontaneity," said the Tibetan lama Anagarika Govinda, and his words are translated daily onto the baseball field. The best ballplayers are the ones who act spontaneously, almost intuitively, with *prajna* (which, interestingly, can mean either "transcendental wisdom" or "intuitive intelligence"). For example: This is what Lou Brock, arguably the best base stealer in the history of the game (A's fans might well argue this), has to say about the right moment to steal a base:

> You just gotta know when that is, which is the part that gets to be intuitive after a while. There's no place for it in the text book. It's a little like knowing what an intimate friend is going to say a split-second before he says it.[2]

What both Stargell and Brock are talking about, quite simply, is spontaneity. In a similar way, the aspiration of Zen Buddhism is to live one's life spontaneously. When Po-Chang was asked to define Zen, he responded, "When hungry eat, when tired sleep." Translated into baseball parlance; just play the ball, don't fight it.

When pitcher Luis Tiant talks about not having to look at the plate when he pitches,[3] he is talking about the same thing as the Zen master in Eugene Herrigel's **Zen in the Art of Archery**, who is able to hit the target without looking at it. He is able to do this because he no longer sees himself as an isolated entity separate from the target, but instead becomes both subject and object within a unified reality. When this state can be achieved, when the archer has become both hitter and hit, perfection of the skill has been realized and the shot falls from the bow like snow from a leaf, perfectly.

This state of enlightenment has been called "relaxed activity," and there is no better phrase to illustrate the ideal toward which the baseball player strives. Occasionally we get glimpses of a ballplayer who has momentarily attained this state, momentarily achieved the ideal. One thinks, for instance, of the defensive play of Brooks Robinson during the 1970 World Series, five games during which Robinson played third base as had no one before him. It was a wondrous display, after which viewers could say with accuracy that Robinson had done the seemingly impossible: had grasped the nuances and mastered the subtleties of his position, and the game as a whole.

Or one remembers the marvelous Willie Mays, who seemed always capable of providing us the exhibition of spontaneous grace. Perhaps the best example of this was his classic catch in the 1954 World Series against the Cleveland Indians.

It was top of the eighth inning, nobody out, Al Rosen on first, Larry Doby on second, and Vic Wertz – who had gone three for four that day – at the plate. Wertz nailed Giants pitcher Don Liddle's first pitch to deepest center field, and the heart of Giants fans sank: Everyone thought that he ball was over the head of the center fielder – everyone, that is, except for the center fielder himself. Head down, Mays raced to the farthest reach of the ballpark, as the ball soared forty feet above his head. As he approached the center field wall the ball started to sink, and suddenly everyone in the stadium knew that Willie Mays was going to catch the ball. Slowing down so as not to crash into the wall – and without ever turning around to face the plate – Mays raised his glove up over his left shoulder, and the ball disappeared into it. And then, still moving away from the plate, he fired the ball back into second base, "the throw of a giant, the throw of a howitzer made human," to send Rosen scurrying back to first. *At no point had Mays ever watched the ball.* He had simply known where the ball was going to come down – had never doubted it for an instant – and made the play that to this day is known simply as The Catch.

Or one recalls Don Larsen's perfect game, in which he needed only 97 pitches to retire the other side, twenty-seven up, twenty-seven down. Or the fastball pitchers at their fastest, before the ravages of the unnatural motion of pitching wear down an elbow, a rotator cuff or a pair of knees: Bob ("Rapid Robert") Feller, Sudden Sam McDowell, Sandy Koufax, Nolan Ryan (and now, perhaps, Dwight Gooden), whose ability to tap the magical force of pure speed left batters shaking their heads and muttering as they made their way back to the dugout. Think, for instance, of Bob Gibson's record seventeen-strikeout game against the Detroit Tigers in the 1968 World Series. After that game, a game in which Gibson seemed able to do no wrong, the Tigers spoke of him in tones that approached reverence. Said opposing pitcher Denny McLain, himself coming off an award-winning 31-win season, "I was awed. I was *awed*." Tiger infielder Dick McAuliffe declared, "He doesn't remind me of anybody. He's all by himself." Commentator Vin Scully was able to concisely portray the intensity of Bob Gibson's excellence in this way: "Gibson pitches as though he's double-parked." For one moment, Bob Gibson had seemingly transcended the limits of the game.

The feeling of transcending the previous limits, of being in perfect synch with the game, has been beautifully described by Pirates pitcher Steve Blass:

> You get so locked in, you see yourself doing things before they happen. That's what people mean when they say that you're in a groove. That's what happened in the World Series game, when I kept throwing that big slop curveball to Boog Powell, and it really ruined him. I must have thrown it three out of four pitches to him, and I just *knew* it was going to be there. There's no doubt about it – no information needed ... all of a sudden you're locked into something. It's like being plugged into a computer. It's "Gimme the ball, boom! Click, click ... shoom!" It's that good feeling. You're just flowing easy.[4]

For a brief moment, Steve Blass had achieved *satori*, the opening into enlightenment. During that moment, Blass experienced the sensation that meditation strives to attain, the state of consciousness in which the individual is "locked into something . . . flowing easy." And it was the baseball, like the meditation, which would provide the medium.

Baseball, unlike other team sports, does not use an external time clock to measure the duration of the game. Time in baseball is measured in inherently human terms, in "outs", and this fact is crucial to an understanding of baseball, and its affinity with Buddhism.

In Buddhism, time is a relative concept, not some perfectly ordered external force imposing itself on us. It is not some cosmic time clock, dividing up the Game into symmetrical quarters, with pre-measured time outs for half-time and commercial messages. A baby experiences time very differently than does an older person. A person in motion experiences time very differently than does one who is stationary. A person experiences time very differently when asleep than when awake. The experience of time, therefore, has to do with consciousness. And, according to the Buddhists, for one who has achieved enlightenment, time will appear to have ceased flowing entirely.

In baseball, time is measured by the performances of the players. And the performances of the players, as we have seen, is intimately related to consciousness. If a team is playing poorly they will make out more often and baseball time will move fairly rapidly. However, if the team has been able to achieve perfection – the enlightenment of which Steve Blass was speaking – they will never make out and time will have ceased to flow.

The lack of a fixed time limit in baseball also adds to the possibility of a come-from-behind win, thus eliminating the meaningless "running out the clock" that so often occurs at the end of a timed game. The old baseball adage "It's not over until the last out" – refined by Yogi Berra into "It ain't over till it's over" – is tirelessly trotted out by baseball fans as an example of the delicate beauty of their game. And yet however antiquated that maxim has become, it has lost none of its truth; several times each year we are treated to the exquisite tension of a come-from-behind rally with two outs in the ninth inning. Whether or not the losing team actually wins the game is not the issue; what matters is that both teams *believe* that it might, and the tenor of the game is grounded in this belief – thus, the game really isn't over until it's over.

Another of baseball's great charms is its translucence. We see it all happening as it happens; it is a game that we can follow. When a groundball is hit to the shortstop he must play it, and the play is there for all to see. He must field the ball cleanly, and he must throw it accurately. And he must do it alone; it is his play, and he must execute it without anyone else's assistance. A player who is unable or unwilling to perform will be, in Roger Angell's words, "searched out, caught in the open, and defeated, and there will be no confusion about it or sharing of the blame." The batter and the pitcher face each other; one stands on the pitcher's mound, the other in the batter's box, but both are standing alone, and each will succeed or fail in the same way – alone.

Once again, to Buddhism: Buddha said over and again that he could only show the way, that it was up to every individual to reach the end through his or her own singular effort. Enlightenment is an intensely personal experience, one that can only be attained through individual action. If we are going to seek some understanding of enlightenment through sport, then a team sport which does not allow great latitude for individual action on the part of every player will not be sufficient.

But a purely individual sport will not be sufficient either. For there to be true enlightenment there must be an awareness of others, teammates in the Game, as it were. Lama Anagarika Govinda has written that "So long as the illusion of a permanent, unchangeable and separate egohood exists, we put ourselves into opposition to the very nature of life." In other, simpler words, it has to be a team game as well. And baseball is certainly that; each player has his own individual position, but each is circumscribed and essentially meaningless without the other. Beyond this when a team is playing well the actions of each individual player will merge to form a unity that is greater than the sum of its disparate parts. A batter has a better chance of getting a good pitch to hit when the runner on base is threatening to steal, thus compelling the pitcher to remove some of his attention from the batter. And vice versa: The base stealer has a better chance to succeed when the batter is willing to "protect" him, by swinging at the pitch – wherever it might be – when the runner bolts for second, so as to distract the catcher. Or the batter might have to hit the ball to the right side of the infield, making out himself but moving the runner along. This is the sacrifice play, and the phrase for it in baseball jargon is suggestive of our discussion; it is called "giving yourself up."

According to Buddhist thought, enlightenment requires polarity; it means being conscious of both the individual and the universal, both of one's own identity and one's active relationship to the rest of the world. It is the realization that all is one, and yet all is not one. Both states exist, and both are equally true. A game that aspires to enlightenment, then, should seek to capture this paradox, the state of simultaneous individuality and universality. It should be a team sport that places great emphasis on individual action – as does baseball.

Baseball is a game of action, not movement, and because of this is often thought of as boring by the uninitiated.[5] Like life, it is twenty minutes of action packed into two hours of game. Its mantra – pitch, pitch, hit, field, pitch . . . – is often seen as being not tranquil, but monotonous. This is certainly an arguable point, and a baseball fan might well retort with the old Buddhist saying that if something is boring you're not looking closely enough. But we can let this argument go untended, for to assert the monotony of baseball is still to admit of its aspiration to enlightenment; according to Buddhist writings, "monotony, far from being an obstacle to enlightenment, is central to the practice." If life remains too interesting at the rational level, one may never be able to break through to a deeper, more intuitive level. A baseball game does tend to be slow-moving at times, but it is a slowness that can provide the same sense of serenity as T'ai Chi, a Chinese form of moving meditation, or the Japanese tea ceremony, in which each move is deliberate and richly textured.

Baseball, though, is not solely confined to unrelenting patterns of slow movement. At times the baseball game is punctuated by brief, staccato flashes of motion; the waiting has ceased and been converted into action, and at once everyone and everything has changed. With the runner at first in motion, the pitch is hit into the alley between right and center fields; one run scores and the batter tries to stretch the hit into a triple. The second baseman moves into short right field to take the throw from either the right or center fielder, both of whom are racing toward the ball; the third baseman moves slightly up the line in anticipation of a possible play at the plate; the two runners steam around bases, and by this time the crowd has leaped to its feet, roaring, in a searing moment of catharsis.

It was the slowness itself that allowed the catharsis to occur. In a faster-paced game the sudden action would get lost in the general movement. Not so in baseball – we *know* when the plays that will make the difference have occurred. The drama of these plays is amplified by the waiting for them. The waiting intensifies the game, gives it a heightened sense of grandeur, so that when the sudden action does arrive, "we rise and cry out. It is a spontaneous, inevitable, irresistible reaction."[6]

And then, just as suddenly, the action is completed. The throw arrives a moment too late to nab the runner, and we are waiting once again. The waiting and the action complement each other, bring out the fine points of the other, and the game would not be whole without both.

These opposites, like the opposed poles of individuality and universality, act in harmony with each other, as part of the polarity that enlightenment requires. During enlightenment the polarity dissolves, and we can see the opposites as unified pieces of what Fritjof Capra has called the "organic whole". This Buddhist definition of existence is similar to Marvin Cohen's definition of each baseball game as an "organic unit" in which each play is inextricably affected by the plays that came before it, and which will in turn affect everything that comes later. There are no exemptions: every pitch in the game has its place.

Every pitch has its place, and so does every play, and every player. And it is in this, the relationship between play and player, that we will ultimately find the answers. The real clues to this game lie in the subtle pleasures that give the game its richly-textured character; the tingle of the bat when it meets the ball just right, the gratifying feel of the grounder as it bounces up and sticks right in the pocket of the glove, the exhilarating sensation of rounding third full-tilt and heading for home, or the luxurious moment when you call time out to wipe the dirt from your pants after a successful slide. It is that moment in which time has no meaning, in which the world is whole and at peace; a wondrous moment in which there is only sensation, and the joy of existence.

FOOTNOTES
[1]As quoted in Tom Clark, **Baseball** (Berkeley, CA: Serendipity Books, 1976). p. 70.
[2]Lou Brock, **Stealing is My Game** (Englewood Cliffs, NJ: Prentice-Hall, 1976), p. 183
[3]In Clark, op. cit., p. 73.
[4]In Clark, op. cit., p. 24.
[5]See Gilbert Sorrentino, *Baseball,* in Kevin Kerrane and Richard Grossinger (eds),
Baseball Diamonds (Garden city, NJ: Anchor Press, 1980), p. 65.
[6]Roger Angell, *The Interior Stadium,* in **The Summer Game** (New York: Popular Lib., 1972), p. 311.

THE VIEW FROM LEFT FIELD

Economic Theories Underlying Major League Baseball

Phillip Stephens

One: Free Enterprise and What it Means

If people merely played baseball in their back yards and city parks, they might buy a ball, a bat, a glove and sneakers, which they pay for once and use without cost thereafter. They might buy a six-pack to cool off with after a few innings. They would get lots of exercise, laughs and fun.

If people visit the ballpark they buy small, but more expensive souvenir bats, balls and gloves, more expensive beer, very expensive hot dogs and pretzels, and put gasoline in their cars that they will consume driving to and from the ballparks, as well as consume while idling during traffic jams around the stadium.

They would also get beer spilled on them and develop lower back pain from sitting on the bleachers. Then they will spend money on detergent or dry cleaning, and doctors.

This is the meaning of free enterprise: getting people to spend money (enterprise) for things they would probably enjoy more doing themselves (for free).

Two: How the Wage/Price Spiral Works

When fans pack the ballparks, ballplayers begin to see themselves as entertainers rather than laborers. So they organize, become free agents, and demand big dollars ($) for their contracts.

(This is not to be confused with free enterprise. Ballplayers are not owners and do not produce profits, but earnings. Therefore they do not contribute to the economy as owners do, who give you products and services like baseball to spend your wages on.)

Owners, who have already raised ticket prices to the limit, recoup their losses to salaries at a profit by selling air time to television. TV networks, who air games free to viewers, recoup their TV contract losses at a profit by selling advertising time to the producers of products in the general market so they, in turn, can recoup their advertising costs at a profit through increased sales. All of which, in theory, should mean that owners simply exchange costs at a profit among themselves, while the fans just sit back and enjoy the game.

Except that the other producers also raise the prices of Budweiser, Doritos, Ball Park Franks, Poulin Chain Saws and Radio Shack TV aerials to recoup their advertising costs completely and profit even more from the increased sales.

This is a corollary of free enterprise (designated FE Prime for you intellectuals out there): If you can find a way to increase profits by increasing sales, increase profits even more by increasing the prices too. Who cares where the money comes from as long as it goes into your pocket?

Three: A Brief Editorial From Left Field

I am a baseball fan who, being physically lazy, would rather sit through beer showers in the bleachers than get sweaty swinging a bat. But I resent the huge corporate profits reaped at my expense so that Ted Turner can sail his yacht, or George Steinbrenner can drive a Mazaratti.

I propose we nationalize the major leagues.

In the Owner's Box

Steve Lehman

Time for a pop quiz. One question, multiple choice. Ready? Here goes: Which individual, group of individuals, or organization(s) really calls the shots in Major League Baseball? (a) Peter Ueberroth; (b) the team owners; (c) the Major League Player's Association; (d) **The MRB**; (e) none of the above.

The answer, of course, is (e), none of the above. Who does call the shots in the bigs these days? Network television. Case in point: For two years now, despite the best efforts of the Cubs to render the issue moot, the question has been hotly debated about what to do should the North Siders end up again in postseason play, since play-off games must, for some not-so-obscure reason, be played at night. Many sane and fair solutions to this dilemma have been put forth, such as having the Cubbies play their home games three hundred miles away in the hostile confines of Busch Stadium, as unsuited a ballpark as could be found anywhere in the world for the Cubs. What prompts such lunacy? $$$, in the form of network TV contracts. And the TV people insist that the weekday games must be played at night to guarantee sufficiently bulging profit margins. But what happens to an NLCS game scheduled on a Monday on ABC during the football season? It starts at 11:00 a.m. Eastern Time! Now I'm sure sure that this makes perfect sense to the network programmers and their accountants. But baseball fans should be outraged. Has the National Pastime degenerated to the point where the same imperative that would force a play-off team into exile from their fans is not important enough to pre-empt a meaningless early season football game (pardon the redundancy)? Apparently so.

The Seventh Babe: The Best of Nine New Rookies

Book Reviews by Harley Henry

(The **MRB** has always printed book reviews as the natural appendage to publishing fiction; the detritus of creative writing, if you will. We've been lucky to have learned reviewers like Harley Henry who wrote this in 1981. —Eds.)

* * * * * * *

In Heywood Broun's **The Sun Field** (1925) Judith W. (for Wigglesworth) Winthrop – New England, Vassar and literary correspondent for **Tomorrow** magazine – is introduced to baseball for the first time. She falls for "Tiny" Tyler, slugging left fielder of the Yankees, whose catches she compares to a god picking a comet out the the sky, and whose strikeouts remind her of "Thor hurling a thunderbolt." She becomes a baseball wife, goes on the road, and reports from an eastern wing that she has abandoned her projected essay on Sherwood Anderson, but has an "excellent article ready (on) . . . 'Tribal Rites in America' which begins with the 'The Golden Bough' and ends with a discussion of the custom of standing up in the seventh inning." When told what playing the "sun field" means, she observes, "It's a fine name and a fine job. All jobs ought to be like that. All of us alive should be set to looking straight at the sun and getting our light first hand instead of having it reflected for us out of little cracked mirrors we call novels."

Though not the first novelist to make use of the "matter of baseball" — **The Sun Field** is as much about feminism in the 1920s as it is about the game —Broun was prophetic of American writers' attempts to plumb the meaning of the National Pastime by finding in it myths and rituals of modern American culture while remaining fascinated with the play of the game itself as an activity somehow essential to human life.

Over the last thirty years American novelists have produced an impressive collection of "little cracked mirrors" which try to reflect for us the cultural and social significance of baseball. While a recent Gallup poll reports that baseball has markedly declined as one of America's favorite spectator sports – from 39% in 1948 to 16% in 1980 – the output of serious baseball fiction has risen sharply over that period. More than twenty novels, and countless short stories, have appeared since Bernard Malamud ushered in what might be called the "modern era" of the baseball story with **The Natural** in 1952. Thirteen of these have come out in the last eight years, including an astonishing total of nine plus two anthologies of baseball fiction in the last two years. The 1970s also produced no less than five full-length studies of Babe Ruth and his times, not to mention a host of other non-fiction works and collections about baseball.

It is hard to say whether this outpouring of writing about baseball is an attempt to rescue the game from mere nostalgia and combat the growing preoccupation with football, or whether it is a symptom of a revived interest in baseball – reflected in the average attendance at major league games in the last five years – as a remedy for what ails American life. In any case, we are also seeing an ever-growing number of articles, books, and college-level courses on the role of sport in America, and there have been at least three Ph.D. dissertations on baseball fiction in recent years, one of which, Walter Harrison's *Out of Play: Baseball Fiction from Pulp to Art* (University of California at Davis, 1980) is a thorough and helpful survey of the development of the baseball novel from the 1880s to 1979. Although writing about writing about baseball seems, given Judith Winthrop's observation, something thrice removed from reality, what follows is a sketchy survey of recent baseball fiction with special attention to Jerome Charyn's **The Seventh Babe** (1979), which I think is the best of the recent crop of rookies in the fictional game.

In four "classic" baseball novels of the modern era Malamud, Mark Harris, Robert Coover and Philip Roth have brilliantly succeeded in allying baseball and its wonderful episodic history with more inclusive cultural frames of references. **The Natural** sees the game and its batsman-hero in terms of primitive fertility myth, Arthurian legend and Jungian psychology in order to point to the American hero's failure in his life outside the game to achieve maturity and wisdom for his task within it. Mark Harris' **Bang the Drum Slowly** (1956) – the best of his Henry Wiggen trilogy – shows a temporary and ill-sorted community (the team) overcoming internal dissension and succeeding (winning the pennant) through its growing awareness of the most profound fact of life outside the game in the dying of one if its players. While Malamud and Harris insist that winning and losing on the field is ultimately dependent on how much and well we understand life off the field, Coover's **Universal Baseball Association Inc., J. Henry Waugh Prop.** (1968) sees the game (or games) as a self-contained universe created by its god-like proprietor for apparently unknown reasons, a view which opens up the possibility for what one commentator has called a "remythification" of aspects of modern culture. In Roth's **The Great American Novel** (1973), the ironic contrast between a team of losers and wanderers in the now-defunct and forgotten Patriot League and the history of America in the last fifty years reveals the progressive degradation of American ideals in the face of the contradictory facts of American life.

The more recent examples of American fiction about baseball make it obvious that Malamud, Harris, Coover and Roth have also recreated a rich tradition in which newer writers can work, using the subject of baseball for a variety of purposes. The newer fiction continues this tradition by mixing fiction with baseball as as metaphor for human (or American) life, and by developing the themes and preoccupations of the earlier novelist, principally the male American's search of an identity in a confused society, his infantilism in relationships with women, his moral confusion as a result of an undue emphasis on winning and success, and the values which might make his life in contemporary America worth the living.

The best recent expression of this tradition is Charyn's **The Seventh Babe**, which has strong affinities with at least three of the classic novels. It is the tale of "Rags" Ragland, a left-handed third baseman, who find himself and his "spot" in American life and the game by being thrown out of organized, white baseball and spending his life in the never-ending game played by the Cincinnati Colored Giants, an outlaw barnstorming team which builds its own ballparks and controls its fate through the ministrations of a witch doctor. Though the Giants "have to clown to stay alive," they are so good that they can mimic for fun any of the great white major leaguers, disdain keeping statistics and play over 600 games a year. In this regard, Charyn's novel might be compared to other recent works which deal with black baseball and/or barnstorming: Jay Neugeloren, **Sam's Legacy** (1973); William Brashler, **The Bingo Long Travelling All-Stars and Motor Kings** (1973); John Sayles, **Pride of the Bimbos** (1975), and John Craig, **Chappie and Me** (1979).

But it is to Malamud, and to a lesser extent to Coover and Roth, that Charyn may best be compared. The Seventh Babe has something of the style and aura of the romance of **The Natural**, and Rags' ability to stay in the game for life reverses Roy Hobbs' sad fate. Like Roth, Charyn is preoccupied with the losers and wandering outcasts of American society, and the Colored Giants, outcasts from "organized" baseball, act out an allegory of the history of American blacks forced to live like phantoms outside the dominant white society of America. The comic extravagance and the criticism of society of Charyn's novel also seems to owe something to Roth. Finally, while Charyn avoids the heavier theological overtones of **The Universal Baseball Association**, Rags' emergence as the "Bossman and Magician" of the Giants and his existence fully within self-sufficient world of the barnstorming team, certainly indicate a debt to Coover.

Red Sox fans will be especially drawn to the opening chapters of **The Seventh Babe**. Charyn makes use of some of the facts of Sox history – Fenway (located in the novel near the mysterious Back Bay Fens where Rags goes to be introduced to lust) with its "Royal Rooters," "Duffy's Cliff," center field flagpole, and the "tunnel" to the clubhouse where the "bad boy" Rags settles his disputes with players and team with his fists. Hollis McKee, the fictional owner of the hapless 1923 Red Sox, clearly resembles Harry Frazee who carried out the "Rape of the Red Sox" by selling off this best players (including Ruth) to the Yankees in order to support his disastrous theatrical ventures. Garland James, the Red Sox's center fielder, seems modeled on Tris Speaker, while the performance of the team duplicates the dismal record of the depleted Red Sox in the 1920s.

In the fictional world, McKee neglects his team to give his attention to a new musical about baseball wives, "Eveline," though ironically none of the Red Sox are married. It is also McKee's preference, as an old Dartmouth man, for college educated players which creates a split on the team between the college boys and the country boys. The owner's other preoccupation is with Marylou and Iva Cottonmouth, the wife and daughter of McKee's late fraternity brother, Judah Cottonmouth, the New England ice king. McKee engineers a marriage between Rags and 16-year-old Iva, making Rags, the youngest of the Sox, the first married man on the team. But after Rags' male pride spurns Iva because she is not a virgin, and Iva rejects Rags because she thinks he is responsible for Marylou's suicide in the mysterious fens, Hollis sets up Rags on a charge of consorting with a gambler and Judge Landis expels the young third baseman (like Joe Jackson and Phil Douglas) from baseball. With the Giants, Rags quickly catches on to the ways of "nigger baseball," having learned it from black ranch hands when he was young. Outside of organized baseball, and, as a member of a "phantom team," outside American history, Rags is barely conscious of the passing years of the thirties. Although the war years make the black players acceptable and Judge Landis offers a reprieve, Rags remains outside the white game. When black players join major league teams and become "invisible" after 1946, Rags does a brief stint with the Browns, where he seems a sort of Rip Van Winkle, but he returns to the barnstorming Giants because "he just didn't care about the major leagues." At the novel's end, Rags, now 72 and for some time reunited with seventy-year-old Iva (who has learned to manage the Giants as well as Rags), plays on and on, apparently impervious to physical decline, thanks to his skills as a magician and the endless nature of the Giant's fluid and wandering game.

Charyn's story is essentially a comic and ironic version of the familiar America tale of the hero's search for identity, maturity and freedom. Born Cedric Tannehill, the son of a copper magnate, Rags shows up at the Red Sox training camp in Sackville Forest, Arkansas, claiming to have been raised and taught baseball in the St. Mary's home in Baltimore and thus deserving to be the seventh player in the majors to be called Babe. Although his real past, which included a brief period at Amherst where he learned a little boxing and less Greek, is subsequently revealed, the fans continue to call him Rags, and he takes on his identity as a left-handed third baseman, refusing to become Cedric again. Slowly and painfully he must add new dimensions to his identity as as player who is primarily a fielder, a deliberate contrast to the typical batsman-hero of much baseball fiction. As the novel unfolds Rags' determination to live as fully and completely as possible inside the baseball identity is marked in various ways, most interestingly by his rarely appearing in anything other than his baseball uniform, the "magical pajamas'" which by the end are the tattered and heavily patched gold and white of the Giants.

He was leather, air and horsehide on a ball. He was knickers and dirty brown grass, the first twist of a double play. He couldn't live apart from a baseball diamond. He was married to a fifty-cent glove . . . He was born in a pile of mud near the pitcher's box. A baseball baby. Orphan Rags.

Unlike Malamud's Roy Hobbs, Rags finally learns enough from his life to be able to exist entirely within this baseball self. His first mentor is the Red Sox's mascot, batboy, and sign stealer, a hunchback named Scarborough, who as a fellow outcast, becomes Rags' baseball "roomie," the only genuine relationship with another person Rags is capable of. Scarborough, who is probably modeled on an actual team mascot of the time, voluntarily goes into exile with Rags and the Giants, eventually becoming one of the team's managers and its first baseman. Rags comes to resemble his fellow black players more and more so that when he encounters Iva during the war years she thinks he is "a Negro from the way he had shuffled in," but "it was only the standard crouch of the Cincinnati Colored Giants, a gesture of suspicion and a patter of flight that were necessary for a team that lived on the run. The kid walked and moved like any other Giant." After Scarborough's death, Rags persuades Iva to rejoin him as his "roomie" only, but eventually they are able to be husband and wife.

Rags' final vision of freedom, the freedom of being in the game and thus outside an over-regulated and enslaved society driven by the need for gain and success, is expressed in his having his "spot" in the Giants' endless game played under their portable light, which cast a "mellow fog" over the playing fields they construct for themselves.

> Refugees from nowhere. You would have thought fifty sheriffs had been chasing them. But no one was on their tail except that bossman-magician. Play your own game, he said. He didn't bother to send out hawkers and criers. What the hell is a crowd! He had Miz Iva and his light.

"Play your own game." Charyn drives this point home in the ending of the novel in which Rags encounters his old teammate, Garland James. While for Rags baseball "wasn't a series of rituals between men in flannel suits," but simply "wild play," for Garland it had always been play-for-pay. Spurning the advances of Marylou Cottonmouth, whom he ought to have married, Garland played dutifully until he no longer had to earn the money to send his brother through school. He took himself out of professional baseball by falling from the Fenway flagpole and became a teacher of Greek and baseball coach (like Smoky Joe Wood) at a New England college.

> What could he declare about his own folly? That he loved Greek and the foolishness of cramming Sophocles into the skulls of boys? That he wanted his center field without the rigamorole and politics of a major-league club? He hadn't fallen off any pole. He'd jumped. To cripple himself and shout "fuck you" to Hollis.

Playing a game appropriately against the "Amherst summer-school pickup team" Rags discovers "Garl," over 80 and consigned to a nursing home. Lured by the siren-like voices in the Giants' fire truck-light generator ("Go with the Giants, go with the Giants") Garland accepts Rags' offer of the center field spot and goes off with the team to play his own game, for once, wondering, "Did you kick old age in the pants when you traveled with the Giants?"

With the exception of Phillip O'Connor's **Stealing Home** (1979), **The Seventh Babe** is the best of the nine long works of baseball fiction which have appeared in the last two years. At the bottom of the order, more revealing as curiosities than anything else, are Marty Bell, **Breaking Balls** (1979) and Robert Browne, **The New Atoms Bombshell** (1980). The former is at least a raunchy imitation of Dan Jenkins' popular football novel, **Semi-Tough**. The latter is a largely boring and formulaic futuristic vision of baseball played by a Chicago team in a domed stadium in Lake Michigan and controlled by a mad scientist from a giant computer center. Although Browne's fears about computerized baseball may be uncomfortably accurate, his sentimental and rather trite ending has man (and woman) triumphing over the machine and playing baseball the right way.

Two quite entertaining novels without many pretensions are Paul Hemphill, **Long Gone** (1979), which deals with the fortunes of a Class D, Alabama-Florida League team in the 1950s, and Ron Powers **Toot-Toot-Tootsie, Good-Bye** (1981) about the final season of an old-time baseball radio announcer, L. D. Fanning, whose greatest moment in life was calling Bobby Thomson's 1951 playoff winning home run. Hemphill's novel touches the bases of nostalgia and humor, the dreary and precarious life in the lowest minor leagues, and the mild, but seedy corruption and prejudice of the Deep South. Although the novel never quite makes it home, it does deal with the hero-manager Stud Cantrell's battle against the color bar in baseball and his being forced to throw the final game. **Toot-Toot-Tootsie** advances the reader from nostalgia for baseball as it used to be, or rather "baseball" as it used to be portrayed on the radio, to a confirmation of our worst suspicions about the electronic media and its willingness to destroy the "radio game" in its quest for ratings; but it stumbles on its flat writing between second and third. In both novels the cast of characters, from Cantrell's girlfriend Dixie Lee Box, to Fanning's broadcast partner, Turtle Teweles, is worth the price of admission.

The fourth of the Henry Wiggen novels, Mark Harris' **It Looked Like Forever** (1979) also glances at the media in Henry's brief career as an announcer on television's *Friday Night Baseball*, but for the most part the novel concerns Henry's struggle to accept his baseball "death" through retirement and the accompanying doubts about his manhood. Although **It Looked Like Forever** is a serious novel about the professional athlete's own version of mid-life crisis, perhaps inspired by the third and final section of Roger Kahns' **The Boys of Summer**, it seems, perhaps like Henry himself, rather tired and dutiful in comparison to the earlier Wiggen novels. Also somewhat inspired by Kahn's portrait of himself as as young impressionable sportswriter is **The Last Great Season** (1979) by Donald Honig, who is known for his two collections of interviews with players of earlier eras of baseball. Honig's novel, told mostly from the point of view of a young sportswriter, is a thinly disguised retelling of Larry MacPhail's creation of the 1942 Dodgers including the ruthless exploitation and near-ruin of Pete Reiser. The jacket cover, which features an unmistakable likeness of MacPhail, suggests Honig's fascination with a figure too-often treated only with suspicion in baseball fiction, the owner. Despite the largeness of the figure of Allie Brandon, the owner, the reader is left wondering about the validity of Brandon's (and perhaps Honig's) belief that baseball as it really was ended with the upheavals of World War II.

All of these novels deal in some way with aspects of baseball largely unexplored by earlier fiction – the lowest minors, radio broadcasters, over-the-hill players, and management – in interesting and entertaining ways. Only O'Connor's **Stealing Home** claims a new position in the field of baseball fiction, the Little League coach, and really does something with it. Benjamin Bunne, the central figure, struggles to find some point to his work, marriage and parenting by coaching his son's team. Although baseball is central to the meaning of the novel, it occupies much less time in this sensitive book than Benjamin's problems outside the game. Although I do not think that it uses and advances the tradition and possibilities of baseball fiction nearly so well as **The Seventh Babe**, **Stealing Home** is likely to become one of the more frequently examined "cracked mirrors" with which we and American novelists try to understand whether, why, and how baseball means something more than it seems to. In the meantime, we might do well to remember Judith Winthrop's advice about "getting our light first hand," and Damon's remark at the end of **The Universal Baseball Association, Inc.** as he raises the hard, white ball, "It's not even a lesson. It's just what it is."

Southpaw Switch: Forerunner of **The Natural** Revealed

(Robert Warde, Professor of English at Macalester College, delivered to this editor a paper of brilliant insight and startling revelation: Bernard Malamud, in his classic baseball fiction **The Natural** owed a considerable debt to little-known author Adolph Regli's short story *Southpaw Switch*. Warde's paper is exacting in its analysis, and must become a major factor in critical discussions of Malamud's work. We give our readers here the text of *Southpaw Switch* by Adolph Regli, followed by Warde's essay. —Eds.)

Southpaw Switch
by Adolph Regli

From **Teenage Stories of the Diamond**, New York, Grosset & Dunlap, 1950

Ernie Grant brushed his lean, hot face against the gray sleeve of his St. Frances uniform and shot a worried glance around the diamond. A nervous quiver coursed through his slim body.

The bases were loaded. He'd given up two singles and a walk almost before the McCormick College fans had settled into their seats for the opening game of the year.

Almost too surprised to cheer, the home college crowd buzzed over "Three-Hit" Grant's feeble pitching against the weakest hitting club in the Upper River Conference. He hadn't retired a single batter. Was the St. Frances mound ace washed up, as rumor had it? Had the accident finished his diamond career?

"Hang in there, Ernie," Captain Bud Elberg shouted from first base. Ollie Tudor added shrill encouragement from third and shortstop Daniels ran to the mound for a quick, hopeful word.

Ernie scraped the rubber with his toe spikes and settled himself for the pitch. Fretfully, he gazed at Jaffrey, the McCormick cleanup hitter, waving a long bat across the plate.

He was convinced now. His pitching arm was dead – the right arm that had whipped the conference into helplessness and given St. Frances two baseball championships. He had nothing left but a glove and a prayer.

Winding up slowly, he tried to rifle a slider past the hitter but it sailed in straight and soft. Jaffrey met it squarely and drove it on a line between left and center. Three runs had scored by the time he had slid into third.

While the McCormick rooters roared their glee, Ernie Grant glanced toward the St. Frances bench and caught coach Milton's signal to Captain Elberg. Seconds later the first baseman stood beside him kicking idly at the dirt, his chin lowered.

"Coach is pulling you Ernie," Elberg said, "Sorry. Your stuff – We all have our bad days fella. Next time –"

Next time! Would there be one? Ernie wondered. He was a senior; a good season would earn for him the most valuable player trophy he wanted so badly. Besides that, several Major League clubs were scouting him. Now he'd have to forget all that.

He said to Elberg, "I've sure put you in a bad hole, bud. I shouldn't have let Milton start me, but I thought – I hoped –"

"Sure Ernie. This is only the opener. Lots of time."

Jack Conrad walked in from the bullpen then and Ernie handed him the ball. "Good luck, Jack. Set 'em on their ears." He started for the bench, head down, his spirits dragging at his heels. Coach Milton met him and lifted a hand to his shoulder."Too bad, Ernie. You've got to face it. I've been telling you."

The lanky pitcher was too dejected to answer. He took a seat beside the small, fidgeting coach and tried to find interest in the game but his thoughts drifted off to the accident of last June.

It was like a bad dream repeating itself – the car crossing in front of the bus carrying the squad to Gaylord to close the season . . . the driver swerving . . . the upset in the ditch . . . the players pitched to the floor . . . the stab of pain when he fell heavily on his right shoulder . . . several teammates cut and bruised.

The doctor told Ernie, "The muscles are torn and a nerve is crushed. It'll take a while to see how serious it is."

"Will it stop me from pitching, doctor?" he asked.

Doubtfully, he nodded. "I'm afraid so. You see, with a dead nerve –"

Ernie saw. He hid his fears while the shoulder healed but because baseball was in his blood, he began to throw left-handed, at first stones, then with snowballs. When the snow was gone, he had his roommate catch his southpaw pitches by the hour. Although he began to develop speed and a good curve, he lacked control.

When St. Frances began Spring practice, Ernie tried to impress Coach Milton with his new delivery but the instructor shook his head. "You're trying something few if any ballplayers have done successfully, switching throwing arms. You were a great right-hander, Ernie. Stick to that; otherwise you're through."

Ernie tried but his right arm would not respond. It had neither power nor snap and only because he had a reputation and St. Frances lacked able moundsmen was he started against the light-hitting McCormick College nine.

"The whole conference will know now that I'm finished," he brooded. Coach Milton jarred him out of his gloom. "You'd better take a shower. I want to talk to you after the game."

"If you don't mind, coach, I'll throw a while with the boys in the bullpen. I've still got another arm."

Milton grunted impatiently. "I've told you a dozen times it's no use, Ernie. You have no control with your southpaw. Control, and your fast ball, made you a great right-hander. That's gone. You're just wasting your time."

"I've thrown this game away for you, coach. I've got to make up for that later. I need more practice."

"If you could hit the size of your hat I'd send you to right field." Milton squirmed for a minute. "I meant to ease into this, Ernie, but you're forcing me to be blunt. I need your uniform for Carl Andrews. He's coming along fast and I've got to make room for him on the squad. I'm sorry, but that's the way it is."

Late that afternoon the St. Frances team took home a 5 to 1 defeat and the dismal knowledge that "Three-Hit" Grant had been dropped. Sorrowfully, the onetime mound star turned in his equipment and then went to Coach Milton.

"I'll be around for the last game, the Gaylord game, coach." He tried to speak gaily. "You'd better have a uniform ready for me."

Milton met Ernie's forced smile with a puzzled glance. "I thought you understood –"

"I missed that game last year – the bus accident you know. I'm making a date right now to get into the next one."

"I don't know – I don't get you Ernie."

"You will, coach. See you later."

During the late April, May and early June weekends, Ernie Grant was rarely seen on the St. Frances campus. With him absent, the college team slipped badly, making hard work for winning half its games while Gaylord led the Upper River Conference.

In the nearby metropolis of Morland, a lean and serious pitcher known as Lefty Hargrave appeared in City Park League lineups. So wild at first that he set a pass record, he nevertheless was stingy with hits. His fast ones broke with sharp hops and dips and few batters dared to take toeholds on his delivery. By the first of June he had won five straight and was the talk of the amateur league. He was silent about his personal affairs and after the Saturday and Sunday games he disappeared from Morland.

On June 19, Gaylord rode into St. Francis talking of a cinch victory to close the conference schedule. Defeat of the champions would be balm for the home college fans in this disappointing season but no one expected a miracle.

The Saints were dressing to take the field when Ernie Grant entered the locker room. After getting greeted cordially by his former teammates, he sat down beside Captain Bud Elberg.

"I wish you were going to be out there chucking with your old stuff, Ernie," Elberg said wistfully, "Jack Conrad is afraid his arm won't last through this one."

"Maybe I can toss a few, Bud. I'm going to the coach now."

"Huh!" Elberg exclaimed."Do you mean it, fella?"

Ernie winked mysteriously and hunted up coach Milton. He found the baseball instructor fussing over his lineup, his thin face creased with worry.

"Well, coach, I told you I'd be around for the Gaylord game. Is that spare uniform ready?"

Milton looked up with an annoyed glance. "Oh, hello Ernie. I-Sorry I can't talk to you now. Drop around later."

"You could use a pitcher, couldn't you?"

"I'd give my right arm – Don't bother me now, Ernie. Later."

"I've been pitching all Spring and my arm's okay. You should see my control."

Coach Milton stood up quickly. "Do you mean – Is the zip back in the old soupbone?"

"The new soupbone," Ernie grinned. "I've finally got my southpaw in shape."

The coach raised both hands and waved Ernie away. "I told you I wasn't interested – See here, Ernie. I've got enough trouble without listening to your jokes. Please."

"All I ask is a chance, coach. When you're in a hole and need a relief pitcher, send me in. I'm ready, I tell you."

Milton wagged his head. "All right, all right, get into a suit if it'll make you happy. For old time's sake, I'll let you sit on the bench but I can't put you in the game."

Gaylord opened the fifth inning with a single and a double and then Jack Conrad, visibly weakening, walked the third hitter to fill the bases. Appealingly, the pitcher looked toward the bench for relief. The visitors were ahead 4 to 2 and now threatened to break the game wide open with a big rally.

While Gaylord fans shrieked for the blowup, St. Frances rooters sat numb, sensing a rout in the making. Even the fretful coach appeared helpless.

In the bullpen since the game started, Ernie Grant stopped warming up to look toward the bench. Here was a squeeze if he ever saw one. The coach had to give him his chance now.

While Milton still hesitated, Ernie walked toward him. The Gaylord crowd yelled for action and the plate umpire turned to call, "Well, coach, what's it going to be? Let's go."

Ernie touched Milton's arm. "I'm ready, coach."

"Do you think I want to throw the game away?"

"I want to win it worse than you do. Give me one inning. If I can't stop Gaylord, I'll take myself out."

Milton rubbed the back of his head nervously. "I'm over a barrel. All right, go ahead. It's up to you, Ernie."

When the announcer called, "Grant pitching for St. Frances," a cheer of hope lifted from the rooters. As he took his warmup tosses, Ernie heard a hum of surprise rustle through the stands. This fellow was a southpaw. This wasn't the famous "Three-Hit" Grant. What was Coach Milton pulling off?

With his teammates shouting encouragement, Ernie faced the batsman. A sudden fright gripped him. His promise to the coach and the need to show an iron nerve as well as a strong pitching arm threatened to give him the jitters.

He threw three balls before he could locate the plate. Then he walked the hitter to force in a run. The score was 5 to 2.

"Take him out!" Take him out!" several fans yelled.

Jabbing his foot against the rubber, he gripped the ball hard as cold anger steadied him. He'd show them. . .

The next three strikes sailed past the hitter so fast he saw only a white blur. Working slowly on the third batter, Ernie made him hit weakly to John Michaels and the second baseman started a double play to retire the side. St. Frances fans voiced their relief in a roaring cheer.

Heartened by Ernie's courageous pitching, his teammates began to fight desperately. Three hits and an error enabled them to tie the count in the seventh and Captain Elberg's home run in the eighth put the Saints ahead 6 to 5. Working coolly, Ernie Grant mowed down the rival batsmen.

Crawford, the Gaylord catcher, opened the ninth with a scratch single back of third. Then two St. Frances errors filled the bases and the visiting rooters pleaded for a hit.

This was the spot. Now, if ever, he had to make Coach Milton and and skeptical fans forget the right-handed "Three-Hit" Grant. Unmindful of the frenzied crowd and ignoring the runners, he pitched with all his heart and mind and good left arm.

He threw nine times, the ball swooping, dipping, breaking across the plate or away from the swinging hitters. Nine pitches and nine strikes. The game was over. Sports writers called it the Upper River Conference's greatest hurling feat.

After the players escaped the delirious fans to reach their dressing room, Coach Milton pushed through the jam of happy players around Ernie Grant to grip the pitcher's hand.

"You're the trophy winner in my book Ernie, no matter what the conference decides. I'd never believe it could be done if I hadn't seen it myself."

"That was one we both needed to win, coach."

Ernie grinned, "Look up the record of Lefty Hargrave in the Morland Park League. He put in all Spring training for this game with Gaylord."

Southpaw Switch:
Malamud's Debt to Adolph Regli

Robert Warde

At last appear
Hell bounds, high reaching to the horrid roof,
And thrice threefold the gates; three folds were brass.
Three iron, three of adamantine rock.
  – Milton, *Paradise Lost*

Descend, ye Nine! Descend and sing,
The breathing instruments inspire.
  – Pope, *Ode on St. Cecilla's Day*

Ernie "Three-Hit" Grant had pitched the St. Frances Saints to nine consecutive Upper River Conference championships, under the nervous tutelage of Coach Milton. Yet, as Adolph Regli's undeservedly ignored short story opens, we learn that Grant's pitching arm is "dead," and he has "nothing left but a glove and a prayer." Even this brief introduction must suggest to any sensitive reader the spiritual profundity and archetypal aspects of Regli's work — a work published in 1950, and one that obviously exerted a strong influence on Bernard Malamud's **The Natural**, a book which did not appear until 1952. The astounding success of this latter novel, and the systematic exclusion of Regli's modest tale from critical circles is merely another instance of the injustices so often wrought by the literary establishment on deserving writers. Some voices on the fringe of the *belle monde* of *lettres* contend that Malamud's debt to Regli is so great, he has used his powerful influence in every way possible to ensure that *Southpaw Switch* remains in obscurity, but such a claim is probably unfair. In any event, with the preceding as background, let us examine Regli's small but perfect "diamond."

The plot is easily summarized. At the end of his second superbly successful college season as a right-handed hurler, Ernie Grant is involved, along with his teammates, in a bus accident that causes irreparable damage to his pitching wing. The next spring, he gamely tries to regain his old form, but is driven from the box by a weak-hitting team, and is subsequently dropped from the squad. Throughout the rest of that season, Ernie teaches himself to throw from the port side, while pitching under an assumed name for an amateur outfit in a neighboring town. By June he has mastered the southpaw style, and returns to his former club in time to save the exciting final game of an otherwise undistinguished year. What, we may ask, does Regli make of this apparently simple narrative?

Grant's story is one of rebirth. When he injures his arm, the doctor tells him that "muscles are torn and a nerve is crushed." The "dead nerve" (and we may take this both literally and figuratively) parallels Ernie's career, murdered in its infancy. When the ill-fated team bus swerved to avoid the car in its path, "players pitched to the floor." The phrase "pitched to the floor" chillingly foreshadows Ernie's future, for his once strong arm will have all it can do to keep the ball from biting the turf (on the "floor" of the infield) between the mound and the dish. Though young in years, Ernie is a "senior," and he wonders if, for him, there will be a "next time." Captain Bud Elberg assures him that "this is only the opener. Lots of time," but Coach Milton insists: "You're wasting your time." The Coach is obsessed with Ernie's "rightness" (which is, ironically, a *wrong* view), even telling his pitcher that he'd put him in *right* field, "if you could hit the size of your hat," a reference to Ernie's swellheadedness, which we will consider later. Milton removes his star from the squad in favor of Carl Andrews, and Ernie seems to be, indeed, "dead."

But notice how carefully Regli prepares us for the Second Coming. " 'The whole conference will know now that I'm finished,' [Ernie] brooded." Even as he announces his demise, the vanquished hero is "brooding," preparing to hatch forth a new baseball life. It is "Bud" (incipient flower . . . cf. Malamud's Mexican, Flores) who claims there is "lots of time," and it is, paradoxically, springtime when Ernie dies. Coach Milton may see his pitcher's switch to the left arm as a "waste," but in *Mor*land (not *Waste*land), amid the greenery of the City "Park" League, Ernie becomes Lefty Hargrave (saying "har, har" to the grave), and on June 19 he is reborn, again paradoxically, during his team's last game. Of course, the 19th is important. Two "nines" (or a total of eighteen) prepare to play ball. "Lefty" becomes the unexpected 19th, the new element in an old compound. Milton remains obtuse, not comprehending Ernie's change. "Is the zip back in the old soupbone?" he asks. But, as Ernie/Lefty says, it's not "old," it's "new," and we might add that it's not a soupbone either; this new bone has plenty of meat on it. Finally, "zip" means "zero." Milton thus says, "Is the `nothing' back in your arm?" Again, Regli's irony becomes apparent, as does the poor Coach's foolishness. Ernie knows he must "show an iron nerve" (not a dead one), and the rest is history. Reborn, "he pitches with all his heart and mind and good left arm." He resurrects himself by using what is "left" him after the whips and scorns of outrageous fortune have done their best to put him away.

Malamud exploits much of the above material, as Professor Earl Wasserman's classic study (*The Natural: Malamud's World Ceres*, **Centennial Review**, 9, 1965, pp. 438-457) make clear. Roy Hobbs "dies" in the spring (via an "accident") and is reborn about one-third of the way through a later season (i.e., around mid-June). **The Natural** documents a quest for the Grail, the bringing of "virility to the Waste Land" (Wasserman, pp. 440-41). Regli presents Milton as a representative of "that portion of the community envious of and antagonistic of the hero's regenerative potency" (Wasserman, p. 442), and the Coach's misused word, "zip," becomes, in Malamud's hands, the vicious dwarf, Otto Zipp, who, like Ernie's "dead" arm, is a cipher, a nothing. Ernie can triumph only when the fans' cries ("Take him out! Take him out!") goad him on ("cold anger steadied him. He'd show them.") Likewise, Roy feels antagonistic toward the fickle fans, and "he took it out on the ball, pounding it to a pulp, as if the best way to get even . . . was to smash every conceivable record" (Malamud, p. 152).

Thus far, we have spoken of physical regeneration, but Regli places much greater emphasis on Ernie's spiritual rebirth. The college pitcher undergoes a moving Christian odyssey. He hurls for the St. Frances Saints. St. Francis (whose name Regli feminizes, for reasons doubtless his own), famous for his love of all things, is especially well remembered for his intimacy with nature, and for his habit of preaching to the birds. He seems a proper patron, presiding over the story's message (Malamud also stresses "naturalness," true love, and birds, thereby accomplishing in a diffuse manner what Regli does far more economically through the use of a single name). The Saints and Ernie are tested when their bus crashes. The offending car "crosses" in front of them, while they are on their way to Gaylord. That is, expecting to encounter a happy and benevolent Lord, the team is crossed (tested, as Job was tested), and must bear this cross through a full season. Playing in the Upper *River* Conference, the Saints endure their suffering by the side of the purifying baptismal waters, while Ernie, knocked from the box, leaves the field "head down, his *spirits* dragging at his heels." Milton says, significantly, "I need your uniform," and the dead-arm moundsman is thrust naked into a new world. He had begun, after his injury, to throw left-handed, "at first with stones," which raises a question as to whether or not he is, in Biblical terms, without sin (compare him to Malamud's stone thrower, p. 193), and "then with snowballs," as his despair draws him into the heart of winter (Regli's narrative economy is again visible. . . the simply "snowballs" tells us all we need to know of Ernie's temporal and spiritual progress). When spring arrives and his uniform is stripped from his back, the chagrined pitcher is not ready for re-baptism. "You'd better take a shower," Coach says, but Ernie insists on putting off contact with the waters of redemption. He plays in Morland on Saturdays and Sundays, the Jewish and Christian holy days, replenishing his soul and his powers. Describing the June 19 game against Gaylord, Regli writes: "Defeat of the champions would be a balm for the home college fans . . . but no one expected a miracle." Yet it is just such a miracle that the risen "Lefty" supplies, applying a healing, anointing oil to the wounds of the St. Frances fans.

The moving tale of Ernie's "land change" gains deeper Christian significance through Regli's deft handling of the symbolic numeral three, and its square nine. "Three-Hit" Grant is chased from the mound when McCormick's Jaffrey drives in "three" runs with a "triple." Later, in June (the sixth, 3 + 3, month), he returns to throw "three" balls to the first man he faces, before walking him. Hitter number two sees "three" strikes, and the next batter grounds into a "double" play; but note, he is the "third" batter to whom Grant has thrown. The mystic number, formerly a jinx, has become Ernie's prime weapon of redemption. In the crucial ninth (3 x 3) inning he throws "nine" times. "Nine pitches and nine strikes. The game was over." The St. Frances "nine" has upset Gaylord, and happiness now reigns in "Earnest."

Three is not only a symbol of Deity (Pythagoras' perfect number), it also suggests man's threefold nature (body, mind, and spirit), the threefold world (earth, sea, air), and the three Christian graces (Faith, Hope, and Charity). Hence, if we add man's nature, the world's habitable elements, the Christian virtues, we get nine, or Ernie's' final "perfect" inning, pitched for his now "perfect" team.

Professor Wasserman argues that **The Natural** moves from "baseball story," to "Arthurian Grail myth" (the *Knights*), and finally to "the core of the novel, where we must seek the psychic and moral flaw within the fertility theme" (p. 443), that is, where we must explain how Roy Hobbs goes wrong. Malamud lifts this pattern, or arrangement of interests, straight from the pages of *Southpaw*

Switch. Regli moves from baseball, to Christian ritual (the *Saints*), to Ernie Grant's personal struggles within both an athletic and religious context (though Grant succeeds where Hobbs fails, indicating, perhaps, that Regli is more optimistic than Malamud). Let us consider the personal side of Ernie's story.

Mention has already been made of young Grant's swellheadedness (Milton's comment on his cap size). He exhibits some of the egotism we also find in Roy Hobbs. His first regret, after McCormick's grim reapers destroy him, is that he won't receive "the most valuable player trophy he wanted so badly," and his second is that word of his failure may get around the league. Indeed, he half admits that it was selfish to let Coach Milton start him in the first place. When he appears in the City Park League he is "silent about his personal affairs," and we are reminded, by way of Professor Wasserman, of the "infantile and self-absorptive privacy to which Roy repeatedly flees" (p. 445). What Ernie must learn is self-control. When he began to use his left arm, he quickly developed "speed and a good curve," but "he lacked control." As Lefty Hargrave, he was "so wild at first that he set a pass record." By June, however, he has mastered his weakness. "You should see my control," he urges Milton, and after the game he can say: "That was one we both needed to win, coach." Ernie has learned discipline in switching from right to left; Milton has learned what a determined man can do. The former gains his insight after sacrificing a limb; the latter achieves wisdom after symbolically offering up his own appendage. "You could use a pitcher, couldn't you?" says Ernie. "I'd give my arm," his coach replies. Both men share the final victory, taking a first, if very modest step away from self-absorption. Regli's narrative opens with Ernie away from home (he "brushed his lean, hot face against the *gray* sleeve of his . . . uniform"). He is a visitor, an alien. It ends with Lefty at home where he belongs, having found himself and marked out his "place." Roy Hobbs may also come to understand the importance of maturity and control, but not before he has struck down the pregnant Iris, ruined his chances, and destroyed his potential "home."

Insight, or true vision, is what Ernie achieves. His eyes are opened after the accident ("You see, the dead nerve–" says the doctor. "Ernie saw."), and he begins with the slow trek toward transformation. After metamorphosing in obscurity, he decides he is ready to share his vision with others and returns to the St. Frances hill ("He'd *show* them"). "I'd never believe it could be done," Milton cries after the triumph, "if I hadn't *seen* it myself."

Ernie's deepening insight, growing sense of responsibility, and improved self-control are linked to Regli's Christian theme by the hero's very name. Just as Malamud plays with monikers (Roy = "roi"; Hobbs = "hobbled"), so Regli puns with Ernie Grant. On the one hand, the gallant pitcher "earns" his rebirth through sacrifice, struggle, symbolic death. On the other hand, it is God who must "grant" the ultimate victory. Thus, a combination of human fortitude and lordly benevolence is needed before the perfect inning can be realized.

Southpaw Switch is a brief work, yet certainly, beginning *in medias res*, it reaches epic proportions. Regli (along with his "coach") reminds us of *Paradise Lost,* and Milton's "thrice threefold" gates of Hell become Regli's nine man team, nine frames, nine strikes, and thrice threefold vision of the heavenly resurrection. Both Milton and Regli create imaginative theodicies, and for the latter, God's ways are beautiful in the extreme. When Ernie thinks of the terrible bus crash, he compares it to "a bad dream repeating itself" (cf. the circular imagery in Malamud), but his own efforts and God's grace break the circle and introduce change (right and left). In the end, as with Pope's "Ode," the saintly nine sing out, and their voices "the breathing instruments inspire." It would seem that Mr. Malamud's breathing instruments received the greatest measure of inspiration.

By Grace are Ye Saved:
Ernie Grant and Christian Redemption

Dave Healy

(Bethel College professor Dave Healy took exception with Warde's reading. —Eds.)

* * * * * * *

Robert Warde's provocative essay on Bernard Malamud's debt to Adolph Regli's *Southpaw Switch* is a valuable contribution to students of literature and baseball. However, in his zeal to credit Regli's "undeservedly ignored short story," Warde is guilty of a misleading overstatement. Leaving his central theses unchallenged – the claim that Malamud was influenced by Regli – I would like to take issue with Warde's explication of *Southpaw Switch,* specifically the contention that the story is one of spiritual rebirth and "Christian ritual."

The religious imagery in Regli's story, most of which Warde accurately notes, is inescapable, as is the conclusion that the story has a metaphysical dimension. But to say that it is on the level a story of spiritual rebirth is not necessarily to say that it embodies Christian ritual. For the fact of the matter is that Ernie Grant's apparent redemption is not redemption at all, at least not in any orthodox Christian sense, since his is a salvation by works, not grace.

Granted, Ernie manifests all the appropriate characteristics of a potential convert. The old covenant is no longer adequate: the "old soupbone" has no zip, the "old stuff" that Bud Elberg wistfully recalls is simply that – the stuff of dreams. And Grant does display the requisite consciousness of sin – "I've sure put you in a bad hole, Bud" – as well as its implications implicit in coach Milton's admonition "You've got to face it!" and explicit in his own desire for atonement:

"I've thrown this game away for you, coach. I've got to make up for that later."

It is worth noting in this regard that Warde's observation about Grant's practicing throwing with stones – that is "raises a question as to whether or not he is, in Biblical terms, without sin" – is on target, but for the wrong reason. Grant is, indeed, not without sin, but his sin is symbolized by having put his team "in the hole," not by throwing stones. A more plausible reading of the stones throwing reference is to see it in Old Testament rather than New Testament terms: the young David doing battle with Goliath. Thus, Grant demonstrates his allegiance to an old covenant representative in spite of the manifest inadequacy of that covenant.

But, one could argue, stone throwing was just a stage. What of Grant's fully developed new arm and new stuff? Doesn't his mature re-emergence as a southpaw signal an embracing of the new covenant?[1] It is tempting to read the story this way, primed as we are by the religious imagery for a full-scale controversy. But even a casual reader of the New Testament recognizes that the central message of the new covenant is that salvation is a gift, "not because of works, lest any man should boast." Furthermore, redemption occurs according to God's terms, not man's.

But Ernie Grant's regeneration is entirely self-achieved. He works at becoming a left-hander. Before the climactic game with Gaylord, none of the home fans expected a miracle. Warde claims that "it is just such a miracle that the risen 'lefty' supplies . . . " But Ernie's victory only appears to be a miracle to the fans and to his teammates. To the reader it is an expected and fitting consequence of Ernie's efforts and thus a tribute more to the Protestant work ethic than to the the Biblical doctrine of grace.

To be sure, Grant is to be commended for his initiative. It is impressive and involved some sacrifice. But the sacrifice is limited, for it takes place entirely on Grant's terms. A more noble sacrifice would have been to give up being a pitcher, to learn an infield position for which his impotent right arm would have been adequate. Ernie Grant's right arm has died and been reborn. But Ernie has not died to self – a necessary condition of the Christian convert. Warde observes that he has learned control. But more than control is necessary for true spiritual rebirth, as the rich young ruler learned. (See Luke 18:18-27) All the way up to the very end of the story one hopes for some glimmer of acknowledgment in the story's penultimate paragraph: "I don't see how you did it!" But Grant replies with a self-congratulatory tribute to his alter ego which makes it clear that the egotism Warde notes has by no means been renounced: "Look up the record of Lefty Hargrave in the Morland Park League. He put in all Spring training for this game with Gaylord."

Professor Warde argues, near the end of his essay, that Ernie Grant's name amplifies "Regli's Christian theme": "On the one hand, the gallant pitcher 'earns' his rebirth through sacrifice, struggle, symbolic death. On the other hand, it is God who must 'grant' the ultimate victory. Thus, a combination of human fortitude and lordly benevolence is needed before the perfect inning can be realized." In the context Warde creates (or contrives), one would doubtless do well to pay special attention to the hero's Christian name. In so doing one is struck by two ironic truths: (1) as I have shown, a rebirth cannot be earned; (2) being earnest might be important, but it is not a sufficient condition of being spiritually reborn. Self-sacrifice is needed. "Only he who loses his life for My sake will find it," says Jesus. Ernie Grant appears to lose his life when he surfaces under a new name in the Morland Park League. But this is merely a means to an end – an end which makes it clear that he has sacrificed only for his own sake. Though consciousness of sin and the desire for expiation appear to prompt his initial efforts to become a southpaw, when the chips are down in the climactic inning Grant's thoughts are exclusively on himself: "This was the spot. Now, if ever, he had to make Coach Milton and the skeptical fans forget the right-handed 'Three-Hit' Grant." These two truths render bitterly and tragically ironic the hero's full name and serve to point us beyond the story's ending. Can we really believe that Ernie Grant née Lefty Hargrave faces the future armed with anything more than the strength of his old ego and new left wing? One is reminded that Young Goodman Brown appeared to achieve victory when he refused to join the satanic revelers in the middle of the forest but that "they carved no hopeful verse upon his tombstone, for his dying hour was gloom."

These observations in no way diminish the impressiveness of Regli's story. But the story is impressive for its dramatization of the American ethic of individualism, work and success – not the Christian ethic of selflessness, grace, and faith. Still, *Southpaw Switch* conveys an implicit affirmation of the Christian message – "many are called but few are chosen" – which, though it may seem severe, is a necessary call to watchfulness, a reminder that things are not always as they appear, and a confirmation of Yogi Berra's timeless observation that "it's not over until it's over."

Notes

[1] In point of fact, any careful reader of the Bible will recognize how absurd the notion of a left-hander symbolizing spiritual maturity or rebirth actually is. The Scriptures are quite clear and consistent in portraying God as right-handed. It is with the right hand that He expresses might and power: "Thy right hand, O Lord, glorious in power, thy right hand, O Lord, shatters the enemy" (ex. 15:6). To be blessed of God is to be on his right hand, and to be cursed is to be on his left (Matt. 25:33-34). Furthermore, the people of God exemplify this truth as well. In conferring blessing on someone, one uses one's right hand (Gen. 48:14). New converts are welcomed into the fold with the right hand of fellowship (Gal. 2:19). And it is clear that there is intrinsic worth in the right hand and intrinsic foolishness in the left: "A wise man's heart inclines him toward the right, but a fool's heart toward the left" (Eccl. 19:2).

The Problem of Righteousness:
A Response to Dave Healy

Robert Warde

Dave Healy is right to modify my explication of *Southpaw Switch* as he does. His thorough and intelligent commentary convinces me that Ernie's victory may indeed by "a tribute more to the Protestant work ethic than to the Biblical doctrine of grace." I am troubled, however, by one element in Professor Healy's otherwise sound analysis. He suggests that in my "zeal to credit Regli's . . . story" I was "guilty of a misleading overstatement," and such is perhaps the case; however, in his eagerness to set the matter "right," Healy himself offers an interpretation of Scripture that seems dangerously simplistic. Frankly, I am not worried about Professor Healy's own perception of things, since I feel sure that he would have tempered his rhetoric in a different context; but his words may well be taken at face value by those readers of **MRB** whose capacity for subtle discrimination does not extend beyond the diamond to the realm of Biblical exegesis. Thus, I am moved to offer a corrective to the prominent footnote that smiles fatly forth as an addendum to Healy's article.

In this note, Professor Healy assures us that "any careful reader of the Bible will recognize how absurd the notion of a left-hander symbolizing spiritual maturity or rebirth actually is." He goes on to demonstrate, through scriptural quotation, God's right-handedness, and he concludes with a passage from Ecclesiastes: "A wise man's heart inclines him toward the right, but a fool's heart toward the left." Here Healy exhibits what students of psychology have come to recognize as "the Benjamin Complex" (from the Hebrew "binyamin" – son of the right hand; hence favorite son). It is obvious that Healy himself is right-handed, and no doubt he unconsciously connects this fact with his own Christian name, David (from the Hebrew for "beloved"). He compares Ernie Grant to the Old Testament David; but while Ernie throws stones with his left arm, David, in the mind's eye of Healy, must surely be pulling back that slingshot with his starboard hand. Goliath is the southpaw.

Now such an instinctive conception of things makes no sense, yet it is precisely this vision of life that has damaged baseball. No one would dream of fouling the game with a left-handed third baseman, shortstop, or second sacker, but right-handed goons proliferate around first base, where they have no business at all, and they have turned one of the sport's most graceful positions into a dumping ground for ex-outfielders and catchers whose legs have gone bad, and who must twist themselves into the most grotesque positions conceivable in order to make the throw to second. Furthermore, why is it that catchers must be right-handed? We all accept the fact, but can someone tell me why we do? Unlike the other three right-handed positions, the catchers' spot would seem to accommodate individuals of either persuasion. In any case, four of the eight non-pitching slots are forbidden to lefties, while right-handers, God's favorites, are permitted to play anywhere. Think, too, of the label attached to portsiders – flaky. All flakes are either left-handed or from California (the state at the left-hand side of the United States, as you look at any conventional map). Professor Healy's well-intentioned note will be understood by many, I fear, as as reinforcement of society's prejudice against left-handers, whereas Healy himself, upon sober reflection, would probably agree that both etymology and a sensitive interpretation of God's word leave no soil in which the Benjamin Complex can flourish. Let us first consider the etymological issue.

"Sinister," the word that designates left-sidedness, has come to mean "wicked, evil, dishonest, or ominous" in our common and woefully corrupted contemporary parlance. Students of language realize that this negative sense of the word derives from the Latin sinister, meaning left-handed or unlucky side – unlucky because the last Roman soothsayers (influenced by the Greeks) always faced north, thereby putting the "lucky" east on their right (the west is always "unlucky," be it the flaky American west, or the much maligned Western Division of the AL and NL). Such students also know, however, that sinister originally meant lucky, not unlucky. It stems from the Sanskrit saniyab, meaning "more favorable"; indeed, early Roman augurs faced south, not north, while making their prophecies, thereby placing the lucky east (where the sun rises, rather that sets) on their left. If there were any linguistic justice in the world (there isn't), that which is sinister would be "good, honest, and encouraging."

So much for etymology. Now what about the Bible? Here we must understand what Healy's comments obscure. The Old and New Testament authors needed to convince us of a contrast between good and evil, and so they gave spatial force to the necessary dichotomy by speaking in terms of God's right and left sides. Today as we stand before Michelangelo's *Last Judgment* in the Sistine Chapel, we do indeed see the damned on God's left hand, and we see them thus traditionally positioned in all Last Judgments. But such an arrangement does not purport to teach us that right is spiritually mature, while left is spiritually blunted. It merely enforces the idea of two kinds of behavior, or of the presence or absence of spiritual insight. The division must be illustrated somehow, and it might as easily be God's left hand that dispenses praise. We can be sure that the authors of the Bible were mostly right-handed (reflecting the usual distribution), and thus we are able to explain their choice. God Himself is surely ambidextrous, however. God bats from both sides, and He loves us all through Christ (a "flake," a lefty, a man out of the common way?). We encounter the following wisdom in *The Gospel According to Matthew:* "when you give alms, do not let your left hand know what your right hand is doing, so that your alms may be in secret; and your Father who sees in secret will reward you" (6:3-4).The passage assumes that one does things with the right hand (an assumption that permeates the Bible), but we can turn it around with no loss of message. Similarly, the anonymous right-handed preacher who compiled this gospel places sheep to Christ's right and goats to the left; he means to underscore a distinction between sheep and goats, not to echo Jesus' preference for right-handed pull hitters (as if Heaven were laid out like Fenway Park).

This brings us back to Adolph Regli. He is subtler than Professor Healy realized, because he employs an imagery that mirrors the Bible, thereby reflecting its ultimate truth. Ernie may not fully lose himself and gain the kingdom of God, but he does show us that a change from that which is "right" to that which is "sinister" is not a change for the worse (Ernie grows, even if he fails to achieve a state of grace). We can reach for spiritual salvation with either hand, and as Gerard Manley Hopkins teaches us in his wise little poem, *Pied Beauty*, God is responsible for "all things counter, original, spare, strange. "Only God Himself radiates a beauty that is "past change" – that knows not distinctions between left and right. As Hopkins says: "Praise Him."

Once There Was a Ballpark

Reviewed by Julian Empson

(Julian Empson, student of baseball and beer vendor at Metropolitan Stadium, was one of the leaders of the Save the Met movement in the Twin Cities. We asked him to review Minneapolis-St. Paul newspaper columnist Joe Soucheray's book on the Met, and for his thoughts on the stadium he fought to save. —Eds.)

* * * * * * *

April 22, 1956 — Charlie Johnson — editor **Minneapolis Star and Tribune**: "The last word in baseball facilities, one that will stand for many years as a symbol of private enterprise at its best."

These words appeared over twenty years ago when local businessmen attempted to raise $4.5 million to put a "ballpark" up in Bloomington. Two decades later, a new corporation (Industry Square Development corporation) raised $14 million to erect a concrete tub on the eastern edge of downtown Minneapolis.

This time, though, private enterprise is after the exclusive development rights to the area round the stadium, and minor problems such as a juvenile-detention center (displaced), no parking (tailgating not very important) and the impact on surrounding neighborhoods (Elliot Park is the poorest neighborhood in the city) do not stand in the way of progress or economic revitalization.

And so we have the collective atrocities of a dome, artificial turf, increased ticket prices and a tax on our beer. Ah, so much for nostalgia and heritage.

This brings us to **Once There Was A Ballpark**, by local newspaper columnist Joe Soucheray. The book is a quick-reading series of past articles, interviews and stories about the Met – its sports teams and the weather. Souch starts off with a high hard one and subtly throughout the ensuing 125 pages nibbles at the corners. While telling tales of past memorable moments, and pointing out the wettest, coldest, warmest, foggiest games of the past, he gives us a chance once again to realize that the elements are still part of the game. Hell, we live in Minnesota and the elements are part of our daily life; why protect us from them?

In that light all of our memories and stories could be added to this book and volumes could be produced for posterity.

My first glimpse of the Met was the 1965 All-Star Game which featured three of my Phillies, Dick (Don't call me Richie) Allen, Johnny Callison and Jim Bunning, along with the blue sky, green grass and the late inning heroics of Callison, who knocked one out to win it 6-5 for the National League.

Twelve years later, I was vending beer in the Met bleachers, after two years of hustling at Veterans in Philly. By this time, Crosley, Forbes, and Sportsman's Park were all leveled and replaced by the round, concrete and plastic seats of modern stadiums. My mother on her first trip to the Vet a few years ago got lost because "everything looked the same."

Well, not to be outdone, the word came down that Minnesota was to be blessed with not only another look-alike piece of crap but one with a lid on it. A few of us simple-minded jocks who believed all that garbage about Minnesota being different — you know, good government, democratic process and a place that listens to the little guy — organized "Save the Met." Today, 5,000 meetings, two runs of T-shirts and still in debt — reality says its ain't no different here than there.

It is still beyond my comprehension why you need a dome so that the threat of rain doesn't scare off 200 folks coming from North Dakota. One of my fondest memories of the Met was a rainout. Fifteen of us huddled together for about an hour in the bleachers and finished off my case of beer. We talked about games we'd seen at the Polo Grounds, Connie Mack, and Ebbets Field. After the game was called and the beer finished, we regrouped outside and sent out for more beer since the rain had stopped and the sky cleared. It was baseball lore at its best and, if not for the rain, it never would have happened.

Soucheray picks as a high point the 9-2 stomping of the New York Cosmos soccer team by the Minnesota Kicks in August 1978 in the playoffs. Pure electricity in the air and afterwards the 46,000 fans are cooled by a quick heavy downpour, but they don't care.

My memories of that game center on how well the erector set Met held together. As I finished my last case (14 that night), I felt a little dizzy, so I hit the last row of seats on the first deck. Something seemed to be moving but I thought it was just too much work in 86-degree heat. As I took my hat off and wiped my head, I looked at the second deck's steel girders and they *were* moving. The damn second deck was swaying back and forth about six inches. Immediate panic was followed by the realization that for all the raps the Met has taken as a junkbox, it was built well and no disaster would take place.

Years from now, I'll be able to pull **Once There Was A Ballpark** off the shelf and relive some of those memories and rekindle some of my own. I picture myself sitting outside playing Strat-O-Matic, wearing my "Save the Met" shirt, and wondering why I live here in a cold Omaha after the Twins have been sent back to AAA and the Vikes are blacked out. I'll come back with a trivia question for Gil. What was the temp at the last home opener? Just my luck though, a gust of wind will blow my cards all over the place and louse up the game, but wind can only be a problem for card games. In real life, it just might push a Chuck Baker smash into the first row of the bleachers. Now, that's what a ballpark is all about.

Calvinisms

Ken LaZebnik

(*Calvinisms,* simply put, is a one-man show about Calvin Griffith. We see Calvin in his office at the Metrodome trying to make up his mind about selling the Minnesota Twins: His life in baseball weighs against his life in business. *Calvinisms* was produced in 1987 at the First Stage Theater in Brooklyn and in 1988 at The Mixed Blood Theater Company in Minneapolis. —Eds.)

* * * * * * *

CALVINISMS

(Calvin Griffith's office in the Metrodome, late in the night of June 22, 1984. It is a small office, jammed with memorabilia and boxes. Beige walls are covered with photographs. A large desk covers much of the floor. There is a bookcase with baseballs and plaques. Calvin is lying asleep on a La-Z-Boy recliner in front of the desk. A TV is on the desk; it's on, although the station it's tuned to is off the air. Telephone rings.)

CALVIN

(stirring awake) Unc. Unc.

> (We see now there is a beer perched on one arm of the chair, a hot dog is nestled on his lapel.)

Tell me, Unc.

> (He lurches up; the hot dog spills on his lap, the phone continues to ring.)

Aw, Christ and every goldarn thing.

> (He sits confused for a minute, then gets up, throws the hot dog into a trash basket and answers the phone.)

Hello. What time is it, Sid? I'm glad you were thinking of me, Sid. I was asleep, goddamn it, what do you think? Sid... Sid... I don't know if I'm going to sell. Sid, I don't know what I'm going to do just yet, but I can tell you one thing, it won't be anything rational.

> (Hangs up the phone. He turns on the light, wipes mustard off his pants. He rubs his face, goes to the TV and flicks around the dial. Most stations are off the air. An old movie is on one channel. He watches for a minute, then looks out, addressing the spirit of Uncle Clark, whom he hopes is hovering about him.)

Are you listening, Unc? Last night on TV I was watching shows. Well, God, the shows that I was watching last night I would turn off because I don't believe in all that stuff you see on TV right now. I can't get any laughs out of it, you know.

> (A commercial comes on. "Are Calvin Griffith's baseball days numbered? Eyewitness News has a special report—are the Twins up for sale? Tomorrow at six." Calvin turns the TV off, pulls out vodka, glass and tonic water. He pours.)

(addressing God) Lord, forgive me. I try to keep it to two. (still up to God) For Uncle Clark, it was one ounce a night. Like it was poured gold. (Out, addressing Uncle Clark.) Unc, you would have sold out long ago. Isn't that right? (pause) (still to Unc) I used to feel it so strong. I'd sit in that La-Z-Boy, and cogitate about some trade, and Christ, Uncle, there you'd be. I get the vibes. Isn't that what you call them — the vibes? You shut your eyes and it comes around, something comes around. Sometimes it's so strong, a feeling one way or the other, like with that Mincher trade. Damn, that was like a Magic Fingers all over my body.

(He sits in the La-Z-Boy and closes his eyes for a moment.)

(To himself.) It ain't coming. You aren't around tonight, Uncle. I can't feel a thing. (Out, searching for a spirit who will listen.) Is anyone there? Anyone listening? Unc? God? Harvey McKay? (To himself.) Jesus, you're over here every goddamn day, maybe you've tapped my office. (Addressing God again.) Lord, I've got to think this thing through. I'm not a praying man, but what does Don Riley say? I'll talk and you listen. (He smiles. He continues, directing his conversation with God in the direction of the audience.)

Unc would know what to do. Uncle Clark Griffith. He's the one who really influenced my life. I've thought of this same thing so damn many times: If Clark Griffith hadn't come along and taken me out of Montreal, what would Calvin Robertson be doing today? Robertson was my dad's name. Montreal is where his baseball career died. In the minor leagues. He was a frustrated man. He had a longstanding love affair with baseball and when she walked out on him he found someone who would never leave him. Except it wasn't a person — it was a bottle. I remember being under one of those old bearskin rugs in a horse-drawn buggy, delivering newspapers along with my father. It was colder than hell, but he had that friend to keep him warm in his pocket. Thank God that horse knew where to go. I'd hear those papers thump on the porch, or then I'd hear a kind of nothing kind of muffled sound when they landed in snow, or a soft rustle if they ended up in a bush. I just kept my head under that bearskin. Next year I started delivering the papers and taking care of the horse and everything. I was eight or nine. At dinnertime my mother would send me out to taverns. I'd go door to door. In those days they had those doors that didn't come down to the floor. I'd go to a tavern, stoop down and peek under the door, and then I'd go to the next beer hall and get on my knees and look in, and on and on. Then I'd find my father. Throwing a baseball or throwing a newspaper — that's what kids do. But it ruined my father to go from one to the other. I was always afraid when my father came home with stink on his breath. The next day at school, I thought I was Jack Dempsey. They made me take recess with the girls because every recess I took with the boys I'd end up in a fight. That was embarrassing as hell to me. When I was ten my mother told me I was going to spend a long summer vacation with my uncle Clark Griffith in Washington, D.C. He was the owner of the Senators baseball team, she said. I said, "I don't know why you're choosing me to go. You need me. I'm the oldest son. I take care of the horses and deliver the papers. I'm the one that does most of the damn work. The only way I'll go is if sister goes with me." So Thelma did. We got to

Washington, D.C. and Clark Griffith calls us in: "Calvin, Thelma – your vacation here is going to be a permanent one. Your father has passed on to Heaven. He is blessed now beyond this world." My father had died of cirrhosis of the liver. That's when my life began. My life began when I was ten years old. How could I have led one life and then gone into an atmosphere so different? I must have had a split personality. I had spent my first ten years with a father that was a stranger to me. Ten years, that's a long time to live with a stranger. And now — you couldn't believe the change. I mean, it was unbelievable. Money. Why, we had money for new clothes, we had an automobile, a nice Franklin sedan — we had a new life. Uncle Clark didn't have to do a goddamn thing for us. We were the poor relations, his wife's brother's kids, and he took us in because — well, that's just the way he was. He adopted Thelma and me and eventually all my brothers and sisters. Uncle Clark had lost his own father; died in a hunting accident when Unc was two. Maybe that's why he did it. I don't know. I thank Uncle every day for what he did. I appreciated what happened to me. Hugged him and everything else.

(He goes to the wall cluttered with photographs. He looks at one in the center, Clark Griffith, circa 1950.)

I did everything in the world to make that man happy. Everything. His eyes could pierce right through you. Look at those goddamn bushy eyebrows. When he got mad at you, it was like they were coming out and pointing at you. Next to God, Clark Griffith was it. I named my son for him. (pause) Damn him. If you weren't such a stubborn jackass — you ought to be here now. This is not a night for a man to be alone, without his goddamned son. If I could just know he wouldn't bankrupt the family. (To audience.) It's no secret. The whole state of Minnesota knows me and Clark, Jr., don't get along. Clark says I wasn't a good father to him. Hell, if I wasn't, I'd have saved a helluva lot of money. I'd have let him go to public schools and learn the hard way. He was spoiled more than anything else. I had to work day and night. He's always felt he could run a ball club better than me. Hell, if I'd listened to him we'd be so far in the red now it'd be unbelievable. He lives by the credit card and I live cash on the barrel. I did everything for him, I gave him everything. I did everything in the world for him to have this ball club, and I got nothing but piss. I wanted him to have it, Thelma and I always planned it that way. Now Clark, Jr. and I don't talk. There are some things you just cannot forgive. How could he do that to Howard? I wanted you here, Clark, but you threw it away. That's right, goddamn it, you threw it away and don't you forget it. You never had to make a payroll. I always put bread on the table. Bread on the table for this family. This is a family-owned business. I've got a family to look after! I can't sell them out. My family intends to own the Minnesota Twins for many future generations. This is a very close-knit family.

(He starts going through a box, sorting Twins sox into one pile, and tube tops — both from promotions — into another pile.)

Hell, I played catch with him and every other damn thing. I can't understand it. I can't understand a lot of damn things. As long as my mind isn't cluttered I don't know why the hell I should worry about anybody else. You're young enough to take care of yourself. Baseball is all I've ever known. I didn't have no East Coast college or easy way. I had to work in the minor leagues. I had to struggle. Uncle gave me opportunity and I thanked him for it. He gave me baseball, and I thank him everyday for it and I'm not going to give up this team to you or any other non-baseball corporation! No sir! You never saw so many non-athletically minded people in your life, Unc. All these MBAs and such. Uncle Clark knew the value of what he had earned.

(He starts looking though photos on the wall.)

I've got this picture up here somewhere. This photograph collection was my uncle's prize possession. This goddamn office is so small. Jesus, we got boxes and boxes of stuff put in storage. I had an alcove in Met Stadium where all these pictures hung. Unc's big desk was there with all these pictures just like it had been in Griffith Stadium. Jesus, our offices here are so Christ-awful small. We got boxes of stuff in storage. (finding a photo in one of the boxes) Here's the oldest photo of Uncle. Clark Griffith on a horse, Nevada, Missouri, oh 1870-something. You know how Clark Griffith learned about honesty in baseball? He loved telling me this story. He'd look at you with those eyebrows. He'd illustrate this, see: "We used to make our own baseballs with one of them, with a spinning wheel, Calvin. We wound our yarn tight and threw buckskin over it. In 1876, Spaulding made a new ball. I mean a professional quality baseball. This was a new-fangled thing and it cost a dollar and a quarter. Money was scarce in those days and this was a lot of money. But we passed the hat and made collections and got our dollar and a quarter. The problem was nobody was free to spend a day to ride off and get the ball. Finally one of the fellows who made a fund-raising speech volunteered to go. In 1876 Civil War marauders were still being caught and hung. You know, real bandits. The tree used for this purpose in Vernon County was right next to the ballfield. We'd hear they'd strung somebody up; the next morning you'd go down to the ball diamond and see if you knew who it was. A fellow volunteered to go get a Spaulding ball. And he rode off and came back with a new ball. On the first pitch with that ball, the batter connected and hit a line drive out into left center field. The left fielder ran over, picked up the ball — and damned if one side wasn't flat as a pancake. That fellow had bought a ten cent ball and pocketed the change. Everybody on that field was hopping mad. They set off looking for that chiseler and there was no sign of him. He disappeared with the money. A few years later, I was laying in bed and I heard the dogs barking. I knew what this meant. One of those Civil War bandits had been caught and hanged. The next morning I went down to the ball field to see if I knew the man. And there was the son-of-a-bitch who had pawned off the dime ball as a new Spaulding. He was swaying in the wind, his clammy eyes looking out over third base like he wanted to argue with the umpire. But that son-of-a-bitch was out of the game. That was my first lesson in the honesty of baseball. It was in Vernon County, Missouri." Boy, if that didn't put the fear of God into you! "Honesty, Calvin, honesty." Yes sir! Yes sir! People can say what they want about me, but I've always been honest. Just like Uncle. They may have said he was tight-fisted, but nobody ever said he wasn't honest. Joe Engels used to say that he'd go in and argue with Unc for five hours about a hundred dollar purchase. Then the next week Clark would give someone a thousand dollar bonus. He was fierce in his convictions. He was sharp. He didn't take no crap. I tell you if the players and salaries and hair make-ups had been like this when Unc owned the team, he would have gotten out so fast it would have been like night and day. I can hear him saying to me, "Why didn't you get out when you had the chance?" Some nights I hear that. Unc was running the Washington Senators up 'til the day he died. He was 85. I'm only 73. Unc had a sign on his desk: "Long life. Sleep plenty, eat moderately and keep your conscience clean." Two out of three ain't bad. Every night Uncle would come home from the ballpark, light up a Robert Burns cigar, drink his ounce of Old Grand-Dad, and take a one hour nap. If the Senators had a night game, he'd then go back to the ballpark. He saw more ball games; he didn't miss a Senators home game for more than forty years. He talked baseball with all the presidents. Every president that was elected from 1924 until Unc died had his photo on Unc's wall before he was elected. Goldarn it, I have those pictures somewhere. Coolidge was in a flag-raising ceremony picture before he was elected, Roosevelt was in another flag-raising thing. Hoover was in a picture taken when President Harding threw out the first ball. Here's Harry Truman, see? Unc started Presidents throwing out the first ball. In 1912, with President Taft. That man was huge. I like my meat, but William Howard Taft was like a cow on hind legs. Damn that photo. It's here somewhere. With my arthritis and everything else, I can't look so good. They operated on my knee last year and removed the cartridge. Here's a picture (on the wall) of the World Champion 1924 Senators. We're meeting President Coolidge at the White House. I've been in baseball sixty years, and this is the only World Champion team I've been associated with. There have been pennants, but this is the only Series winner. Here's me — see, that's me. I was twelve years old. I was the batboy. That Series was decided by a pebble. Earl McNelly hit the ball and here's Muddy Ruel scoring. The ball hit a pebble and bounced over Lindstrom's — the third baseman's — head. The celebration was unbelievable. They used to keep the balls back then in the ground behind the umpire. It was my job to collect them after every game. The fans came pouring out of the stands after that last out and I was jumping up and down. I was so goddamned happy. We won, Unc! We won! We're the champs! There's Muddy and all of them, and Walter Johnson. Then I saw those fans grabbing up the baseballs. Hey! Stay away from those balls! Those baseballs are the property of the Washington Senators! I cried when they stole those balls from Uncle. It was the happiest day of his life, and I was crying. Unc, there was nothing I could do.

(Pause. He goes behind the desk and gets a Dictaphone mike.)

Jean, have them go down to the hardware store and get some more picture mounts, you know, those hooks you can nail to the wall. Just the hooks. The hooeys are still on the back of the pictures. And take home some of these socks. See if the Dairy Queen people can get a return on them. Or ask Jimmy – ask Jimmy...he can put them in the booths and everything.

(He goes to drawer of the desk, gets out some crackers and a can of Cheez-Whiz. He sprays Cheez-Whiz on a cracker. A big gob of it drops on the floor. He looks for something to wipe it up with — can't see anything. Finally he takes a pack of Twins socks, opens it, and uses a sock to clean up. Painfully:)

Christ almighty, who'd think I was a catcher? They've taken out so much cartridge. I was a pretty damn good catcher. Best at George Washington University. None of this one-handed Johnny Bench crap back then. Johnny Bench was the greatest catcher of the last twenty years, and he set the art of catching back thirty. You see all these kids stabbing at the ball with one hand, like they're spearing fish. Uh-uh. That's the stupidest thing I ever seen in my life. Johnny Bench could do it because he had super reflexes and a superior throwing arm. These kids imitate him and they do it just because they don't want to bang up their pinkies. That's right! Shake hands with any old catcher — it's like grabbing a slug of pig iron. They're all gnarled up. Get your body in front of that pitch. Don't spear the goddamn thing.

(He moves to illustrate and groans.)

Ah, Jesus, and everything else. I was a good catcher. George Washington University. Summers while I was in school I was traveling secretary and treasurer of the Chattanooga farm team. The Lookouts. Uncle sent me there to learn the ropes. In 1937 I became president and treasurer of that team. I was making $250 a month. At the end of July we were two games out of last place. Our manager was Red Meat Bill Rogers. Red Meat Bill Rodgers was a crazy man. Son of a bitch ate raw meat. In Birmingham, Alabama, we went out to a restaurant together. Nice place. Water on the table, cloth napkin kind of a place.

Waitress comes over to take our order, he says, "I'll have a steak just like you got it." "Pardon?" "Just bring me the piece of meat like you got it in the kitchen." So they bring him out a plate with a raw steak on it. Son of a bitch ate a raw steak. I got up — I couldn't stand it. I had to leave. I thought I was going to urp right there. Ever since then I can't stand underdone meat. Well done. That's the way to have your steaks. Bill Rodgers would go hunting with us. He'd kill a deer — hang the deer up on a tree, cut the guts out, eat the heart and the liver right there. No kidding. Same thing with a bear. Like I said, the club was two games out of the cellar. It wasn't performing up to our expectations. Uncle let Red Meat go and made me manager. I loved managing. I had them work out extra. The first day I managed we lost a doubleheader in Nashville. But we won 12 out of 15 when we got back home and nearly made the play-offs. I'll never forget that year and those next ones with Charlotte. I was president, treasurer and manager of the Charlotte Hornets in the Piedmont League. Class B ball. Our catcher Al Evans broker a finger, and then so did his sub. Then two more guys caught — and they both broke fingers, too! I'm desperate. "Jimmy," I said, "I know you're an infielder, but we're out of luck. Would you put on the tools of ignorance?" "Yes, sir, coach!" Our pitcher was one of those fellows we got in a Cuban canebreak — Roberto Ortiz. He had an incredible fastball. I mean, it was terrific. And we're in Charlotte with that night ball and those kind of soft lights. Jimmy gets behind the plate. Ortiz winds up. Batter swings. Faint click of the bat — foul tip. Jimmy jumps up, his middle finger is purple and swelling like a balloon. Catcher number five busts his hand. We're out of catchers. I say, "Jimmy, give me that gear." I hadn't caught in six years. I had never played professional ball. But we were in a pennant race, and by God I was going to keep my team in it! Griffith was now catching for Charlotte. I got down and looked up at that big Cuban. He was a huge man. Ortiz threw faster than any man in the league. I flashed one finger. Give me your heat. See what you've got. He went into the big wheelhouse delivery and then — bang — that ball was on me before I knew it. It skidded off my glove and hit the screen in back of the plate on the fly. The ball stuck in the wire mesh. I went back to get it. The fans started moving back a couple of rows, away from the line of fire of home plate. I threw the ball back to Ortiz. "Rock and fire, amigo." The next pitch popped into my mitt like a marshmallow. He threw a light ball. And the next. And the next day I caught again and got a hit. I kept on catching until Evan's hand healed up. Newspaperman asked me why did I do it. Call it superstition if you like. All I was trying to do was put the pressure on the jinx. Boy, that Ortiz was something else.

(Starts fishing for more Cheez-Whiz)

We had lots of Cubans. Unc always said it was cheaper than building a farm system; use the talent you've got access to. Hell, he saw more folks turn out to see Cool Papa Bell play in D.C. than came to see the Senators. He thought about signing him, but the American public wasn't ready to accept that. Particularly in Washington, D.C. I ain't no racist. No more than you are. Rod Carew was like a son to me.

(Pause. He sprays Cheez-Whiz on a cracker, very carefully this time. He eats.)

He was like my son.

(He gets out vodka and tonic, pours another one.)

It's not good for a man of my age to eat alone. Hard on the indigestion system. I know Uncle Clark wouldn't approve of my lifestyle. But he didn't have TV. (He turns on the TV. Everything's off the air. As he flicks through the dials:) We're a close-knit family. (He picks up the Dictaphone.) Jean, get those tickets to New York changed. I'm going to stop in Toledo that night. (Stops Dictaphone.) They had a fight there, you know. Wasn't nothing like the fight we had in Durham. Durham, North Carolina, 1938, we played the Bulls in a doubleheader. We bombed them the first game something like 15 to 4. The second game their pitcher was Everett Hill. He was trying to get some revenge and he was brushing back some of our players. Ellis Clary came up to bat, our shortstop. First pitch was a little inside. That's O.K. The second pitch was a fast ball right at where Ellis' head was. He ducked and the thing missed him by an inch or two. Ellis was hotter than hell. He steps out of the box, puts some dirt on his hands, says, "I'm going to get that so and so." Next pitch was right over the plate and Ellis bunted it down toward the first baseman. The pitcher Hill covered first base and ended up in right field. I mean Clary ran into him like a diesel truck and sent him flying. Here comes the people down the slopes. The fans poured out on the playing field. The benches emptied. We had about 200 people on the playing field — and still had about 1800 up in the stands watching. I ran out there. There was dust getting kicked up. "Break it up! Break it up! Look, it's the cops!" Our guys started after them. Police rushed down on the field. Safety director Crown yelled, "You sons of bitches." He got punched and spiked by a couple of our guys. They were working him over pretty good. There were some players around me rolling in the dust. I could barely see across the diamond. Then I saw some big son of a bitch grab Jake Clarendine my catcher. "You let go of my man!" And I socked him on the nose. It was the chief of police. It took three policemen to carry me off the field. They put me in the slammer for three or four hours. I had to post $200 bail... Didn't bother Uncle Clark. He was a fighter. He never gave in. There's nothing wrong with being a fighter. I loved managing. I learned the ways of ballplayers. I learned how they feel about things and what their problems are. I begged Clark Jr. to spend time in the minor leagues but he wouldn't do it. He'd say things are different now.

He'd say, "Dad, you ran those minor leagues teams. You were in charge. But these days the whole minor league structure is push-buttoned from the major-league level. There's no profit in going to the lower minors." You can't learn a ballplayer's heart from behind a desk, son. All the law and business classes in the world won't tell you why a player's not hitting. No book ever tells you that with a man on first you give the bunt sign. The things you learn on an overnight bus stop, in dingy hamburger stands, on ten inch planks that are supposed to be dugout benches and dressing rooms in trailers — well, those are things you absorb in your heart. There's no way you an put that learning in a book. You learn the soul of a ballplayer. Inside every ballplayer there's a little angel. Sometimes that angel sings every morning and lightens that person's heart and he comes up to the plate with an inner certainty that he's going to connect with the pitch and drive it. It's meant to be, because he can see that ball so clearly, down to the rotation of the stitches, down to the American League stamp rolling over and over in slow motion — that angel inside him is in tune with the heavenly spheres. The sun, the moon, the earth, the ball the pitcher throws — they're all crystal clear. You love to see a player when that angel's singing. He floats along the base, he flies in the green grass of the outfield — he has soft wings inside him. A bad manager is a killer of spirits. He strives with those inner cherubim and fights with them because he wants to run the show, not some godburned ballplayer. Now, mind you, some ballplayers are born without those angels and some are born with devils inside. You've got to find those ones and cast them out. Get 'em out of here. You've got to find men with that spirit inside of them, those bright quick angels. I don't know how you know, but it ain't rational. After some years of living with ballplayers on the bus, playing cards, hearing their jokes — you just know which ones got bright angels inside them. Look at that team of '65 — what a flock of spirits was in that team. Kitty Kaat, Allison, Earl Battey, Jim Perry, Tony Oliva, the Killebrew. That team floated. You got to love baseball with your heart and soul. You give your soul to it and then it opens up souls to you. You see right through the jersey of men and know their hearts. I don't know exactly how you put together a good ball team, but I can tell you this — it ain't rational.

(Pause. He wanders over to shelf.)

I loved managing. I always wanted to be a big league manager. But my uncle advised me against it. He said there was no security, that I could do better in the front office. I always respected my uncle. I would never go against his wishes. When he asked me to come up and work in the Senators' office, I said, "Yes, sir!" No questions asked. That was 1941 and I handled concessions. Don't let nobody fool you — baseball is a business, least it is to the Griffith family. This is how we make our living. We don't have McDonald's or ships or breweries, we got a bottom line here and business is business and the bottom line is the bottom line, that's all there is to it. Concessions — that's where you make some money. Every adult who stops in the ballpark is going to spend an average of three dollars or so on his wiener and beer and everything else. Boy, don't let anybody tell you wieners aren't important. Hot dogs are essential to baseball — those things pay a lot of bills. I don't think there's anything better in the world than a ballpark frank with mustard and a big beer. Hell, watching a ball game and the lights are on up above you and maybe you can see the moon and you got a winning team with maybe a rally going in the fifth inning and here comes that vendor flapping the lid on his metal frank heater and shouting, "Hot dogs! Hot dogs! Get your hot dog!" — it makes me salivate just thinking about it. Of course, I've got to watch my diet now (he heads for the Cheez Whiz and crackers). Doctor won't let me eat too many franks and beers. Oh lord, in 1941 I'd get those good franks with mustard. Uncle Clark always said I had a good mind for concessions.

Lookie here. Here's a copy of the Green Light letter from President Roosevelt. He wasn't much of a baseball fan, but he liked Uncle Clark. Everybody in Washington loved Uncle Clark. He saved baseball in 1942. That's right. We had a war then, and you may recall that in World War I baseball halted operations early one summer. People thought it was unpatriotic to be playing a game during wartime. Well, here comes those Japs and Germans and people thought, "Maybe we shouldn't be playing ball." The rest of the owners were scared to death. In those days it was a livelihood for the owners. What could they do if the government put the nix on baseball? They were so scared they couldn't think straight. Uncle Clark marched into the White House. He was Mr. Baseball in Washington, D.C. He marched in there and said, "Mr. President, I think we should keep on playing ball during this conflagration. We have all these wartime workers and it's our duty to provide them with leisure activities. We don't want to give in to the Japs and Huns on the battlefield, and we don't want them running our lives over here. If Hitler thinks he can stop Americans from playing ball, he's got another think coming!" And FDR gave him this letter, the Green Light letter, saying yes, baseball should go on. He was made Baseball Executive of the Year for that, and it's right. See, I've got the certificate right here on the wall. That one ain't lost.

He had some bad teams over the years, but he never had money like the Yankees. People, they said: "Washington — first in war, first in peace, last in the American League." But Unc never had barrels of money. Early on, the Yankees bought their way to a pennant. Hell, they bought Babe Ruth. If that Red Sox owner hadn't needed money for his Broadway show, the history of baseball might have been different. But Uncle never had that kind of money. He had to play people like Germany Schaeffer, Nick Altrock, Al Schacht — crowd pleasers, comical men. He played Zeke Bonura. Defensively, as a first baseman, I can't recall seeing a worse major league player. Ever. But he was in the top echelon of hitters. He used to hit the ball so fast through the infield, it was unbelievable. See, that's what makes a good hitter — a ball rolling slowly thought the infield will most likely be an out. A ball going through the infield a little faster will have a better chance of going through. A .300 hitter hits balls that travel through the infield *fast*. And how do you get a ball to travel fast? Bat speed. That's all it is. The faster your bat is moving when it hits the ball, the faster the ball's going to move back. It's just like swinging a golf club. The faster the club head is moving when it hits the ball, the further the ball's going to go. Banana Nose — Zeke Babana Nose Bonura — his ground balls were like rockets on the Fourth of July. We thought Unc had got rid of Zeekus for good in the winter of 1938. I mean, his fielding was pathetic. Unc sold him to the Giants for $25,000 and two guys named Joe. Zeke came back to the Senators in strange circumstances. He was a holdout the spring of 1940, he hated the Giants and Bill Terry. He shows up in Florida, all fat and out of shape, he shows up in the stands at a Senators exhibition. He comes up to Unc and says, "Poppa Griffith, I want to play for Washington again. I want to be a Senator again. I'll even pay $1,000 toward my purchase price out of my own pocket." Unc shoved Zeke away. I mean Unc had written in the newspaper that "Zeke is a no-account. In 50 years in baseball he's the worst and most overpaid ballplayer I've ever seen." That's strong words, but Zeke kept coming around to Senators games. Unc would tell him he had Jimmy Wasdell on first. The season opened and Uncle told the press he wasn't even thinking about Zeke. "Give Wasdell a chance, the kids' in a slump." Well we lost the first 4 games and we had no hitting power at all. Wasdell was completely overpowered, he couldn't hit his body weight. So Unc calls up Horace Stoneham, owner of the Giants, and says, "I know Zeekus isn't happy with you. I'll give you $10,000 for him." "Sold." So there you are — Unc repurchased, for $10,000, the fellow he sold for $25,000. The press got all hot about it because they said Unc lied to them about not wanting Bonura. They don't understand. They want you to tell them the truth, but sometimes you just can't say it. You've got to do certain things. I don't talk about certain trades. I don't want to be talking about a ballplayer and then have to keep him because then if you do that you're talking about wanting to get rid of this guy, that guy. Well, you show no support to him and he's going to let you down. Anyway, I wouldn't say I wanted to trade players if I really wanted to trade them. That would take away from my bargaining position. So you see, Uncle Clark was right in not talking about the Bonura deal. He was trying to make ends meet and keep ballplayers happy and everything else. He had to play every angle he had to keep that team going. He traded his own son-in-law. My sister Mildred married Joe Cronin, who was manager and one of the best shortstops who ever lived. When Tom Yawkey offered Unc $250,000 and a shortstop for Joe, why Unc had to consummate that deal. He had to think of his team first. What was best for the team, the Washington Senators. I'm sure he'd approve of my moving the team. People just didn't support baseball in Washington. I had to move. Uncle kept things going year to year, we'd make a little money by selling a player or cutting a corner, but it was precarious, let me tell you.

Everybody loved Uncle Clark. He was elected to the Hall of Fame in 1946. In 1948, they had a day for him at Griffith Stadium. President Truman came out there, they gave him a plaque and everything else. After Connie Mack retired in 1950, Unc was the dean of the American League. People said he was hanging on too long. He was 80 years old. Hell, they say that to me and I'm only 73. What do you do after baseball? Connie told Unc, "When I get off that bench, I would not have anything to think about. I would be a much older man." Connie stayed on that bench until he was senile. Uncle Clark was still president of the Senators when he was 85. He was very old, and you'd think he couldn't pick up things. He'd sit there with this kind of a blank expression on his face and you'd swear he had no idea what was going on. But then, an hour later, he'd ask you a real good question and you'd realize he'd heard everything. He was one of the most gentle persons who ever lived. Never had a cross word for anybody. Just like an angel, always calm. He was strict. He would talk to you in a voice that was very calm. He had a way, a personality that was strong. He and I had conversations every day. You could learn just by watching Uncle Clark run things. No matter how dumb you were, something always broke off and you retained it. That last year, in 1955, he'd bring me in to his office in Griffith Stadium. He kept it a little bit darker and a little bit warmer those days. He'd be listening to the Lone Ranger. He loved that show. He had a big old radio right in his office. When the Lone Ranger came in, he turned off phone calls and everything else. He used to have a painting of the Lone Ranger in his office and they gave him one of Tonto's arrows. He said that idea of one lone man, unknown to most, righting wrongs, just touched him somehow. He had a big old moose head on the wall, and all these photographs. We have crates of them in storage. This office is so goldurn small it's a joke. We have 25 boxes in storage.

One day he called me in. He sat behind that huge desk he had — we had it out at the Met, you couldn't get it in here. He sat behind that big oak desk and his eyes looked very blurry, like he couldn't focus right. His wrist was skin and bone, but still pretty strong. He motioned me over to sit next to him. I pulled up a chair. "Unc — what is it?" "Calvin, you've had enough schooling to take over." "Unc, don't talk that way. You're going to be around for a long time." "Calvin, you've been through hard times. I haven't always had the team I wished for. You've had to work hard." "Uncle every moment with you has been a joy to me." "Hard times will turn to good, Calvin. Hard times will turn to good." (Pause) When they put his body in the earth, I couldn't hardly believe it. He was one of those people you thought would last forever. I couldn't imagine life without Uncle Clark. I should have learned nothing lasts forever.

> (He sits in the Lazy, puts his head to his hands. He gets another drink. He turns on the T.V. and flips from empty station to empty station. He flips through the test patterns for a minute.)

I like some T.V. shows. *Dynasty, Dallas, Dance Fever.* I love to see those nimble bodies move. If I see people making up or getting back together with each other, I cry. But if anything gets sad, I turn it off. A friend in Japan got me a deal on this TV set. (He flips it off) I ship stuff to him. I've got this box here — **The Sporting News**, **Golf Magazine** — I ship it to him. That's $75 out of my own pocket. I've got some friends. See, I've got a baseball over here signed by Richard Nixon. He was a big sports fan. (going to baseball shelf) I've got some balls here signed by movie stars, too . . . ah, Gary Grant and the other actor, Charles Heston, and... oh, who else? Ali, Ali... I don't know how to prounounce his last name. He's the fighter. Ali Muhammed, that's it. Here's Ike. Eisenhower was a tremendous baseball fan. I used to come back from spring training and see President Eisenhower at a function and damned if he didn't know more about the team than I did. He sent me a card after Uncle Clark died. Uncle Clark died October 27, 1955, and I was elected president five days later. We called a meeting of the whole family. The club had a debt of about $100,000 and controlled about 100 players. We decided to start building a farm system. We raised the price of our tickets by 25 cents and paid off the debt while getting a little money to invest in young players.

Lots of people in Washington were fans. Huey Long had two season tickets. But see, Congress would let out in June and then a whole bunch of people would leave the city. There was nobody behind us there. We'd sell season tickets to the coal miners union and TWA and that was about all.   Chesterfield cigarettes were the radio and TV sponsors and we got $100,000 a year. The first year in Minnesota we got $750,000 from radio and TV! The American League got tired of playing to small crowds in Washington. I'd hear from the other owners. The Yankees one season took only $39,000 out of there the whole year. Boston got $24,000. Baltimore got $14,000. The lowest was $9,000. The teams in the American League wanted a change. Every year I'd be approached by people, like the people from the Twin Cities. The papers would get all excited because they'd say, "You're going to leave Washington." "It's been my hope that the Washington team would be able to operate in the nation's capitol where the Griffith family has its roots. I have never questioned the loyalty of the Washington fans. I'm seeing this group from Minnesota as a courtesy. The only move I want to make is to a better stadium in Washington, D.C." I had to say that. I'd be cutting my own throat to tell people that I was considering moving. Who'd come to see the Senators then? One year I wrote a letter to the papers saying I'd stay. But I had to move. The fans weren't supporting the team. And every year Charley Johnson from Minnesota would come to the winter league meetings. And he'd talk to me and everything else. I'd say, "Charley, St. Paul and Minneapolis have been fighting for years. Who's making the offer here — St. Paul or Minneapolis?" See, they both wanted the Senators. And then there was the American League. I couldn't move without the approval of the American League and they didn't want me to do it. Baseball depended on the reserve clause. This was when it was as family owned business and you couldn't run up these huge deferred payments. The congress had given baseball special exemption from anti-trust laws. It seems like a different lifetime. Things were so different then. People had a way of working together; it wasn't every man for himself, like today. See, you didn't want to get Congress angry by leaving Washington D.C. without a team. But we were in a hopeless situation. There was no parking . We couldn't build parking lots because the real estate around our stadium was too expensive.

(He pours another drink.)

The people in Washington, D.C. didn't support the Senators. There are some decisions you make that you don't want to make, but you make them because you have to. You know what I mean? Circumstances, things, events happen and you have to make a decision. And you listen for that feeling inside you, that glow, that tingle of magic fingers. Sometimes you never get it. You do what you think you have to do, but there's a sort of empty feeling in your stomach, like when you don't get enough dairy products. I sat up night after night in my La-Z-Boy. I know Uncle would have approved of what I did. I had to do it to save the Griffith family from financial disaster. In 1960 the National League expanded, and the owners of the American League met and we decided we were ready to expand. I said I was ready to move out of Washington and they could put a team in there. For seven years I'd been wooed by Minnesota. Now I knew it was time for me to see what they really had. October of 1960, the league was meeting in New York. Wheelock Whitney, Gerry Moore, Bill Boyer and Charley Johnson came up. October 26, 1960. I met with Bill and Gerry and we talked a long time. I didn't know what decision to make. I tried to think what Uncle Clark would do. Finally I stood up and I said, "I'll move to Minnesota in 1961 if you can promise me: You'd increase the seating capacity of Met Stadium to 40,000; guarantee a paid attendance of 2.5 million for the first three years; give me 90% of the gross of concessions; agree on a 7% rental charge for the stadium; arrange bank credit to get the new deal going after the move to the Twin Cities; and throw in $250,000 to cover expenses of moving from Washington. I'll give you until 8:45 tomorrow morning to give me your decision." They left the room and I sat there, contemplating what I had done. I was moving the Griffith family out of a city they'd lived in for 30, 40 years. People in Washington would be mad as hell. But I had to get my due. I have learned that if you run for a popularity contest, you don't achieve things. You must make a few mistakes in this world if you want to accomplish things. I must have made a few — I have been criticized pretty good. The next day Joe Cronin told reporters: "The American League today has decided to expand to ten teams for the 1961 season. We have approved the transfer of the Washington franchise to Minneapolis and St. Paul."

Moving to Minnesota was the best decision I ever made. Those first few years at the Met were like paradise. We got big crowds at the park all the time, everybody was so goldarn happy. We drew over one million each of our first four years. We hit 1.4 million in 1962 when we finished second. I got a license plate that said "TWINS" on my car, and people would drive by me, honking their horns and waving and smiling . Not like later on, when they'd give me the finger. You know what that's like, to be driving your car with maybe your wife or somebody inside and have some total stranger drive up next to you and give you the finger? Back then, everybody was happy. We had a good contract with Midwest Federal — we had some money finally. We built up a good farm system. We had the moon rising like a goddamned orange over the scoreboard and some stars in the sky and maybe you'd see a plane go by in the night, all lit up like an ocean cruiser of the air. Everything seemed to hang suspended in those bright lights on a summer night. You wanted the world to just stop right there and let you live in your shirtsleeves with a hot dog in one hand and a beer in another. Just stay like that forever, with those Twins coming up to the plate: (he picks up a mini souvenir bat, crumples up pieces of paper and starts swatting them) Zoilo — bingo! Single up the middle! Rich Rollins moves him over to second. Bobby Allison — single to left! runners on the corners. Come on, Harm. The Killer — a tremendous blast into the upper deck! Home run! Earl Battey — double to right! God damn it, we had a *team*! Camilo and Kaat — we were on our way to '65. Oh, what a team that was. We had finished in 2nd place in 1962 — but we slipped down to 6th at the end of '64. Sam Mele asked me to do a couple of things; I said O.K., let's try it. We moved Killebrew in from left field to the infield. I hired Billy Martin and Jim Lemon as coaches. We wanted to use more speed. Billy Martin taught our team how to run the bases. Oh, what a year! 1965. Everything was right. See (getting photo off the wall) here's the All-Star Game that year. Met Stadium was filled to the rafters. God, that season was beautiful. That was a team. We had All-Stars on the roster — Earl Battey, Harmon, Tony, Zoilo, Hall, Mudcat Grant — all on the 1965 All-Star team. That year started off bad. Versalles loafed in an exhibition, so Sam fined him $300. Then Sam nearly punched umpire Bill Valentine — he got a five day suspension and a $500 fine. Killebrew had an elbow dislocated. Here's the photo where they've all got their arms crossed. Sandy Valdespino, there's Bob, Johnny Sain — he was pitching coach, Johnny Klippstein, he still lives in Minnesota; Dave Boswell, Andy Kosco, Kitty Kaat, Jim Perry, Mudcat Grant, Al Worthington. We had a hell of a pitching staff that year. Look at that back row — Rich Rollins, Earl Battey,Versalles — you know, I had managers tell me to dump that guy. But I stuck with him, even in 1961 when he jumped the club for a month because he was homesick. When he first got here he couldn't speak a word of English. The only thing he knew how to order at a restaurant was bread and Coca-Cola. There's Jimmie Hall. They called him The Wedge — forty-three inch shoulder, thirty-four inch waist. He got that from driving a plough horse on a North

Carolina farm. Harmon Killebrew and Tony Oliva. You don't find that kind of talent all on one ball club anymore. 1963 Jimmie Hall hits 33 home runs as a rookie. 1964 Tony Oliva hits 32 home runs as a rookie. They were all in their prime 1965. Look at how young Tony looks, before his knees got all messed up. Oh, that was tragic. I got the DH rule put through the American League for Tony Oliva. It broke my heart to see him trying to run out to the outfield, his knees hurt so goddamn much. And don't let nobody say to you that I called Rod Carew a damn fool for signing a contract. It was Oliva. He came in one year saying he wanted a two-year contract. I told him he was a damn fool — that he'd win the batting title that year and then he could come in and ask me for a big raise the next. But no, he wanted a two-year contract. I told him, "You sign contract, that's it. That all (lapses into imitation of Oliva's speech patterns) money you get for next year." He says, "OK, OK." So we gave him a two-year contract. Sure enough, he wins the batting title. I was in my office that winter, and Tony sticks his head in. "More money? More money?" And he ran away laughing. He knowed he'd been a damn fool. But I never said that about Carew. Carew was like a son to me.

(Looking at photo again.)

That was a hell of a team; we were on top from July 5. We won 102 baseball games. That day we won the pennant — things went through my body. All kinds of electricity, because it's something I have dreamed about all my life to be president of the club that won the pennant. That's the most thrilling part of anything that's ever happened to me, winning the pennant in 1965. We went into the World Series and Buzzie Bavasi of the Dodgers predicted they would sweep us in four games.

The sun dawned that first day over Met Stadium and I was already there I was so excited. They were pitching Don Drysdale against us. It started out as a tight game — then Zoilo hit a three-run homer, he singled in another run, and with a 7-1 lead, Zoilo stole second base. Oh, the Dodgers complained about that. I'll tell you why — it's because they were embarrassed because the Twins had kicked their butts. We won the first game, but the second game proved we could play. It had rained in the morning and the field was wet. Bob Allison was playing left field, Ron Fairly was on first base for the Dodgers. Batter slashes a line drive down the left field line. Allison gets a good jump; the grass is slippery, but here he comes, on his horse. He gets near it, but I can't see how he can catch it. He dives. Full extension, backhand: Just off the ground in fair territory, the ball plops in his glove. He skids on the muddy turf far into foul ground. The ball stays in the glove. He gets up and makes a strong throw into second base, keeping Fairly at first base. Harmon called it the greatest catch he'd ever seen. There are times when you love baseball so goldarn much — its like dessert. How could that come together so perfectly? The arc of the ball as it was hit, the angle of Allison's dive, the ball and glove meeting at the last possible instant, the ball suddenly smacking the glove and changing direction as Allison carries it across the foul line — there's something God-given, beyond reason when that happens. Scientists could tell you just why a ball hit off the bat like that would go just there, and how Allison got a surge of adrenaline that increased his speed; but how and why those two phenomenons collide so perfect; why those lines meet not a moment too soon, not a moment too late, that's God given: That ain't rational. (He looks at picture of the 1965 team again.) I believe if you look it up you'll see we didn't win a single game in Chavez Ravine that year. That's where the Angels played in these days, and it just wasn't our kind of ballpark. We got out there and dropped those next three games and Koufax shut us out in game five and that hurt. It was one of the all-time great Series. We got back to Minnesota and Jim Grant pitched a great game to tie things up at three games apiece. The seventh game, the last game of 1965, we sent Jim Kaat up against Koufax. Koufax was pitching with just two days rest. Lou Johnson hit a home run for the Dodgers and they were ahead 2-0. In the fifth inning of that final game, Frank Quilici, who batted all of .176 that year, doubled to left. Rollins walked. Then Versalles pulled a shot along the third base line. Their third baseman, Gilligan [Author's note: Jim Gilliam to most.] – you know, that Junior Gilligan – made a sensational play and doubled up Quilici. It was still 2-0 with one out in the bottom of the ninth. Killebrew singled, so we had the tying run at the plate. Koufax reached back and struck out Earl Battey and then he reached back some more and Bob Allison went down swinging. That was it, the end of a great Series.

(He paces a bit, looking for his glass of vodka.)

Goddamn arthritis. I'd like to be running the Twins when I'm 85. What do you do when you retire? I'd most likely crawl into a shell and die. Bear Bryant said when he quit coaching he would die overnight, and I think he died within a month. That's the way I feel. If I got out of baseball right now I would have nothing to do. When you have nothing to do things get monotonous. Your mind wanders. You lose friends. As soon as you quit you practically become nobody.

(Finds vodka glass, goes to refill it.)

We had a great team; we should have won in 1967, too. We should have won the pennant with that team. Spring of that year I insisted on promoting a kid from Class A ball up to the majors. I had remembered when we first signed him. We had him come to Yankee Stadium for a tryout. He got a bat and we had a pitcher throw him some. Lord Jesus — the line drives started popping like the Fourth of July. I said, "Get that kid off the field and sign him before the Yankees see this." And in 1967 I made them play Rod Carew at second base. He's done alright since. Lord, I was sick to death over not winning in 1967. You don't get that many chances in baseball to win a pennant. We went into Boston up by one game with two games left. We lost in 1967 because of the enthusiasm of the Boston fans. If we'd played those two games in Minnesota, I know we would have won. But that year was Boston's miracle season. That happens in baseball sometimes — genuine miracles. You're in the game fifty years and you think you have it figured out, and then some goddamn thing happens — like that pebble in 1924 bouncing a ball over Lindstrom's head, or Ron Jackson getting a double in the clutch — miracle things, things that have no sense behind them — and you say, it surpatheth understanding. There was no way the '67 Red Sox had a better team than we did, but they beat us those last two games. Their fans stayed right in their seats in Fenway Park after the game, and they broadcast the game from Detroit over the loudspeakers. There was 30,000 people in front of an empty diamond, cheering and booing like the game was being played right there in front of them. Detroit lost — Red Sox win the pennant. (shrugs) You've got a round ball and a round bat and you're supposed to hit it square. You explain it to me.

Sam Mele didn't do anything with team that next year, so I had to make a change. I had sent a guy to the minors to manage for a year, so he'd get some experience, and in 1969 I called up Billy Martin. Those two years he managed the Twins was like sitting on a powder keg. It's just he's so unpredictable. Did you hear he broke up a urinal the other night? He went berserk or something and took a baseball bat to a urinal! Maybe Billy Martin was the big bang. Maybe 1970 was when everything started turning inside out. Flood took the reserve clause to court. The National League had all this artificial turf being laid. I went to the All-Star game in Cincinnati in 1970. The ball went through the infield so fast at times the infielders didn't have a chance to catch it. I saw Brooks Robinson jump in the air to get out of the way of one ball. Pete Rose said that artificial turf would add as much as twenty points to averages. That's not a sure test of baseball. Baseball is supposed to be played on grass, that's no secret. They forced me to come indoors here. They would have run me out of town if I hadn't. They promised me the moon and didn't come through with a damn thing. But here I am. I am here. I've got to try and relax and think this damn thing through. I used to tell Tom Kelly he was too tense. He could never relax. I'd tell him, "Tommy, go out and get yourself a bottle of goddamned whiskey and a woman, and tomorrow you'll go four for four." Now I know, Tommy. Relaxing's not as easy as its sounds. I don't have a bottle of whiskey here and let's not talk about women. It's harder to move out of this office than it was to move out of my house in Lake Minnetonka. I keep in close touch with my family, Clare and everybody. (Looking at framed **Sporting News** article hanging on the wall) "Land O' Lake's Cal's Bread 'n Butter." There's so little room in here. I had to hang a picture of Uncle's coffin out in the hall. This ain't pertinent no more. (Taking down the framed story.)

Clark Jr. went to Dartmouth and everything else. I paid for the best schools for him. "Calvin and Clark II — two generations in diamond dynasty". Oh, dear. I paid for law school and everything. He wanted to go to law school and then he got sick or he said he was sick. Let me tell you *I* was sick when I got that tuition bill. He was out swimming in Lake Minnetonka and I'm inside urping. Jesus. Bill Veeck's been saying Clark Jr. should be the next commissioner. I can't say how that would work out exactly because it would depend on who he'd hire for staff. Clark Jr. never was much of one for keeping office hours. I never fired him. He fired himself. Just like Billy Martin. Billy Martin said he didn't want to manage so I said fine. You would have thought I fired Hubert Humphrey. People got all riled up. They hung me in apathy. This was about a man that beat up Dave Boswell, one of his own pitchers. The only kind of fights that help a team are ones held on the field. That didn't help our pennant chances. That team did OK the next year without Billy Martin. They came damn close to being in the play-off. The year after that — 1972 — nothing ever seemed settled after that. That was the year of the first ballplayers' strike. The owners agreed unanimously not to submit to arbitration, and that included Earl Warren, LBJ and President Nixon. Let 'em strike. The players haven't got a dime invested and they want all the profits. We've always gone out of the way to try to help them out. We've allowed wives and family to travel on our charter plane without charge. We've arranged for parking places for wives. We've done a number of things we're not obliged to do — it's been a one way street. (pours another drink) Most lawyers are paid to get people out of trouble. Our lawyers are paid to get us in trouble. The trouble is, we baseball people can never be trusted to do anything sensible. We were going along fine for about 60 years is all, and then we agreed to this collective bargaining crap. The old reserve clause was fair. We didn't have all this hospitalization, pension fund, termination pay, grievances, arbitration. Most of this stuff makes me sick. Players weren't being deprived of a damn thing under the old reserve clause. Who pays the bills, the players or the ball club? Free agency has been the ruination of baseball. Players don't have the same feeling for the game, the same desire they used to. It's become too commercial. Players seem to be interested only in what you pay them. It's this "me generation" crap. Today a ballplayer, very few of them, will take the time to autograph. Very few of them will go out to do things around the city . So, therefore their popularity is not like it used to be. We talk to them about doing things like this. I'm not a person that will beg anybody for anything. If you don't want to do it, that's it. It's up to the individual. When we first came out here, I used to go and stand up on my automobile and watch ballplayers go out the gate and watch which ones stopped and autographed balls or scorecards. And when I saw all this I used to be a little more lenient with them in their salary negotiations than the guy that just pushed by you. So why do people stand up for these players? Why did people get mad when I try to be rational and save money? And I never sold a player just for the money. I told Charlie Finley, "Charlie, if you want to trade

Vida Blue, go ahead, but make sure you get something in return. You can't play money at third base. You can't play money at shortstop. You've got to have ballplayers." And to have Clark, Jr. on the committee that screws us to the wall! To have him wandering around the office, telling us that we should do this and that; that we should advertise. You spend $300,000 a year telling people, "C'mon out and see us, we're great." Then you win five out of fifteen and you make yourself look like a horse's ass. I think if you have a good product you don't need to advertise it. And if you have a lousy product it isn't any use to advertise it. Nobody's going to want it. We got rid of our advertising. You hear that son? Because I'm running this ball club. You have to have charisma to really do this and do that. People howled when I traded people away — Blyleven, Campbell — he got away, Carew, Hisle, Soderholm, Bostock, Ford, Goltz, Landreaux, Koosman — we got our money's worth for all of them except for maybe Campbell. We're millions and millions ahead of the game by not signing these people. Hisle had one good year out of four. Goltz won seven and lost about 18 and was making about $450,000 a year. He's got a million eight coming to him. They're prima donnas; that's what the modern athlete is. Ballplayers used to sit in the dining car and discuss baseball when they traveled by train. Now they get on a jet and 80 percent have attache cases and some kind of musical box with earphones on. The money is so easy they don't have to struggle or become students of the game. The talent has become watered down. The players wear gloves that are like nets. They just look at the ball and it's caught. They were better hitters back in the olden days, too, because they would stay after a game and take batting practice. A player today wouldn't think of staying after. Sports owners don't owe an athlete anything. The athlete owes everything to the sport he's participating in. I mean the payrolls are ridiculous. Steinbrenner regulates salaries for everyone. Most of these owners sign these players to such ridiculous salaries just because they're afraid of their image with the fans if they don't. They're egotists. They've got so much money. But nobody knew who they were before baseball. Who the hell ever heard of Ted Turner or Ray Kroc or Steinbrenner? If I have the smallest payroll in the majors, I'm proud of it. It shows I'm not a horse's ass. I know in a lot of people's minds I'm cheap. But they never had a pencil or a pad in front of them to sit down and try to analyze how to make a payroll. The people that have to make payrolls say that Calvin is a good business man. I have had compliments. In the **Tribune** they had a survey. I don't know if you saw that one or not, where I was respected more than I was hated. And of course they run it on the day of the newspaper strike. They had 25,000 circulation that day instead of having 600,000. So that's the reason why people call you cheap.

(pours another drink)

I think I've been the most crucified man in Minnesota. After that Waseca speech I was crucified. The newspaper was going so lousy that it needed something to stimulate it. I almost cried when I read the story. That was the biggest frame-up that ever happened. That S.O.B. Coleman is more racist than I am. The words were misunderstood, taken out of context. I had had a couple of drinks and in answering questions from the group I was trying to be funny. At times you try to be comical and try to get a laugh and that's it. I did get quite a few laughs. I didn't say anything that requires an apology. Even the president at the Lions Club told me that everything at the meeting would be off the record. I stood up just like this, see, and people asked me questions. What was the worst trade you've made? Sometimes you trade because you have to, cause the manager and player just don't get along. I hated to see Jim Kaat go. Conswega — I called Frankie Lane up and said the manager can't get along with the man — what can you give me? I finally got $10,000 for him, which was terrible. How do I feel about Jerry Terrell? I'm glad he's a favorite son of yours. It's a disgrace to major league baseball that Jerry Terrell is on a club. What about Butch Wynegar? He was playing hands with his wife during spring training, and instead of running around the outfield he did his running around the bedroom. Now love is love. But it comes pretty cheap for young ballplayers these days and I think they should take advantage of that and wait to get married. Why did I move the Senators to Minnesota? It was when I found out you had only 15,000 black people here. Black people don't go to ballgames, but they'll fill up a rassling ring and put up such a shout it'll scare you to death. It's unbelievable. We came here because you've got good hardworking white people here. (He drinks some more) I had a couple of drinks, but I wasn't intoxicated. I have better sense than that. No siree! (obviously, by this time he's a little drunk) Lord, people acted like I had shot Martin Luther King. Newspapers wanted me to get out of business. Hell, I was being comical. You can't do anything these days. Nobody tries to help anybody out or be generous. It's just grab for whatever you can get. I'm no bigot. When we sign a prospect, I don't ask what color he is. I only ask, "Can he run? Hit? Throw?" After this season, I'm going to ask one more question — "Can he field?" We've made so many errors this season . . . ah, never mind.

Dump on Calvin. Calvin is a dinosaur. Well, from what I see on TV a dinosaur is a pretty powerful animal. They were around a long time. And I'm going to be, too. Nobody was coming out to the ballpark. This is a family business. This is my business! You think I can afford to lose money, year after year? No — I've got to balance the books — it's all I've got. If the Minnesota Twins go belly up, Calvin Griffith goes belly up. People told me that Waseca crap hurt attendance. A losing ball club hurts attendance. And I did not call Carew a damn fool. The one I called a damn fool was Tony Oliva, like I told you. During the All-Star game in Chicago last summer, I saw Carew and Oliva in the lobby of the hotel. I said, "I'm happy to finally see you two guys together. Now, Rodney, you remember I supposedly called you a damn fool? Tony, you tell him the story."

Tony said, "He no call you a damn fool. He call me a damn fool." So I finally got the damn thing straightened out. Thank God for Howard Fox. Vice-President. He stood by me. More than my own son. Damn, Clark — you stubborn, proud big-headed son of a bitch! I kept telling you you had to be more humble. You carry yourself around here with your Dartmouth College and Jap prints in the office. All those non-baseball books in there — Spanish lessons and theatre friends. That was the last thing you did to please me — took those non-baseball books out of the stadium. And after the Smalley and Wynegar deal — when me and Howard saw you in the hall — "Why wasn't I consulted about this?" "It was a baseball matter, it wasn't a business matter." "Like hell. They're an investment, Dad. You're buying people's confidence." "I'm buying a shortstop and catcher that hits .240 between them. For over 2 million dollars. That's the stupidest thing I ever heard of." "They're leaders, Dad." "Baloney," says Howard. "Dad, you're letting go of good players to balance the books. You're letting Howard Fox run this team." "Don't you talk to Howard like that." "You're destroying the Twins, Dad. Dad, I'm ready to take over. Let me take over now, before you ruin yourself and the team." Howard says, "Shut up, Clark." Clark says, "To hell with you!" and pushed him down. "Get out Clark. That's it. I'm running this ball club and if I want to trade you or cut you, I will." End of conversation. End of talk. We pass each other sometimes in the hall. He don't say nothing. I don't say nothing. We stare straight ahead. He still draws his salary, though. He still comes around to pick up his check.

Everything's changed. This office is so goddamned small. No windows, anywhere in here. Plastic grass. Plastic roof. They forced me to come here. They would have run me out of town if I hadn't. I'm too old to move. Pack up all those boxes and crap. Just moving here from the Met was too much. I had no choice. I was losing money. At least here I could have an out; three years of sub-par attendance and I could get out. But Thelma wants to sell so bad. And the salaries and all. Ron Davis got all that money in arbitration — he won three ball games! Three ballgames and they give him the moon. I was so sick about it I felt like vomiting. He is no more entitled to that kind of salary than I am to being President of the United States. If I had to pay him that much money for a whole year, I know deep down in my heart I would die a slow death. I don't want to sell, but I can't keep paying these salaries. I'm not going to be a goddamn fool about it and get involved when the Twins are $5 million in the hole or something. I'm not that stubborn. And now I have no one to give the Minnesota Twins to. I have no one to give my baseball team to. (pause) I was thinking tonight, I have to think this thing over like a Dutch oven. And I needed to talk to someone. I could talk to myself, but I don't want to be that kind old person who talks to themselves, because I've seen some people do that who are not my kind of people. I'm not that far gone. Uncle Clark has left me for a while. Then I thought, well, for two or three thousand years, when people are lonely, they've been talking to someone. In the depths of isolation a man has someone he can talk to. So. So, I've been talking, and it feels like someone is out there, listening. And I think that person loves baseball as much as I do. (pause)

Everything ends. That's what your silence means, doesn't it Lord? (pause. gets out Dictaphone) Jean, tell Tom to call a press conference for tomorrow at three. (puts Dictaphone down) Have you ever had a check for 31 million dollars in your hands? (phone rings. Calvin looks at it, as if he knows who's calling. He waits two rings, then picks its up) Hello, Sid. Who else would be calling this hour of the morning? Well, Sid, there's going to be a press conference at three. Yes, I have to sell. It's the only rational thing to do. I'll talk with you after the conference. Stick around. Viola's pitching tonight. I hear it's going to be quite a ball game.

LIGHTS FADE OUT – THE END

An Interview with Calvin Griffith

Jon Kerr

Over 60 years of baseball experience has passed him by. From team mascot of the old Washington Senators, to concessionaire, to minor league manager to major league owner and mogul, and now finally (in a sense) back to being a team mascot, Calvin Griffith has seen just about every bounce the ball can take.

In his now almost hidden, backroom offices at the Metrodome, Calvin has time in an interview to reminisce about the days before corporations became baseball owners and agents negotiated contracts, and most of all about the great ballplayers of days gone by.

* * * * * * *

You had a chance to see a little bit of Cobb, Ruth, certainly Walter Johnson and a lot of great old players over the years. How would you compare the old players with modern ones? If you had to choose an all-time team who would be on it?

You can't pick an all-time team, because there have been so many great ones up there. What is the differential? Who would you like to have — DiMaggio or Williams? You want both of them, you know what I mean? Either one of them would be the star of your team.

I have tried to put down an all-star team — the ones that I've seen. But after you put it down, you say what the hell, it's practically all American League for the simple reason I never saw the guys over in the National League that much.

Hornsby, hell, I imagine he'd have to be on anybody's all-star team. But all I can go by is his batting average. He was one of the greatest right-handed hitters we ever had in baseball.

If you go way back you get into who was the greatest center fielder you ever saw — Tris Speaker or Ty Cobb. Tris Speaker, Grey Eagle, he played so short – right behind second base. He could go back on the ball greater than anybody else there ever was in baseball.

Better than Kirby Puckett?

Yes. He played much shallower. And his lifetime is much more superior. Kirby has been great, no doubt about it. But these other guys played 15-20 years. Is Kirby going to be able to come up to their batting averages in 15-20 years? He may be better! He's the kind of ballplayer like a Pete Rose. People will pay just to come see him play.

Oh gee it's hard. You get a Lou Gehrig at first base, George Sisler, Jimmy Foxx — he was just OK with the glove, but he'd kill you with the bat.

Then there's a fellow nobody ever heard of, Joe Judge. He was a first baseman with the Washington ball club. He was a marvel with the glove. And he was a left-handed hitter who didn't even know when there was a left-handed pitcher in the game. Why they alternate hitting in the game today, I don't know. It's surprising how many right-handed hitters hate to hit against a left-handed pitcher because their fastball is moving away from the center to left on them.

How about Rod Carew?

Naw, he didn't play there long enough.

The shortstops, you got Lou Boudreau, Joe Cronin, Joe Sewell.

You were close to Joe Cronin weren't you?

Yeah, he's my brother-in-law.

And the greatest defensive third baseman was Ossie Bluege. All the oldtimers say hell, "You see (Brooks) Robinson diving at the ball here and there. Ossie Bluege would be in front of the ball – he didn't need to dive."

I saw Ossie 'cause he was with the Washington ball club (1922-39). He was such a natural he didn't even get his uniform dirty. He used to throw batting practice from the screen behind home plate and let everybody hit it as hard as they could. How many ballplayers would dare do that?

Sounds like an Ozzie Smith of today.

That's right, yeah. Uh, Pie Traynor – they say that he was one of the real great ballplayers. I only saw him in the World Series of '25.

There's so many, so many great ballplayers. You try to make comparisons with today and . . . Differences in the ball too. Back in the old days we used to have baseballs with oil on them. Today the ball is bound so hard little men are hitting home runs now. Back in those days a homerun was a homerun. Now you got guys hitting home runs that they're lucky to hit balls out of the infield.

Do you think the change in the ball was the main thing? There was a change in strategy, too.

Back in those days they used to play what they called the "old Army game." I'd get one run ahead. I'd try to get two runs ahead. I get two runs ahead, I try to get three ahead. It makes good sense. That's the way Casey Stengel played.

You mean one run at a time?

Yeah. If you get one run at a time you may end up having a big inning. But today they steal bases when they're ten or fifteen runs behind. Now its unbelievable how many bases they steal.

Other things have changed too — the DH, expansion. Has that diluted talent?

It's watered things down. There isn't 24 major league ballplayers on any ball club today. I don't know how they're even thinking of expansion.

These ballplayers today sign four, five year contracts and no matter how lousy he gets he still gets paid. The golfer, bowling — they have to go out there weekly to earn theirs.

Do you think that makes ballplayers less hungry?

I think so. What incentive do they have?

Of course the flip side to making that much money is that ballplayers may be taking better care of themselves longer — look at the Niekros, Graig Nettles, Pete Rose. . . .

How many Carews are there? Or Pete Rose, Nettles? They have special bodies. When a ballplayer becomes 35, fellow, you better damn well be careful. Because they can deteriorate overnight. But there is certain ones that carry on.

How do you think George Brett, Wade Boggs, Kent Hrbek or the other great ballplayers of today would compare to past eras?

You have to put them into practically the same category — eventually. Brett is one of the great hitters, good fielder, runs well. He's good, no doubt about it.

Boggs, he's just a hell of a hitter and he's developed into a hell of a defensive third baseman. He's strictly a line drive hitter like Sam Rice – who hit I don't know how many singles — only 13 [hits] short of 3000 .

How about pitchers? Have they changed much with the addition of sliders and other pitches?

They talk about the slider. To me, the slider was still used back in the late '20s. Back in those days they called it the "nickel curve."

Then they had the spitter. The spitball pitcher wouldn't throw it more than 10-15 times a game. We had one, Allen Russell, on our Washington ball club. He used to have that damned slippery elm up in his locker and chew on it.

Then they had the screwballs, the really good fastball. I was talking to Bob

Feller the other day. He was clocked up at 115 m.p.h. You don't hear of anybody doing that now.

And I don't know if pitchers are as smart. You don't see any Eddie Lopats, Bobby Schantzes, Whitey Fords. I remember Killebrew used to bat against Stu Miller and I'd say we should just take him out of the lineup for a week, it'd screw him up so much.

What do you think your uncle, Clark Griffith, would think of the changes today – not only the ballplayers, but the game itself?

Well, he would have gotten out of baseball practically right away after the creation of the union. You don't know your ballplayers anymore. You don't get down and talk to them on contracts.

The ballplayer's a damn fool to let these agents negotiate and take part of their money. When it comes to money everybody gets smart. They could do it themselves.

How about the changes in ownership?

In the old days you wouldn't have a lot of people at meetings. Now you have all these attorneys and people who like to hear themselves talk. I think in the olden days people took the well-being of the game more seriously. When they had a league meeting, the owners all attended. They all attended the World Series. Very seldom do you see that anymore. Baseball is just a hell of a business now.

Anything else, like the ballparks, that your uncle would have a reaction to?

He never even dreamed of having domed stadiums, etc. But he always said that one of these days you're not going to have ballparks anymore. You're going to have studios and film all these games. It may come to that.

Calvin's Silent Partner:
An Interview with Thelma Haynes, 1986

Jon Kerr

She is both Calvin's sister and former co-owner with him of the Twins: Thelma Haynes might well be Calvin Griffith's alter-ego. Quietly diplomatic, with a slight Southern accent from the years she lived in Washington, she graciously welcomes a visitor to her lakeside Eden Prairie, Minnesota home. Despite failing health in her mid-70s, Haynes still takes pride in her well-known white, bouffant-style hairdo.

More socially adept than her younger brother Calvin, Thelma was chosen to accompany him in 1922 on the initial visit to Clark Griffith which began their lives in baseball. Often overlooked by sportswriters and the public, Haynes became a silent yet equal partner with Calvin after their uncle's death.

Her obvious resentment at changes in Twins' management style – symbolized by recent slights to fellow Griffith family members – is tempered by her fond memories of life in baseball's old aristocracy. "We were just one big, happy family" is how Haynes summarizes the 60-plus years she and her surviving brothers (including Jimmy and Billy Robertson) ran the ball club. "We were all in it together."

* * * * * * *

You have been a longtime partner of Calvin's. I mean the two of you came down from Montreal together to Washington. How did that happen?

Well my grandmother and my aunt wanted to bring Calvin back for a vacation. The Griffiths wanted us because they never had any children. And my father had been very ill and there were seven children in the family. The last ones were twins so we were all little doorstops.

So anyhow Calvin wasn't very anxious to go. But I was always wanting to go someplace. So we came together.

So you're the one who actually wanted to go to Washington to join the Griffiths?

Yes. Calvin and I came and we've had a wonderful life. While we've been a family that was reared in two different households, we've stayed very, very close together for the holidays and the Griffiths never showed any partiality — we were all treated alike. 'Course when they died, Calvin and I came into the ball club.

What was it like being the only girl in an all-male baseball world?

Well I think it was a fabulous life. When I was young the ballplayers didn't have enough money to get married early so we always had a lot of young ballplayers in spring training camp. We did things as a group and I was probably the only girl with maybe eight or nine or ten of 'em some nights that we'd go to Harpers and drink Coke and dance to the jukebox.

Were you a big baseball fan then?

Oh yes. We loved the game. We were about five or six I guess when we were initiated into the game. My father was a big baseball nut in his day. I guess it just came naturally.

Calvin was obviously being groomed for a major role by the Griffiths.

That's because he was the only boy that would have come into it. Mr. Griffith had a brother whose son was named Clark. Had he lived I think he may have been the one who inherited the team. They were crazy about this nephew but he went in for a simple tonsillectomy and died. He was 21, I think.

Calvin was a batboy, then he worked in concessions, and he managed a minor league team. Did you have any kind of a role like that?

I was Mr. Griffith's secretary for a number of years. Then in the summertime, when the team was on the road, I would drive and Mr. Griffith and I would go down to the Princess Anne club at Virginia Beach and we would scout the Portsmouth club and the Norfolk club and the Charlotte club. So I knew boys on all the clubs that way and when they came up to the big leagues we always had a very close relationship with them.

Did you ever make any scouting predictions that you were particularly proud of?

No, not until my husband came into the office and he was a handsome young man . . .

This was Joe Haynes.

I was secretary and I wrote on his card "very good looking prospect" and underlined it — never thinking that I'd end up marrying him.

How long did he play with the Senators then?

Well, my father (Clark Griffith) always said "if you marry a ballplayer he's gotta leave." So when my sister married Joe Cronin he was traded to Boston. Then when Joe and I were going to get married my father had us wait for one year till he got started, then he was traded to the White Sox.

Why did your uncle have that rule?

Well, it was hard for anybody in the family to be on the team. I had a brother, Sherrod, on the team in Washington and the fans and the press would not be very nice. But it was funny how you could never win. When Joe used to come back with the White Sox they used to yell, "Put Haynes in, we need some runs."

How was it being a baseball wife?"

We were all very clubby. Particularly when you played day ballgames because you'd go out at night. The wives would go out together shopping and things during the day.

When did you get back involved with the Senators organization?

My husband came back to coach. But I didn't get back into the office until Mr. Griffith died in '55. Then I joined the board of directors and my husband became executive vice president.

When was the structure set up with you and your brother (Calvin) sharing the stock inheritance?

Well, it was always talked about, you know. Mr. Griffith owned more stock than anybody involved. We were into an agreement that one of us couldn't sell out stock without the other. We knew that without the other part of the 51 percent, my stock wouldn't be worth anything. Calvin's wouldn't either.

We were well trained along that line. The Comiskeys and then the Connie

Mack family had had a lot of trouble and ended up losing the ball club. That was always quoted to us, "You'll be like the Connie Mack family if you start fussing." (laughter).

How did it happen that Calvin became the spokesperson and you were in the background?

Oh, I didn't mind. Only that he made all the money. Mr. Hartman (Sid) kept writing about how much money I was making. I just wish he'd have made up the difference between what I made and what he was quoting.

Between you and Calvin, there must have been some things you disagreed about in running the team.

Well I never got involved really in the ballplayer part of it. I always felt if they were paying him, he should know more about it than I did.

When the team moved to Minnesota, did you have feelings about that?

It was hard. When Calvin told me about it I said, "Well, looks like the Antarctic region to me. But if that's where we've got to go to make a living, that's fine with me."

But we've had a good time in Minnesota. I think the people have been the sort that we are — sort of down-to-earth and realistic. I think we've made a lot of good friends here.

There've been some controversies over the years . . .

With Calvin? He's so outspoken and says things that he thinks he's being funny and other people don't think it's funny and it comes out sounding entirely different.

Like the Waseca speech?

Oh, I had a hemorrhage. I couldn't believe it. And I know he didn't mean it in that context. He was being sarcastic. Because when the people did come to Washington to try to prevail on us to come to Minnesota they used the fact that there weren't many colored people in Minnesota as one of their selling points.

The problem that we had run into in Washington was that the ballpark was in a very black district and people were getting their tires cut up all the time and things like that — not that whites don't do the same things, I don't mean that. But it just was a district that was hard to control and we didn't have parking facilities like we do out here, you know.

Calvin had always said — which he shouldn't say — that colored people don't seem to want to come to ballgames. But they don't seem to come to ballgames anymore. They seem to prefer other sports. But that's to their liking, you know.

Did you ever give Calvin any advice on his speeches?

I just told him, "Don't talk too long."

The decision to move into a dome stadium — did you share Calvin's feelings on that?

We were sold on the idea, and in fact we were forced into it whether we liked it or not. They were going to build the stadium and you have to go where you have the facilities to play.

A lot of people still say to me, "We liked it out at the Met. We like to sit outside at the ballgames." And I say, "Well, you just didn't sit out at enough of them."

It's been reported that you maybe thought the team needed to be sold a year or two before Calvin did.

Calvin always thought things would turn around. I'm a little more of a realist. We were lucky to hold out as long as we held out.

Do you feel sad at all not being a part of baseball anymore?

I miss it, especially the association with baseball players and their families. I haven't been to many games because I've been sick the least year and a half. I listen to a few games and watch a lot on TV. My father always thought that housewives were the better fans. I don't know. But I'm just glad to have been part of a game that brings pleasure to so many people that can't get out.

And finally...

The More Things Change . . .

The newspaper article on the following page is reprinted from the **Sioux Falls Argus-Leader** of March 9, 1920. Clearly, the more things change, the more they stay the same . . .

Big League Clubs Lose Money, Increase Prices at Gate, Asserts Griffith

Washington. Mar. 9. —Clark Griffith, Washington baseball magnate and owner, believes in enlightening the public — the baseball public — on the financial difficulties attending the conduct of a big league franchise.

"All expenses of the game have doubled in the past few years and yet the magnates have kept the admissions down until this year," says Griff. "There is nothing to do but increase the receipts or get out of the business. It is doubtful if the majority of us could make a living at the old schedule of admissions and it is a certainty that few of us would receive any returns on our investments.

"Last year the Washington club made $20,000 and out of that we had to pay a tax of $3,000. That is on an investment of $300,000. But that was baseball's banner years. Previously we had lost money season after season — one year as much as $43,000.

"The increase in the price of admissions probably will make the receipts from 15 to 20 per cent greater this season — if the attendance is as big.

All Expenses Greater.

"But we are paying much bigger salaries — every club is. I have calls for the expenditure of $6 a day for each player's room and meals while on the road. Bats cost $1.50 now. Formerly they were 75 cents. Balls cost twice as much. Bus hire is greater. Labor on the grounds and for office and park attendants is twice what it used to be. In fact, everything costs twice as much as it did.

"I don't believe there is one real fan in a big league town who wouldn't be willing to fork up the extra $10 it would cost him for attending practically every game of the season if he was told it was either pay more or lose the club. That is what it means to a fan who attends 70 out of a schedule of 77 games.

"Increases in salaries have been exorbitant. Many of the demands were unjustified.

"There are few ball clubs making money. Chicago and Detroit in the American League and New York and Pittsburgh in the National are financial successes. The others have their difficulties.

"Some of the losses have been great. I'm one of the poor men in baseball and I couldn't stand the losses that some of the big fellows have to stand.

"And yet the big fellows keep on in hopes they will turn the club into a success — some of them have lost as much as $100,000 a year."

THE END

Base Paths II: The Best of the Minneapolis Review of Baseball, 1987-1991
will be published by Wm. C. Brown in the spring of 1992.